Praise for Sirona Knight's DREAM MAGIC

"Magic is the art of making your dreams come true. In *Dream Magic*, Sirona Knight has conjured a unique and useful guide to spells that will help you make your dreams come true. This artful addition to any magical library will show readers how to transform and fulfill their lives with the divine power awaiting us in the realm of dreams."

—Phyllis Curott, Wiccan priestess, attorney, and author of
*Book of Shadows: A Modern Woman's Journey
into the Wisdom of Witchcraft and the Magic of the Goddess*

"Oh, there is that 'other' life we live, in our dreams, between the worlds. Sirona spins the mystic silver thread, rooted in a lovely spellbook to bring us in balance with that 'other' life. Accessible, easy to absorb. Try some."

—Z. Budapest, visionary activist and author of
Grandmother Moon and *Summoning the Fates*

"Sirona Knight has done it again! *Dream Magic* provides everything necessary to make your problems evaporate right into thin air. All you have to do is pull up the covers, snuggle into bed, and dream a little dream . . ."

—Dorothy Morrison, award-winning author of *Everyday Magic*

"Sirona's brilliance shines brightest yet with *Dream Magic*. She shares ancient mysteries in a way that translates exquisitely into the twenty-first century. In this book Sirona reminds us that our imaginations are our key to realizing our fullest potential. Such an amazing array of detailed step-by-step doable spells that will put the reader in charge of their dreams has never appeared in book form before. With this book Sirona establishes herself as one of the best authors in this field."

—Michael Peter Langevin, Publisher and Editor, *Magical Blend*

"Dare to dream—this is *Dream Magic*'s ultimate message. By learning how to use our dreams' spiritual essence we can truly reclaim the night and put it to good use, manifesting love, prosperity, peace, and pleasure for our waking hours. Sirona Knight's dream rituals, spells, and down-to-earth advice makes this a welcome, if not essential, bedside book to warm our dreams, and help them come true!"

—Patricia Telesco, author of *Magick Made Easy*

"I found this book to be an excellent guide to working with the subconscious mind through dream imagery. It is both enchanting and practical. *Dream Magic* is filled with the magic of youth and the vision of aged wisdom."

—Raven Grimassi, author of *The Wiccan Mysteries*

"Sirona Knight has a unique talent for explaining things in a way that is communicative, relaxed, and easy to grasp. I recommend this book for anyone wishing to delve further into the magic of dreams through her simple practical methods that span across different traditions and resources."

—R. J. Stewart, author of the bestselling *Merlin Tarot* and many books on meditation, music, and magic

"*Dream Magic* adds new meaning to the old phrase 'Let's sleep on it!' Sirona has combined magical spellcraft with the Dream State to bring a waking merging with the divine. With reading ease, her book explains the steps in which we can first bring our conscious thought into our dreamtime, and then bring the world of our dreams into our waking reality. If you can dream it, this book can help you realize your dream's potential reality and the reality of your dream's potential."

—A. J. Drew, author of *Wicca for Men*

DREAM MAGIC

DREAM MAGIC

NIGHT SPELLS AND RITUALS
FOR LOVE, PROSPERITY,
AND PERSONAL POWER

Sirona Knight

HarperSanFrancisco
A Division of HarperCollins*Publishers*

HarperCollins books may be purchased for educational, business, or sales promotional use. For information please write: Special Markets Department, HarperCollins Publishers, Inc., 10 East 53rd Street, New York, NY 10022.

HarperCollins Web site: http://www.harpercollins.com

HarperCollins®, 📖 ®, and HarperSanFrancisco™ are trademarks of HarperCollins Publishers, Inc.

FIRST EDITION

Designed by Lindgren/Fuller Design

Library of Congress Cataloging-in-Publication Data
Knight, Sirona.
     Dream magic : night spells and rituals for love, prosperity, and personal
power / Sirona Knight.— 1st ed.
        p. cm.
     Includes bibliographical references.
     ISBN 0-06-251675-2 (pbk.)
     1. Magic. 2. Incantations. 3. Dreams. I. Title.
   BF1621.K55 2001
   135'.3—dc21   00-031972

00 01 02 03 04 ❖/RRD(H) 10 9 8 7 6 5 4 3 2 1

Dedicated to Gwydion the Harper.
To Michael and Sky for their love, light, and laughter.
And to all the dreamers everywhere.

CONTENTS

Contents

☾

chapter three
Dream Magic Components ☾ 29
*Basic List of Items Needed ★ Candles ★ Essential Oils ★ Incense
and Resins ★ Herbs ★ Crystals and Gemstones ★ Dream Stone ★
Color Correspondences ★ Magical Symbols*

☾

chapter four
Love Dream Magic ☾ 44
*Bridget's Eve Love Wish ★ Lover Attraction Spell ★ Candle Magic
Love Spell ★ Linked Souls Dream Charm ★ Beltane Love Spell ★
Finding Your Soul Mate Spell ★ Loving Partner Dream Charm ★
Lustful Encounters Love Spell ★ Moon Fertility Magic ★ Dream
Lover Charm ★ Love Poppets Dream Spell ★ True Love Spell ★
Moon Mate String Magic ★ Forest Grove Love Adventure ★
Mending a Broken Heart ★ Lover Protection Spell ★ Crystal Dream
Castle Love Spell ★ Love Magic Charm Bags ★ Lovemaking
Placket Magic ★ Flying Free Love Adventure ★ Romance and Love
Pentacle ★ Magical Symbol Love Charm ★ Dream Knot Marriage
Spell ★ Samhain Love Magic Spell ★ Holiday Mistletoe Ritual ★
Canceling a Love Spell*

☾

chapter five
Money and Success Dream Magic ☾ 90
*Wildflower Success Spell ★ Creating a Dream Magic Money
Crystal ★ Green Underwear Money Spell ★ Money Placket Spell ★
Lucky Coin Charm ★ I Got the Job! Spell ★ Dream Water Spell ★
Money Trail Dream Magic ★ Bindrune Prosperity Charm ★ Apple
Abundance Spell ★ New Moon Dream List ★ Success Story
Charm Bag ★ Money Mantra Spell ★ Mojo Money Dream Bags ★
Candle and Coin Abundance Spell ★ Dragon Riches Dream Spell ★
Wendrune Money Spell*

Contents

☾

c

chapter nine

Divine Dream Magic ◐ 216

APPENDIXES

INTRODUCTION

On my thirteenth birthday I received a diary from my mother and a book of magic spells from my best friend in high school. I remember sitting in my room each night, writing in my diary by candlelight, recording first all the things that had happened during the day and then all the thoughts, desires, and dreams that I had at the time. One of those dreams was to write books. One night I read a section in the book of spells on candle magic, and so I did a spell where I stuck a pin through the wick of a lit candle. I imagined myself writing a book for the largest publisher in the world.

Here I am, older and wiser, acting out this dream while sharing my insights and spells on making your life more complete. I didn't realize at the time of the gifts that the mating of a diary, representing my dreams, and a book on magic, representing my initiation into magic, would result in this book on dream magic, techniques for making your dreams really come true!

The spells and rituals in this book can be done in any order. I suggest you do one spell or ritual per night. Depending on your own desires, you can do love magic one night and a spell for finding the perfect job the next. Every technique gives you all the items and instructions you will need for doing successful dream magic.

An essential ingredient in dream magic is merging with the divine energy. Merging occurs naturally during sleep. By merging with divinity, you invoke this energy in your magical dream pattern. In this book, the term I use to refer to this divine energy is *Oneness*, a term that is not specific to gender or exclusive to any spirituality. Oneness represents the infinite whole, a collective consciousness that takes on divine proportions. This is expressed in the phrase "From the One comes the whole of existence, and from this infinite whole comes Oneness." By merging with Oneness in dream magic, you reach into this infinite whole and move this energy into your pattern. Each of us is part of the whole of Oneness and thus is connected with it. This connection is accessible through dream magic, and it provides the conduit for making things happen.

Oneness is open enough to include all divine energies that you might want to use in your dream magic. Feel free to use the deities with whom you feel the deepest connection. Again, this is the beauty of dream magic—it's open to everyone, and everyone can benefit from the techniques.

Magic is the process that makes your dreams come true. This connection between dream and magic creates an alchemical union between the formless and form, which takes place within and without your being. Dreams are the channels through which the unconscious enters consciousness while at the same time connecting into divine Oneness. Through dream, you build your castles in the air in your mind's eye, allowing your imagination to soar, and then you use magic to create foundations under these castles, thereby actualizing your dreams.

The dream magic techniques contained in this book are easy to use and are grouped together by subject. Chapter 1 lays down the basics of dream magic, including spellcasting and timing in relation to the astrological and lunar correspondences. Chapter 2 moves you through the steps for setting up a dream altar and calling in your dream guardians to help make your magical patterns successful. Chapter 3 is an overview of the components used in dream magic, such as candles, essential oils, crystals and gemstones, and magical symbols.

Chapters 4 through 9 are filled with night spells and rituals, together with suggestions for making dream magic work in your life. Chapter 4 deals with love dream magic and includes an array of techniques for improving your love life. Chapter 5 offers techniques for bringing money and success into your life, including instructions on creating a dream money crystal, making mojo money dream bags, and using green underwear to generate money. Chapter 6 reveals ways to use dream magic to empower yourself and become the person you want to be. Part of this includes moving the negative energies out of your life and replacing them with positive ones. Chapter 7 covers health, beauty, and wellness dream magic, including making a healing placket, letting go of grief, and bringing out your inner and outer beauty while living a long, healthy life. Chapter 8 gives spells and rituals that are practical in the sense that they bring you a great vacation and nice neighbors and show you how to make better decisions. Chapter 9 moves into the realm of divine dream magic and gives techniques for twinkling with the faeries, starwalking, shapeshifting, and becoming one with the divine energy.

chapter one

Modern Dream Magic

Dreams are the source of creativity. They are expressions of experiences that are seeking to become real. When you practice dream magic, you do not just focus on what your dreams mean, you use magical techniques, in the context of your dreams, to help them come to fruition. This book challenges you to step into the river of dreams and purposefully and actively use dreaming for making magic.

Basics of Dream Magic

Dreams, for most people, have three basic aspects. The first aspect is the sensory experiences that you undergo each night while you sleep—images, sounds, and feelings appearing to your consciousness. While each person's dream experiences are different, many aspects are also similar, thus giving rise to the field of dream interpretation, the subject of countless books and theories.

The second aspect of dreams is akin to a shamanic experience, where you have a dreamlike experience while in a waking state.

Like the Australian aboriginal "dreamtime," this aspect of dreaming has to do with moving into an Otherworld, where time and space seem to drop away. A prime example of this sort of dream-like state is when you become so engrossed in thought that you don't even notice someone walking into the room and saying something to you. It might take a few moments to come back to the present time and place, giving the impression that you traveled somewhere else while it was happening. Often you will receive a vision, message, or other useful information from the dream experience. Within terms of magic, this part of dreaming relates to "merging," a process where you enter a divine state of being and are One with all things. The practice of merging will be discussed further in the section on spellcasting and creating magical dreams.

The third basic aspect of dreams stems from the old saying "Dreams can come true." It is possible to use dreaming to achieve a particular goal that you strongly desire and expect to come true. Many times this goal is notable for its beauty, excellence, and ability to satisfy a heartfelt wish or ideal. Having an expectation and desire for a specific goal not only is a major aspect of dreams, it is also the cornerstone in magic. Without expectation and desire, there is no magical pattern and, for the most part, no forward movement. Your dreams, in the form of expectations and desires, are often the things that get you through the night and each day! It's the magic that makes your dreams come true.

Each morning when you get up, you have expectations about how the day is going to progress. These expectations are like a basic dream that you have about how things will turn out in the future. In the case of a day, if you drive to work, you expect to arrive safely. If you are working on a contract or project, you expect and intend for this to come to fruition and be successful.

The basic misconception regarding dreams is that somehow they aren't real—that somehow you should disregard your dreams and go on with your life as if they don't exist. This attitude negates your expectations and desires and says the experience you have each night should simply be cast aside. I disagree with this old-school attitude. Your dreams are energetically and experientially very real, and this book shows you how to tap into their power to enrich your life. Dreams are fields of energy in the form of creative sparks that need to be kindled, fine-tuned, nurtured and fed, and brought into full flame. The magical dream spells and rituals presented here are intended to do just that and to help make your dreams come true!

Common Misconceptions About Magic

People commonly hold three basic misconceptions about magic. These misconceptions often unjustly influence their attitudes toward magic. If you view pentacles as Satanic or think that old ladies dressed in black fly around in the sky on broomsticks—when they aren't turning handsome young men into toads—you're not likely to want to use magic. These images are sensationalized and couldn't be further from the truth.

The first misconception of magic is that it is done by stereotypical witches—ugly, unbathed old women with warts on their noses who wear pointed black hats and ride broomsticks through the sky. I have met thousands of witches in my life, and none of them comes close to fitting this Hollywood stereotype. People who believe in and practice magic are young and they are old, they come in all sizes and from all walks of life. What brings us together are the beliefs both in the power of the mind and in a synchronistic divine power that can make magical things happen.

The second misconception stems from the idea that people practicing magic worship Satan. This idea is at best far-fetched to the point that if people didn't believe this misconception, I wouldn't even address it, but unfortunately it continues to rear its ignorant, ugly little head. The folks that I know who practice magic use a variety of divine energies, from the Celtic Mother Goddess Kerridwen to Mother Mary to the Norse Father God Odin.

Wicca is the modern revival and renewal of a nature-oriented, Earth-spirited tradition that stems from the Old Religion or Goddess Religion, often referred to as the Mystery Traditions. The actual origins of contemporary Wicca owe much to Charles Leland, Gerald Gardner, Aleister Crowley, Doreen Valiente, and Alex Sanders, among others. Today Wicca has evolved away from the "old-school" attitudes of its founders to a more "new-school" perspective that is open-ended and eclectic.

The majority of Wiccans are tolerant of different points of view and lifestyles, and most are dedicated to the responsible stewardship and protection of the Earth and to the positive evolution of human consciousness. An appealing tradition whose main focus is to relink humanity with itself and nature, Wicca is all about self-discovery, personal growth, and empowerment. It values participatory revelation and celebratory action that lead to a more expanded understanding of oneself and the universe. Through myth, ritual, spellcasting, poetry, music, lovemaking, and working in harmony with the Mother, the sacred Earth, Wiccans awaken the divine within and the magic of every moment.

The wonderful thing about magic is that is inclusive rather than exclusive, meaning that you can include and incorporate any deities that you have rapport with into the magical process. In the craft there is a saying, "Positivity engenders positivity, and negativity engenders more negativity." Satan is basically a Christian concept, and as a deity, he is the embodiment of all negativity and evil. If you were doing a magical work, why would you want to invite in the embodiment of evil? Talk about self-sabotage!

To see the full absurdity of the propaganda that has been slung around about witches being associated with Satan, let's go back to exactly what Satan is historically and mythologically. Satan originated as a Semitic demon whose name meant "opponent" or "adversary." It's interesting to note that Satan has no direct correlation with the Underworld Gods of other mythologies such as the Greek Hades and Norse Hela or the adversary Gods such as the Norse

Loki and the Celtic Morganna. None of these deities is inherently evil in the way that the Christians portray Satan. In this sense, Satan becomes a uniquely Christian concept, with definite political and economic overtones.

For their image of Satan, embodiment of all evil, the Christians of Europe appropriated the Horned God of the Old Religion. The Horned God went by the names of the Greek Pan or the Celtic Kernunnos or Herne, to name a few, and was not in his original form evil in any way. He become evil only when the Christians imported him into their mythology to symbolize all the evil the world. In fact, German Christian folklore says that Satan is so busy running the world that he has to send in his grandmother to help out. The Christians made the Horned God their Satan so that they could claim that anyone who worshiped the traditional Earth-spirited Goddesses and Gods were worshipers of Satan and therefore, by connection, evil. In this way early Christian fanatics could justify the inhumane massacre of those they called "pagans," which meant everyone who was not Christian, much the same way as Moslems call non-Moslems, "infidels."

Fortunately, those backward times are in humanity's past, and today things are changing for the better with regard to spiritual freedom. Today those of us who practice the art and craft of magic proudly call ourselves pagan because we know through our experience that the pagan path is one of empowerment, compassion, tolerance, and hope for the future.

Most of us who practice magic believe in the divine union of the Goddess and God. This union stems from perfect love and perfect peace (trust), and from this union everything is created, both animate and inanimate. This "everything" is what I call "Oneness." Nothing exists outside of Oneness. From Oneness came the whole of existence, and from this whole comes Oneness. It is ever beginning, ever flowing, and ever ending, and it connects everything together into One.

The third misconception is lighter in tone. It involves the idea that practitioners of magic wave a magic wand, chant a few magic phrases, and presto, kaboom, abracadabra, the magic just happens, manifesting itself out of thin air, usually with no further effort on the part of the person doing the magical work. Ah, if it were only that easy!

Magic is an art and craft like any other. It is a skill that requires effort and practice. You learn how to read and create energetic and physical patterns. The more adept you are reading and making patterns, the more likely your magical spells and rituals will be successful. If you want to get a better-paying job, then putting together a great résumé and applying to the companies you want to work for helps you succeed. You can wave your magic wand all you want, but you must put some thought, effort, and energy into magic making if you expect to reap the rewards.

Spellcasting and Creating Magical Dreams

Each night spell and ritual in this book is formatted into three parts: an overview of the adventure, the items you will need, and step-by-step instructions for spinning the spell or doing the ritual. It is essential that you read the entire spell prior to starting so you know what you will be doing and which items you will need to gather together. Make sure you have everything you will need, including matches, because once you begin doing a magical work, which often involves doing certain things in a particular sequence both before you go to sleep and while you dream, you don't want to have to interrupt the flow. In this respect, preparation before doing dream magic is a key element for successful magic. This is because magic is about creating energetic patterns, and once a magical pattern begins, it has a flow that can be enhanced and amplified for maximum effect. If you break up the flow, you fragment the energy, making your dream magic less effective.

Every spell and ritual involves three basic steps. First you set your expectation, then you fill it with your desire, and finally you merge with the divine, to help your goal or desire become a reality. Together, these three steps move the energy of the spell into physical reality, causing it to happen. Let's look at each of these steps in turn.

In the way that preparation is essential, expectation provides the foundation and platform for creating magical dreams. Sometimes we use the word *expectation* interchangeably with *intention,* but close examination shows there is a difference between them. Expectation is what you expect to happen, while intention is what you intend to happen. The roots of the two words are also very different. *Expect* comes from the Latin *exspectare,* meaning, "to look forward," whereas *intent* comes from the Latin *intentus,* meaning an "act of stretching out," as if to grab hold of something. Intent, in both a legal and linguistic sense, refers to your state of mind when doing something and usually involves concentration on a goal. The word is used in the context. We hear people say, "It wasn't so much what he did but his intention that was the problem." This implies that mistakes are all right as long as they're not what you intended.

By contrast, the word *expect* infers a high degree of certainty and involves the concept of preparing for and envisioning a particular outcome. In terms of dream magic, an attitude of expectancy means having a clear image of the outcome you desire and then setting the stage for this outcome to occur. A large part of having a clear image or expectation requires knowing what you want. If you do not know what you really want, you take the chance of winding up with something that is not to your liking. In this way, you are working against yourself and creating problems rather than patterns. By having a clear expectation and knowing what you want, you move toward an outcome that is more in accord with your true desires and deepest dreams.

The second step in creating a magical dream pattern is desire, which means how much you want something to happen. Once you have a clear expectation of what you want, then you move into a state of mind where you mentally and emotionally map out the steps required for your desired outcome. In the case of a deeper and more sensual relationship with your partner, you look at all the steps needed to make this a reality. As you go over each step mentally and emotionally, paint it with your desire for your magical dream and energetic pattern to be successful. Use all of your senses to see it, feel it, taste it, smell it, hear it, and intuit it. Be passionate about your magic making!

Once you build your desire while doing a magical work and it reaches the point where you feel you are about to burst with energy, the time has come to merge with your goal. Merging with the goal and the overall pattern will generate and direct the energy toward making your dream a reality. When you merge, you become One with divine energy, whatever name you give it. In this way, merging is the key to successful dream magic because it bridges worlds and dimensions. Merging imbues your magical patterns with divine power, helping you build energy and move it toward your expected and desired outcome. The more energy, the better the results.

When you merge, you receive divine assistance by strengthening your connection to the divine energy inherent in all things. In the craft, you are encouraged to merge with Goddesses and Gods, Oneness, or elemental energies to receive help, wisdom, and protection. For all practical and magical purposes, you become One with these divine energies. They are not separate from you, any more than your dream world is separate from your waking life. Everything is connected into One. Always keep this in mind when doing magic.

Spellcasting and rituals enhance and give form to the overall pattern of your dream magic. When you cast a spell or do a ritual, you use certain materials and tools in ritualistic ways to move energy toward a particular outcome. By adding these materials and a formula for using them, you add sensory input to your wish; you lend a method to your magic. The purpose and goal of your spell needs to be clearly understood and then enhanced with magical components such as candles, oils, incense, stones, and photos. All the materials and tools you will need for a particular spell or ritual are listed, making it much easier for dream magic making. After you become familiar with a ritual or spell, feel free to alter or add components and change the invocations to make the work more personally appealing.

Nine-Point Dream Magic Checklist

1. Write down the kind of spell you are doing, for what purpose, and what your expectation is for the spell or ritual. Your writing becomes your own special Dream Magic Journal or Book of Shadows.[1]

2. Note the date and time you cast the spell or performed the ritual.

3. Note the significant corresponding astrological facts such as sun sign, moon phase, and so forth.

4. Select sponsor Goddesses and Gods, power animals, elementals, guides, or other allies to help you in your work.

5. Prepare the area in which you will be doing your magic.

6. Gather together all the items you will need for the night spell or ritual.

7. Cast the spell. Be sure to have this book close by so you can refer to it while you are working.

8. Write down the results of your efforts. Remember that with some spells and rituals, it may be necessary to wait awhile to enter this information into your journal.

9. Write down any additional comments, suggestions, and other notes.

---

[1]Most practitioners keep a book of spells, rituals, and notes as well as magical instructions, prayers, invocations, and the like in a binder, loose-leaf notebook, or bound blank-page book. Most Books of Shadows are highly personal collections.

Dream Magic Timing

Most of the dream magic spells and rituals in this book are best done on certain nights of the week, times of the year, and phases of the moon. For easy reference, I have included the following sections on what times are the best for doing the various types of dream magic. Different times exhibit different energies. Knowing the best times to create certain magical patterns adds to the power of the pattern and increases its chance of success.

Astrological Correspondences

The zodiac, which circles the Earth, has astrological correspondences that translate into energies that can be used for magic. The following is a list of these correspondences.

ASTROLOGICAL CORRESPONDENCES
Aries: Fire, strength, persistence, assertiveness
Taurus: Creativity, love, tenacity, self, brashness
Gemini: Polarities, communication, ideas, compromise
Cancer: Flow, emotion, home, mother
Leo: Power, father, ego, prowess
Virgo: Organization, structure, healing, orientation to detail
Libra: Balance, love, creativity, oneness, relationships
Scorpio: Desire, transformation, astuteness, mystery
Sagittarius: Perception, expansion, travel, knowledge
Capricorn: Practicality, discipline, order, steadiness
Aquarius: Knowledge, mysticism, the unknown, individuality
Pisces: Dreams, intuition, feelings, divinity, beliefs

Moon Phases

Each phase of the moon has its own special energy that enhances your dream magic spells. The following is a brief overview of each phase of the moon.

MOON PHASES

Full Moon (night of the full moon): Highest moon power, dreaming, love magic, protection, initiation, fertility, creativity, prosperity, inspiration, healing, psychic ability, divination, high magic

Waning Gibbous (night after the full moon to seven days after the full moon): Banishing negativity, diminishing addictions, easing stress, help through divorce, ending relationships

Waning Crescent (seven days after the full moon to the new moon): Overcoming obstacles, getting rid of pain, discovering or uncovering deception, banishing negative energy

New Moon (night of the new moon): New relationships, new jobs, new beginnings, letting go of the past, neutralizing spells, banishing, binding, justice

Waxing Crescent (first day after the new moon until seven days after the new moon): Growth, protection for animals, change, help with business affairs

Waxing Moon (seven to ten days after the new moon): Forward movement, friendship, luck, psychic abilities, increased growth, prosperity, commitment

Gibbous Moon (ten to thirteen days after the new moon): Psychic awareness, divination, fruition, completion, patience, growth, harmony

Esbats

The esbats are the thirteen full and new moons of the year. As with the moon phases, each esbat has its special natural energy. The following are the names of the moons from Celtic tradition, together with the primary qualities of that specific moon. The moons are counted from the Winter Solstice, which usually falls on December 21. The first full moon after that date is the Wolf Moon, the second is the Storm Moon, and so forth. If the full moon and Winter Solstice fall on the same day, use an ephemeris to find out which comes first astrologically. If the moon is exact on the day of the Winter Solstice rather than on the eve before, then it is considered the first full "Wolf" moon.

ESBATS

Wolf Moon: Unity, dormancy, potential, clairvoyant dreams

Storm Moon: Intensity, duality, and polarity (as above, so below)

Chaste Moon: The threefold trinity of the Maiden, Mother, and Crone and Son, Father, and Grandfather; purification

Seed Moon: The four elements of manifestation and using elemental energies; planting seeds

Hare Moon: Control of the self and physical reality

Dyad Moon: Time and space, multidimensions, shapeshifting, and boons

Mead Moon: Lunar fertility, lucid dreams, spiritual connection

Wort Moon:[2] The yearly cycle; the beginning, middle, and end

Barley Moon: Wisdom, knowledge, harvest, and skill

Wine Moon: Prophecy, divination, inspiration, and healing

Blood Moon: Maternity, fecundity, ancestral communication

Snow Moon: Divine, royal, or noble purpose and intention

Oak Moon: The lunar cycle, rebirth and transmigration

The Eight Sabbats of the Sun

The eight sabbats, also called "the Great Days," follow the path of the sun as it moves through the annual changing of the seasons. Like an eight-spoked wheel, equally divided, the year is divided into eight equal parts with a sabbat marking each part. The solstices and equinoxes make four of the sabbats. The other four are situated evenly between the first four so that, for instance, Bridget's Fire is halfway between the Winter Solstice (Yule) and the Spring Equinox (Hertha's Day). Magical spells and rituals are tra-

---

[2] The "wort" represents a type of plant, such as pennywort. Also, in brewing beer the infusion of malted barley combined with hops and other grains produces a wort, which is combined with yeast.

ditionally performed on the eve of the sabbat. The designation of each sabbat is as follows:

THE EIGHT SABBATS OF THE SUN
Winter Solstice (Yule): At 00.00 degrees Capricorn
Imbolc (Bridget's Fire): Feb. 2 or at 15.00 degrees Aquarius
Spring Equinox (Hertha's Day): At 00.00 degrees Aries
Beltane (May Day): May 1 or at 15.00 degrees Taurus
Summer Solstice (Midsummer, Letha's Day): At 00.00 degrees Cancer
Lughnassad: First week of August, or at 15.00 degrees Leo
Autumnal Equinox (Hellith's Day): At 00.00 degrees Libra
Samhain (Halloween): October 31 or at 15.00 degrees Scorpio

Days of the Week

The days of the week correspond to the divine energies of the deities from whom they received their name. Wednesday derives its name from the Norse god Woden, also called Odin, who is known for his quest for knowledge, learning, and the mystical arts. The following is a listing of each of the days of the week and its energetic qualities. Use these qualities to make your dream magic rituals more powerful and your spells come true.

DAYS OF THE WEEK
Sunday (Sun's Day): Divine power, success, ambition, healing, tranquillity
Monday (Moon's Day): Beginnings, emotions, employment, flow, psychic abilities, childbirth, home, mysticism
Tuesday (Tyr's Day): Courage, strength, sexual energy, passion, steadiness, war
Wednesday (Woden's Day): Communication, knowledge, learning, creativity, mental ability, acting, writing
Thursday (Thor's Day): Legal matters, political power, expansion, wealth, luck, power

Friday (Freyja's Day): Love, romance, beauty, nature, the creative
  arts, music
Saturday (Saturn's Day): Property, inheritance, agriculture,
  structure, resolution, departure

The Elements and Directions

The four directions of north, east, south, and west relate to particular aspects of magic making. North is the home of the Gods and Goddesses, the ancestors, and divine power. Mental power, mastery, invention, and initiating patterns are all associated with the east. The south embodies transformation, the creative fire, and pure power, while the west represents emotions, feelings, and intuition.

Each of the four directions also corresponds to a specific element: earth is associated with north, air with east, fire with south, and water with the west or with all directions. The fifth element, spirit, is associated with the center and all directions. These key elements are integrated into the night spells and rituals in this book. When doing rituals and spinning spells, each element is represented on the altar. Earth is the bowl of salt or soil, air is the incense, fire is the candle, and water is the chalice filled with liquid.

The magical tools on your dream magic altar also reflect the elements. The element should be able to create the tool associated with it. For example, fire is necessary to forge metals, so the athame, or knife, is associated with fire. The bowl is made from clay, or earth.

One easy way to enhance your connection with the elements is by associating them with areas of your being. Verbally remind yourself that you are the elements. You can energize and empower yourself by chanting, "My flesh and bones are the earth; the earth is my flesh and bones; we are one. My breath is the air; the air is my breath; we are one. My eyes are the light; the light is my eyes; we are one. My emotions are water; water is my emotions; we are one. I am spirit; spirit is me; we are one." The more you practice this simple chant, the closer your rapport with the elements.

c

chapter two

Creating a Dream Altar

An altar enriches your spiritual life by offering a sacred space where you can spin spells, celebrate ritual, and ask for divine guidance and help. Approaching the altar, with its candles, incense, and tools, instantly evokes feelings of mystery and magic.

The word *altar* means "high place," which is symbolic not so much of altitude but of attitude. As a spiritual threshold to the divine energy of Oneness, an altar represents something that moves beyond this physical reality to a connecting place where the sacred and mundane meet. Because of this connection, your dream altar provides a focus and the means for gathering, patterning, and directing energy, the main activities of magic.

Your Dream Magic Altar

Your dream altar is the magical working surface that holds your tools, components, and other items you will use in magic making. Approach it with respect and a little ingenuity. Any sturdy surface in your bedroom will work, such as a bedside table, bureau of drawers, trunk, desk, or fireplace mantle. Place your altar in the north quarter or corner of your bedroom. North is the realm of midnight, deities, dreams, and magic. Accordingly, most people sleep and dream better lying from north to south.

Setting up a dream magic altar readies the stage for a year of magical dream adventures, guaranteed to enrich your life. First, gather together all the items you want to include on your altar. Then spread an altar cloth out on the altar surface, and arrange your altar tools and other magical components. The altar cloth is usually made of a natural material such as linen, cotton, silk, or wool. It can be any color, although midnight blue, black, silver, and white are natural choices for dream magic. You can also embroider or paint magical symbols such as stars and moons on your altar cloth.

The left side of your dream altar is the creative, nurturing side, dedicated to the Goddess, while the right side is traditionally the active, power side, dedicated to the God. Customarily, a statue or other image representing the Goddess is placed on the left side of the altar and an image of the God on the right side. You perform your invocations and gestures before these images, and you turn toward their direction when casting spells and doing rituals.

It's best to keep your altar fluid, changing it to reflect the different seasons, phases of the moon, your hopes and desires. In the spring you can dress your sacred dream altar with flowers such as daffodils and tulips, and in the winter you can place pine cones and pine or fir boughs on it. Also be sure to place all the items on your dream magic altar so that you can conveniently reach them, even in a darkened room.

Your Astral Dream Magic Altar

After setting up your bedroom altar, the time has come to create your astral dream magic altar. But remember, unlike a physical altar, your astral dream altar is fueled with your imagination, and thus it remains unhampered by physical laws. Your astral dream altar is a connecting place where you can enter and depart from the dream world.

To create your astral dream magic altar, you will need a small smooth white stone, a bowl of saltwater, and an active imagination. First, place the stone carefully in the bowl of saltwater for a few minutes to clear it of any unwanted energies. Rinse the stone with cool water for one minute, and after drying it hold the stone in your receiving hand (left if you are right-handed) while you sit or recline in bed. Empower the stone by saying,

> *Magical altar seen but not seen,*
> *Sacred stone table of my dreams,*
> *May I stand before you tonight,*
> *Beneath the starspun moonlight.*
> *So be it! So dream it so!*

Now close your eyes and visualize the stone becoming larger and forming into a natural stone altar resting in a sacred grove of stately oak trees. See and sense yourself standing in front of your astral dream altar, placing each of your imaginary altar tools on it one by one. Start simple, and then make your astral dream altar and magical tools more elaborate and unusual over time.

After laying your dream tools out on your astral altar, mentally connect them with a thread of brilliant white light. Move your attention and the radiant white thread from one object to another, filling them with light. Continue connecting the tools together with light, and as you do this sense yourself filling the stone in your left hand with the image of your astral dream magic altar.

Now lie back and continue to hold the stone in your hand. As you drift to sleep, repeat silently, "Dream it so." In the morning, give the stone a place of honor on your bedroom altar. Anytime you want to return to your astral dream altar, simply hold the stone in your left hand, close your eyes, and imagine yourself standing in front of your astral dream magic altar.

Dream Magic Altar Tools

Infused with the sacred energies of the Goddess and God, your magical tools are energetically alive. The implements you gather together, consecrate, and use regularly in magic become more than just symbols that trigger whole-brain activity. On a grander scale, they become essentially alive and a part of you while being energetically imprinted with your energy signature.

In dream magic, you can use physically tangible altar tools on your bedroom altar, and you can also use imaginary or energetic altar tools in dream state. Some of the spells and rituals in this book are designed to make use of altar tools both in spinning spells and doing rituals as well as in dream. The following is a basic listing of dream magic altar tools for your reference.

DREAM MAGIC ALTAR TOOLS

Athame: A double-edged knife purchased new for magical work. A symbol of creative fire, the athame is used to cut the sacred circle and can also be used practically to cut magical foods, to inscribe candles, and to carve runes on items. The athame's edges are often dulled for magical use to avoid accidents. (Remember to keep all knives in a safe place, away from young children and away from the edges of your altar table.)

Bell: A feminine symbol of the Goddess, the bell is rung during magic making to create the optimum vibration or frequency.

Bowl: Traditionally made of clay, the bowl corresponds to the north and the earth element. The universal purifier, salt, usually dry, and sometimes mixed with water, goes into the bowl. You can also use soil in your bowl.

Cauldron: A womblike, three-legged pot with its opening smaller than its base. The cauldron represents the Goddess and the water element and is usually made out of black cast iron. Candles can be set inside the cauldron and allowed to safely burn out.

Chalice or Cup: Symbol of water and the west, the chalice or cup holds water or wine. It is a vessel made of lead-free metal, stone, clay, or glass that represents the loving cup of the Goddess.

Dream Magic Journal or Dream Book of Shadows: This is your private dream journal that you write your dreams down in. The best time to do this is just upon waking and before you start moving around. If you prefer, you can use a small, handheld tape recorder for dream recall.

Drum: A bridge to the spirit or Otherworld. A magical tool of vibration and sound that is associated with the elements of air and earth. Also it is excellent for enhancing magical focus and merging. The head of a drum is sometimes broken when its owner dies as a way to free the person's spirit.

Incense Burner or Censer: Representing the fire and air elements, the incense and incense burner are almost always used in magic. A burner large enough to burn small papers is best. You can use a layer of sand or pebbles inside the burner as a base for the charcoal block(s). Pot pads, handles, or a chain are advisable if you are going to move the burner while it is hot.

Robe: Your magical skin, made of any fabric, color, or design. Reserve your robe for dream magic spells and rituals. When you put your robe on, you automatically move into a magical frame of mind. You can also work "skyclad" in your bedroom, wearing nothing at all.

Wand: Associated with the east and the air element and traditionally made from the wood of a fruit-bearing tree, wands are usually no longer than the length of your forearm. Considered the most ancient of tools, the wand is used in magic to bridge dimensions and direct energies in specific patterns.

Consecrating Your Dream Magic Altar Tools

The best time to consecrate your dream magic altar tools is at dusk or midnight on a sabbat or full moon. Before doing so, be sure to smudge the tools thoroughly with sage and cedar to clear out any unwanted energies. You can also wash your dream magic tools with dew before sunrise just before a full moon or a sabbat to cleanse them of any negative energies.

The easiest way to consecrate your dream magic tools and other items used in magic is by merging deeply with the divine energies of the Goddess and God, with the intention of imbuing the tools with the elemental qualities they embody of earth, air, fire, or water.

To consecrate the bowl, fill it with earth, hold it upward toward the north point of your sacred space, and say three times,

> *Generous and divine powers of earth,*
> *Fill this tool with your sacred energy;*
> *I ask this in the name of the Goddess and God,*
> *Blessed be! So shall it be!*

To consecrate your incense burner, hold the censer upward toward the east point of your sacred space and say three times,

> *Generous and divine powers of air,*
> *Fill this tool with your sacred energy;*
> *I ask this in the name of the Goddess and God,*
> *Blessed be! So shall it be!*

To consecrate your candleholder, hold it upward toward the south point of your sacred space and repeat three times,

> *Generous and divine powers of fire,*
> *Fill this tool with your sacred energy;*
> *I ask this in the name of the Goddess and God,*
> *Blessed be! So shall it be!*

To consecrate your chalice, cup, or cauldron, hold each one of them upward toward the west point of your sacred circle and say three times,

Generous and divine powers of water,
Fill this tool with your sacred energy;
I ask this in the name of the Goddess and God,
Blessed be! So shall it be!

To empower your tools even more, pass them through or sprinkle them with the corresponding element. For example, pass your candleholder through the flame of a candle, or sprinkle water on your chalice. When doing this, say,

With this element,
I consecrate this tool to the Goddess and God.
Blessed be! So shall it be!

You can also rub scented oils on your tools or set them out in the moonlight to empower them even more.

Another way to consecrate your dream magic altar tools is by merging and becoming One with the Goddess or God and asking the deity to impart her or his divine energy and aspects into the object you are focusing upon. Actually imagine the power of the Goddess and God pouring into the object, and then use your breath to physically pulse the divine energy into the item by breathing in and sharply exhaling through your nose. Do this at least three times and, for better results, nine times. Your breath and focused intention are the carrier waves that move the energy into the tool, thereby consecrating it and making it sacred.

Yet another way to consecrate tools is by sprinkling cool vervain tea on them. Sacred to the Roman moon Goddess Diana, vervain is called the enchanting herb and is reputed to be able to empower any magic making. It protects against negativity, both within and without, and is used in home and house blessings as well. It can be found at most health food stores and tea shops, through mail-order catalogs, and over the Internet. Or you can grow your own.

Smudging Your Sacred Space

You can purify your sacred space by smudging. The smoke of an herbal mixture of sage and cedar, sometimes blended with lavender, copal, or sweetgrass, cleanses your bedroom, altar, tools, magical components, and yourself of unwanted energies.

Smudge sticks are available at most health food and metaphysical stores and are relatively inexpensive. You can also grow or gather sage and cedar, dry the herbs, and either tie them in sticks or use the loose dry herbs for smudging. For a smokeless alternative to smudge, use sage and cedar oil in an aromatherapy diffuser, or put three drops of both sage and cedar oil in a pan or bowl of boiling water.

To smudge your bedroom, begin by lighting the smudge stick and blowing on it softly until it starts to smoke. Hold the burning smudge over a fireproof bowl or dish because a certain amount of the burning herbs will drop down as thick, hot ash. Allow the smoke to waft over your altar. Pass each of your altar tools through the smoke three times. Move in a clockwise circle around the room with the smudge and say,

> *May the Goddess and God*
> *Protect and bless this sacred space*
> *And rid it of all negativity.*
> *Blessed be! Blessed be the Gods.*

When you finish smudging the room, altar, tools, and yourself, douse the stick in water to put it out completely.

Drawing a Sacred Dream Circle

A place between worlds, the sacred circle allows you to relax into magical states of consciousness. Within the sacred circle, you can achieve a higher awareness, creating a connection to the divine and Oneness. A sacred circle acts as a vortex of light, setting up an energetic plane of communion between you and the Goddess and God. Drawn also as a means of protection from negative influences when you spin a spell or do ritual, the sacred circle is indispensable in dream magic. This is especially true since you are most vulnerable to psychic and magical energies when dreaming.

When you draw the sacred circle, feel free to work with Goddesses and Gods from other spiritual pantheons. The reason I have selected Kerridwen and Kernunnos is because I have the strongest rapport with the Celtic Goddesses and Gods. To successfully draw your sacred dream circle, you will need a compass, athame, and a bowl with salt in it.

Begin by determining the four directions of your bedroom by using a compass. Generally the altar is placed in the north point, so you can use it for a reference point and dispense with the compass. After determining the directions, start in the north point and, spinning clockwise very slowly with your arms stretched outward to your sides, imagine a clear, cobalt blue light washing out the entire room. As you do this, say aloud,

May all evil and foulness be gone from this place.
I ask this in the Lady's name.
Be gone, now and forevermore!

Starting and ending in the north direction, the direction of deity, use your athame to draw a clockwise circle around your bedroom, and be sure to include your altar and sleeping area. As you do this, see and sense a blue-white flame flaring from out of the blade like a laser beam, creating a bright energetic circle. If you don't have an athame handy, you can also use your wand or your dominant, power hand for this purpose. Just imagine the light flaring from the tip of the wand or from your fingertips.

Next, purify the four corners with salt by taking a pinch of salt from the bowl, tossing it gently toward the north point, and saying,

Ayea,[1] Ayea, Kerridwen!
Ayea, Ayea, Kernunnos!
Ayea, Ayea, Ayea!

If you prefer, you can use a sprig of greenery dipped in saltwater in place of the pinches of salt. After purifying the north point, repeat this process at the east, south, and west points, in that order. At each point, sprinkle a pinch of salt and repeat,

Ayea, Ayea, Kerridwen!
Ayea, Ayea, Kernunnos!
Ayea, Ayea, Ayea!

Then face the altar and say in a firm voice,

I consecrate this dream magic circle of power
To the Ancient Ones, to Goddess and God,
May they bless this circle with their presence.
Blessed be! Blessed be the Gods!
Blessed be all who are gathered here.

Knock nine times on the altar with the handle of your athame, in three series of three. Your dream circle is now set in place. While working magic in the circle, move clockwise, not widdershins (counterclockwise).

Calling In Your Dream Guardians

Like the traditional Watchtowers and four Wards, which are the lesser Goddesses and Gods who watch over the corners of the

---

[1]Pronounced "eye-yay."

sacred circle. These deities can be very helpful during magic-making. They weave a protective shield around your circle. Your dream guardians are ancient beings who protect you during night spells and rituals by standing guard at the four corners of your sacred dream circle. What sets them apart from traditional Watchtowers is that they not only stand guard while you are making magic, they also specifically watch over and protect you during sleep and dream.

Called the Ancient or Old Ones, these watchful guardians were originally the lesser Goddesses and Gods, whose task it was to watch over Earth and all the celestial realms. A different dream guardian rules and guards each gate or portal of the four elemental directions leading to the Otherworld.

Once you set your sacred dream circle in place, you call upon your dream guardians to stand guard at the thresholds of each of the four corners. They remain there until you release them.

Begin by facing north toward your altar, and then stretch your hands upward toward the moon and stars. Merge with the earth element and say,

> *Dream guardians of the north,*
> *Generous powers of earth,*
> *Protect the dream door of the north Ward,*
> *And guard this circle and all within.*
> *Come, I summon you!*

Now turn and face eastward, and stretch your arms toward the night sky. Merge with the air element and say,

> *Dream guardians of the east,*
> *Generous powers of air,*
> *Protect the dream door of the east Ward,*
> *And guard this circle and all within.*
> *Come, I summon you!*

Next, turn toward the south, stretching your arms upward once again. Merge with the fire element and say,

Dream guardians of the south,
Generous powers of fire,
Protect the dream door of the south Ward,
And guard this circle and all within.
Come, I summon you!

Then face to the west, and stretch your arms toward the moon and stars. Merging with the powers of water, say,

Dream guardians of the west,
Generous powers of water,
Protect the dream door of the west Ward,
And guard this circle and all within.
Come, I summon you!

Now stand in the center of your sacred dream circle and say,

Dream guardians of earth, air, fire, and water,
Grant me your power and protection tonight!

Your dream guardians are now set in place. A quicker way to set your dream guardians in place is to use four dream guardian markers. Positioned in the four directional corners of north, east, south, and west, around your sacred circle, these markers are magical symbols of your dream guardians. By consecrating them as dream guardian markers, and also by merging with the elements as you put them in place around your sacred circle, you can set your dream guardians in place without verbally calling them into the circle.

You can use four clear quartz points for markers. They can also be made out of wood or metal and then painted or inscribed with symbols of the four directions or inlaid with crystals and gemstones such as quartz, citrine, garnet, and moonstone. Wood markers can be consecrated with scented oils. By being used again and again in spells and rituals, your dream guardian markers increase in power and can be used to strengthen, focus, and amplify the energy in your sacred dream circle.

Cutting the Little Gate

Once you have set your dream guardians in place, it is customary to cut a "little gate," which is an energetic gate through which you can enter and exit physically without disrupting the magical energy of the circle. Cut this gate just below the east point of your circle either with your athame, holding it in your power hand, or with a sweeping gesture of your dominant hand. Be sure to close the little gate each time you enter and exit the circle. Do this with a sweep of your athame or power hand. I suggest that you cut the gate at your bedroom door, if possible, so you can easily come and go when doing night spells and rituals.

Pulling Up the Sacred Dream Circle

Once the spell is spun or the ritual completed, it is time to pull up your sacred dream circle. Do this by spinning counterclockwise while imagining the blue-white light of the circle being drawn back into your athame, wand, or hand.

Releasing Your Dream Guardians

After pulling up the circle, it is time to release your dream guardians. Start at the north point and say,

> *O generous powers of earth, depart in peace.*
> *Many blessings and thanks for your presence.*

Then face east and say,

O generous powers of air, depart in peace.
Many blessings and thanks for your presence.

Next turn to the south point and say,

O generous powers of fire, depart in peace.
Many blessings and thanks for your presence.

Then face west and say,

O generous powers of water, depart in peace.
Many blessings and thanks for your presence.

When using dream guardian markers, pull them up in the same order as you laid them down: north, east, south, and west. As you do this, merge with the elements and thank them for their presence, protection, and blessings, asking them to depart in peace.

After you are done releasing your dream guardians, knock three times on the altar with the base of your wand. Your night spell or ritual is now complete.

Note: It is crucial that you release your dream guardians when you are finished making magic. They are set in place specifically to guard your sacred circle, and to leave them in place is not only disrespectful of these energies, it is also pointless. It's egotistical to think these ancient energies are just waiting around to do your bidding. They come because they want to, because they are attracted to your field of energy and are willing to help you. They aren't willing to be divine victims of misuse.

c

chapter three

Dream Magic Components

Spell and ritual components enhance magic making by influenc-
ing your senses. Some components affect you visually, such as
symbols, colors, photos, the moon, stars, and written words. Some
are also kinesthetic, which means you can touch them and imprint
them with your personal energy. Kinesthetic magical components
include ritual tools, talismans, and stones. Auditory components,
such as invocations, chanting, singing, music, and drumming, are
also powerful additions to night spells and rituals, as are gustatory
items, which are things you taste and ingest, such as food and
beverages. Olfactory components are particularly effective in
magic because your conscious mind does not automatically filter
them. Examples of magical components that influence your sense
of smell are things like incense and essential oil. Intuitive components are more elusive and include things that represent a divine
or magical experience you have had, such as ritual jewelry. Often
magical components combine several sensual qualities in one,

affecting more than one sense at one time. For example, scented oils are both olfactory and kinesthetic and often influence your intuitive sense as well.

Basic List of Items Needed

Before doing each of the night spells and rituals in this book, be sure to gather together all the components you will need for the specific work. Always make certain you have all the items listed, plus matches or a lighter and a cloth to wipe your hands when using oils.

In addition to your altar and ritual tools, you will need some other items that you can easily gather together. You can purchase many of these items from markets, health food stores, drugstores, discount stores, new age shops, metaphysical stores, gift stores, department stores, mail order houses, and over the Internet. I encourage you to grow the herbs and flowers yourself. The following is a basic list of items you will need to perform all the spells in this book.

BASIC LIST OF ITEMS NEEDED

Almonds
Amethyst
    (tumbled)
Aloe vera juice
Answering
    machine
Aventurine
    (tumbled)
Apples
Barley
Bay leaves
Beads
Belt
Book of love
    poems

Buddha figurine
    (small)
Candleholders
Candles
Carrier oils
    (almond, olive,
    and sesame)
Cashews
Chalice
Charcoal blocks
Chocolate candy
Citrine (tumbled)
Coat hangers
Colored fabric
Colored felt pens

Compost
Computer
Cornucopia horn
Dictionary
Dollar bills
Dragon's blood oil
    (an essential
    oil)
Drawstring
    pouches
Drum
Elephant figurine
E-mail service
Envelopes
Essential oils

Feathers	Mirror	Silver anchor
Flashlight	Mushroom	charm
Flower seeds	Music	Silver bell
Flowers	Pecans	Silver chain
Fruit-bearing tree	Pebbles	Silver crocheting
(outdoors)	Photographs	thread
Fuzzy blanket	Plastic straws	Silver dollar
Glass jar with lid	Pot of soil	Silver needle or
Gloves	Potted fern	pin
Glue	Purple pouch	Smudge
Gold cup or	Quarters	Socks
chalice	Quartz crystals	Spices
Green bow	Quartz (tumbled)	Springwater
Green jade	Quill or ballpoint	Stapler
Green malachite	pen	Star confetti
Green moss	Ribbon, cord, or	Stone from a
Green sock	string	natural setting
Green underwear	Rice	Straws
Handkerchief	Ring	Sunflower seeds
Herbs	Rolled oats	Tape
Honey	Sacajawea dollar	Walnuts
Horseshoe-shaped	Saltwater	White and colored
magnet	Scissors	paper
Incense and resins	Sea salt	Wildflower seeds
Juice or wine	Seashell	Wire cutters or
Lotus oil	Sesame seeds	pliers
Matches	Shoes	Wire hangers

Candles

Candles have been used as part of spiritual rituals and ceremonies since the earliest times, primarily because they symbolize the power of light. Candles speak a mystical language. The words are expressed by the flickering and dancing flame, the billowing of the smoke, and the popping and crackling of the hot wax. Candle chatter and the direction of the flame denote magical communication. Each candle is unique and reflects its own personality when lit. Communicated by the fire element, the candle's personality is sometimes seen in mystical traditions as a small salamander encased within the flame.

It is important to be fire safe when using candles. Always use a fireproof holder and surface on your altar. Since in magic-making candles are almost always allowed to burn down completely on their own, and since you are using them for dream magic and may be letting them burn while you sleep, fire safety is essential! Metal candleholders withstand heat better than glass ones, and fireproof surfaces such as ceramic or metal are helpful.

When used safely, candles are a powerful change element, and candle magic provides a valuable and potent tool. The magical quality of a candle extends into the energetic realms, and its flame touches something deep within your being. The flame of the candle represents the spirit's highest potential while the smoke carries your wishes, prayers, and desires to the divine.

Different parts of the candle and candleholder represent certain aspects of being. The flame of the candle symbolizes the soul, while the wick, when lit, is the vehicle of transmutation. The halo of the flame symbolizes divinity and Goddesshood or Godhood, while the body of the candle represents the physical properties and, when lit, embodies all of the elements.

Candle magic can be as easy as dedicating a candle to a special God or Goddess. Making a simple dedication by lighting a candle in memory of an ancestor or a friend who has died is a form of candle magic. Birthday candles are still used for making magical wishes, and dreams still come true during romantic candlelight dinners.

Candles can be found just about everywhere. They come in all colors, shapes, and sizes. I have discovered amazing bargains on candles from stores that discount their products under a dollar. Gift, health food, and metaphysical stores all carry beeswax candles. Sweet smelling like honey, beeswax candles are ideal for magic making because they are biodegradable and can be buried. Also, bees were sacred to the Goddess and are still considered divine messengers. Unfortunately, beeswax candles are rather high priced. But, fortunately, you can order sheets of beeswax from bee supply stores and roll them up yourself, which not only saves you money but also empowers the candles as you make them. Match the color of your candle with your magical goal. Please refer to the color table later in this chapter for guidelines on the color of candle to be used for particular night spells or rituals.

I work primarily with votives and tapers because they are reasonably priced and easy to obtain. Beeswax tapers are my favorites. Not only do they smell honey sweet when they burn, they are natural and biodegradable. Also, once a year I make my own candles. You can do this, too, using beeswax, paraffin, natural dyes, or color crayons. Old milk cartons, toilet tissue rolls, or deep bowls filled with sand work great as molds, or you can buy premade candle molds from an arts and crafts supply store. Handcrafting your own candles for candle magic can be fun and particularly powerful. During each step of the process, merge with the ingredients and the procedure, placing your magical intention, expectation, and desire into the candle itself.

Before using candles for magic, it's always a good idea to wash them in cool saltwater to rid them of any unwanted energies. You can use a quill, ballpoint pen, awl, toothpick, or any other pointed tool to inscribe candles. Make sure you consecrate the tool by dedicating it to the Goddess and God. Then dress the candle with oil. When applying scented oils, rub the oil from the center of the candle body outward toward the candle ends. A word of warning: Always wipe any oil off your hands before lighting candles or incense!

It is also worth repeating: Make sure you provide a fireproof holder and surface for your candles so they can burn down in complete safety and without being disturbed. If you don't want to leave a candle burning when you are sleeping, snuff the candle out with a snuffer or with your wet fingers, and then light it again the next night so it can burn all the way down. Once it is completely burned, bury or discard the candle appropriately. Beeswax candles can be buried, while those made from synthetic materials are best put in a brown paper bag and placed in the garbage. One option is to keep the candle ends and then sort them by color, melt them, take out the old wicks, and make a new candle from the wax. A final note is never to use broken, chipped, or cracked candles for magic. The quality, color, and scent of a candle all add to its magical power, so broken, chipped, or cracked candles result in equally flawed magical results.

Essential Oils

The art and craft of making and using scented oils for magical purposes dates back to well before the rise of the Egyptian dynasty. Essential oils are concentrated essences from aromatic herbs, resins, and plants. Their fragrance and qualities have been extracted through steam distillation. Oils create a magical state of awareness, stimulating the body, mind, and spirit. You can also create a magical state with a particular oil or blend of oils. For example, make a dream oil using a blend of lavender, sandalwood, and vanilla oils, and use this scent in baths, on altar candles, for anointing in night spells and rituals, in sachets and charms, for consecrating magical tools, on every note you write, and on every gift you give. In this way, the scent immediately puts you into a magical state of awareness.

Oils are very potent, and care must be taken when using them. Be sure to make a skin patch test before using any oil on your skin. If you have any adverse reactions, immediately apply pure lavender oil or jojoba oil to the area to soothe the skin. Then discontinue using the oil, and try another carrier oil or brand. If certain oils irritate your skin, an option is placing a drop or two on a cotton ball and carrying it in your pocket.

The best place to purchase essential oils is from health food stores, since there you are more likely to find quality oils. A lot of inferior oils are available that are best avoided. Since oils are frequently used to anoint your body, use only pure essential oils. You can make a bottle of essential oil last a long time by mixing three, seven, or nine drops of the essential oil with a carrier oil. I prefer edible carrier oils such as sweet almond, sesame, or extra-light olive oil. Jojoba oil also works well. When you are pregnant, lavender essential oil is a good choice, using sesame oil as a carrier oil. Use only fresh oil. Add a few drops of wheat germ oil as a natural preservative if you find your oils do not keep well.

The basic fragrance oil formula is simple. First put the crushed or powdered herb, flowers, or resin in the oil, and then cap it. Charge the oil for magic by rubbing the vial between your palms until the oil is warm. As you are doing this, see a bright light of energy moving from your hands into the oil, empowering it for magic. Focus on the properties you want in the oil. Wait a few nights or a couple of weeks, until the fragrance is to your liking. I find that resins such as amber work best in oils when you use tiny pieces of the resin. The pieces float to the bottom, and the oil ages nicely like a fine wine, becoming even more magically potent.

If you don't want herbs and flowers in your finished oils, put the herbs or flowers in cheesecloth and suspend them by a string in a wide-mouthed bottle. I also suggest straining your finished products if you plan on keeping them for more than a few weeks.

The best bottles to store your oils in are dark brown bottles with a dropper top. I save all my brown herbal tincture bottles just for the purpose of storing my essential oils. Be sure to sterilize containers before using them by running boiling water over them, and be sure to label the bottle with the date, the type of oil, and the formula.

Incense and Resins
Made by blending together herbs, spices, resins, gums, and oils, incense fills the air with harmonious magical vibrations and opens the higher centers of consciousness. For thousands of years

incense has appeared on altars as an offering to the Gods and Goddesses. It was burned in temples to purify the worshipers, and it also represented the messages and prayers of the faithful rising toward the heavens.

Incense comes prepackaged in sticks, cones, and blocks, and it can be bought just about anywhere. You can also use loose herbs, flowers, and small pieces of resin laid directly on a smoldering charcoal disk. These small disks are available from health food stores and metaphysical shops. Be careful not to burn your fingers when lighting the charcoal. I suggest using a pair of tweezers to hold the charcoal disk while lighting it. I also recommend using a lit candle rather than a match or lighter to light the charcoal disk.

Set the lit disk into the bottom of your incense burner. Use a thin layer of pebbles, sand, or clean soil between the burner and the charcoal block. This will protect the burner. You can use powdered incense formulas prepared beforehand, or you can sprinkle herbs on, a pinch at a time. Be careful not to smother the lit disk. Then add drops of oil and place small pieces of resin on the burning herbs.

If you are sensitive to smoke, an option is to substitute essential oils, using an aromatherapy diffuser. Putting a few drops of essential oil in a small pan of boiling water or on a lightbulb also releases their powerful and magical fragrances.

Herbs

Nature communicates her mysteries directly to us through color, smell, taste, sound, shape, and texture as well as through subtle energies. Herbs are one of these mysteries—simple treasures for our use.

The ancients were familiar with the magical power of herbs, and the Hindus called them *yantras,* or sacred objects. People of all cultures found aromatic plants could be used for magic, medicine, and seasoning, and this herbal lore once formed the nucleus of medicine. Today herbs can be used in magic with incense and oils or in sachets, plackets, charms, and teas and on candles.

Because herbs are such hardy, common plants, they grow almost anywhere, under most any condition. Their natural herbal strength can be used to strengthen your magical night spells and rituals. The natural qualities of herbs can help you focus and send specific kinds of energy toward your magical goal.

To charge herbs for magical use, put them in a bowl, and hold your power hand over the bowl. Imagine bright energy and power coming from your hand and being absorbed by the herbs. Then mix the herbs with the same hand, and merge with their natural energies. Be present with the plant spirits, and thank them for giving you their power for your magic.

Like herbs, flowers also have magical qualities and uses and can be charged with energy. In Victorian times, flowers were used as a romantic language between lovers, to express feelings and intentions. Sending or bringing your beloved flowers reflects this tradition. The texture, shape, season, scent, and color of a particular flower, plus the traditional use of flowers, determines the flower's magical properties. Use your intuition when selecting flowers for your bedroom altar.

Growing your own herbs for dream magic spells and rituals imbues them with even more magical power. I would encourage everyone to grow herbs and cultivate a healthy connection to nature. Be sure to avoid using any metal (especially iron) garden implements, cooking pots, utensils, or containers when working with herbs and flowers, except when using them for incense. When gathering herbs, take no more than one-third of the foliage of a plant, and take only bits and pieces of bark from trees. Always treat plants with respect, thanking them for their natural gifts.

Crystals and Gemstones

Crystals and gemstones are gifts of nature, gifts revered and used by the ancient Chinese, Egyptians, Sumerians, Native Americans, and Celts, among others. Considered the holy water poured by the

Goddesses and Gods from the skies for the protection and blessing of humankind, crystals have long been used for magic around the world because of their energetic properties. A number of alchemists, wizards, sorceresses, and magicians throughout history have known and applied various knowledge of the alchemical science of crystal energies.

Physical form, we now know, is made up of energy. Everything that exists is an external manifestation of an energy form, a rate of vibration. Quartz crystals and gemstones have extremely high and exact rates of vibration, which can be manipulated precisely to augment, transform, amplify, store, and focus other rates of vibrations. This makes them powerful tools for magic!

According to modern science, quartz crystals and gemstones consist of naturally balanced, solid-state energy fields. These energetic field properties can be harnessed for spiritual and magical purposes. By using crystals and gemstones, thoughts can be amplified and transformed, intensifying your magical field of intention and enhancing your dream magic abilities and powers.

Dream Stone

Your own dream stone is used in some of the night spells and rituals in this book. First, select the kind of stone you want to use as your dream stone. I would recommend a piece of clear quartz, amethyst, rose quartz, or citrine as your first dream stone. To clear out any unwanted energies in your dream stone, place it in your left hand, covering it with your right. Next imagine a clear pool of water in your mind. Breathe in deeply, seeing and sensing the clear water washing out your dream stone, and then pulse your breath out sharply through your nose, as if to set the image in place in the stone.

To program your dream stone, repeat the clearing process, only instead of imagining clear water in your dream stone, imagine what you want in it, from spiritual clarity to prosperity or maybe a new relationship. The choice is yours.

After programming the stone, hold it in your nondominant or receiving hand (left if your are right-handed) as you sleep, noticing how it affects your dreams. Check out different types of stones, programming them for various things while again observing their effects on your dreams. You can also intentionally bring your dream stone into your dreams, using it for energizing, traveling, and healing. As you drift to sleep, simply repeat to yourself,

> *Dream stone of light,*
> *Dream with me tonight.*

Keep this stone next to your bed, under your bed, or in your pillowcase in a natural fabric bag for cushioning, or hold it in your receiving hand at night as you drift to sleep. The power of the stone entrains your dreams, just as your energy entrains the dream stone. The following is a list of stones you can use for dream magic, along with their properties.

DREAM STONE

Agate: Grounding and balancing your dreams, self-confidence, balance

Amethyst: Divine communication, wisdom, banishing nightmares, dream protection, mental clarity

Citrine: Dream messages, mental clarity, dispelling negative dreams, empowerment, remembering your dreams

Clear Quartz: Ultimate dream magic stone, spiritual connection, divine guidance, healing dreams, divine dreams, time travel, astral travel

Diamond: Divine inspiration, remembering your dreams, amplifying dream energies, protection, magical dreaming

Herkimer Diamond (an extremely hard diamond): Propitious for all kinds of dream magic, stimulating higher awareness, filtering out negative dreams

> *Jade:* Helpful for dream protection, calming your mind, enhancing
> your dream awareness, encouraging prosperity and abundance
> *Pyrite:* Wealth, prosperity, abundance, plenty (make sure your piece
> of pyrite holds together and doesn't flake apart)
> *Rose Quartz:* For dreams of love and romance, enhancing dream
> creativity, divine inspiration in your dreams, personal
> attunement, promoting flexibility in dreams
> *Turquoise:* Skywalking, dream wisdom, actualizing your dreams,
> dream communication with your ancestors, devas, and
> elemental beings such as faeries

Color Correspondences

Color plays an essential role in magic and in dream, just as it does in your everyday world. Color reflects light. In our very visual world, color influences everything you see and affects the way you act and feel. It can be used to strengthen your magical field of intention. For example, the color green promotes growth, prosperity, and harmony, while cobalt blue is used for protection and healing. The following correspondences can be used as a guide for incorporating color into your magical spells and rituals. Remember to use your intuition, and select the colors you feel are the best ones for the dream work at hand.

> **COLOR CORRESPONDENCES**
> *White:* Divinity, inspiration, spiritual guidance, motivation, power,
> ritual, positive power, perfection, purity, love, peace, protection,
> Oneness
> *Gray:* Wisdom, merging, cosmic consciousness, creative life force,
> balance, mastery, mystery
> *Black:* Protection, banishing negative and harmful energies, ending
> relationships, the shadow self, sleep, dreaming, mystery, the
> ethers, night, all of the elements

Blue: Divination, dreams, travel, healing, loyalty, psychic protection, cleansing, clarity, harmony, peace, moving energy, emotions, higher wisdom

Purple: Psychic ability, ancestral lore, respect, sacredness, consecration, active protection, divine dreaming, higher wisdom, spiritual healing, leadership

Pink: Friendship, love, play, healing emotions, children, kinship, kindness, compassion, romantic love

Rose: Divine love, enlightenment, divine communion, nirvana

Red: Passion, sexual energy, the physical body, dynamic force, vitality, virility, courage, blood, healing, rebirth, determination, power, animation, intense desire

Orange: Pleasure, joy, generosity, success, happiness, gladness, mirth, ease and comfort, prosperity, plenty, the hearth, home, friendship, happiness, meditation, fair play, justice, productivity

Yellow: Imagination, knowledge, learning, teaching, studying, mental agility, understanding, cognition, truth, fact, comprehension, communication, perception, happiness

Green: Creativity, birth, spring greening, healing, ambition, prosperity, abundance, money, regeneration, renewal, growth, nature, good luck, fertility

Brown: Earth, pets, animals, potential, nurturing, birth and rebirth, home, common sense, stability

Gold: Higher wisdom, expanded awareness, creativity, wealth, strength, security, the sun, solar power

Silver: Dreaming, lunar and stellar power, ancestral communication, emotions, peace, divine insight, prediction, clairvoyance, astral travel, divination

Magical Symbols

We use symbols to communicate on a daily basis. Whether you are aware of it or not, you are continuously encircled by symbols and signs, and your dreams are filled with them. Volumes of books have been written solely on the subject of dream symbols, most of them valuable only to those few individuals with the same cultural, social, and environmental associations as the author who penned them. The reason for this is that symbols often mean different things to different people. Each of us places our own valences on the symbols around us, including magical symbols. For example, some people think that a black cat is bad luck, but my personal experience has been just the opposite, so I consider black cats lucky, loving, and helpful.

As you can see, symbolism occurs with the process of association. Your mind uses symbols to arouse these associations so that a complex concept is encompassed, for example, by a word, song, sign, gesture, body position, or picture. This is particularly useful in magic, for instance, drawing a pentacle in ritual to bring divine protection, power, and elemental rapport.

Magical symbols are an important part of the art and craft, and like all symbols they have a layered quality, representing collections or clusters of thought and feeling. One thing gives meaning to another, with personal experience adding another valence to symbolic representations. Symbolic association stretches the capacity of thought and expression and becomes a channel for conveying universal and mythic concepts. When people for hundreds, if not thousands, of years focus on a symbol, it gives it magical power. A very real field of energy is created around it. Whenever you use that symbol, you are tapping into that energy. In this way, symbols go beyond definition and take on magical proportions.

The power of magical symbols stems from their ability to influence your subconscious and unconscious minds and thus alter the way your conscious mind perceives the world. A magical symbol stands for or represents a combination of divine and elemental energies and triggers a powerful response in you.

Magical symbols and dreams are the perfect fit, with magical symbols acting as focal points in dream magic and giving greater power and depth to your spells and rituals. They are used primarily as a magical shorthand and to consecrate tools as well as in ceremonial magic, in forms of divination, and to build power. In every moment the Goddess and God impart their wisdom in the form of symbols and signs. It is up to you to watch, listen, and learn.

You can use the traditional magical symbols drawn here, or create your own. Many of those who practice the art and craft also use a magical symbol in conjunction with their signature for protection and empowerment. I strongly recommend doing so. Also, I suggest you familiarize yourself with the meaning of specific magical symbols before using them, in order to use their power correctly. The following are a few of the magical symbols you can use in your night spells and rituals.

Pentacle	New Moon	Travel
The Triple Goddess	Waxing Moon	Ankh
The Horned God	Full Moon	Owl Goddess
Earth	Waning Moon	Bird Goddess
The Circle	Moonrise	Gift
Female	Moonset	Candle
Male	Love	
Altar	Craft Sign	

c

chapter   four

Love Dream Magic

The first step in loving another person is understanding who you are as a person. Before delving into the spells and rituals for finding and attracting love, first take some time and think about your own characteristics, needs, and desires. By doing so, you begin to understand the qualities of the person who would best match your own needs and desires and also the nature of the relationship you would want with this person. People often put the needs of others before their own, with the best of intentions, but this is not practical and only creates frustration and resentment in the long run.

You can use your dreams to explore who you are by thinking about who you are in your dreams. Now compare this dream image with the image you have of yourself in your waking world. How close are these images? What are the similarities and differences? Your dream image is as much your genuine self as the face you put on each day. There is essentially no separation between your dream self and waking self. This is a key in actualizing your dreams and aspirations, which is what dream magic is all about.

Once you have a better understanding of who you are, the next step is to begin seeing yourself in a relationship with a person who fulfills your needs and desires. Again, you can use your dreams to experience different types of relationships with different people, transporting yourself ahead in time and seeing how a particular situation may unfold. In this way, you can use your dreams to try things on and get a sense of how they fit. Often it is wise to feel and act things out in your dreams first, then act them out in waking reality.

Love dream magic, like all magic, works best when it is done for the greater good and not against anyone's will. It is most effective when you influence events to unfold as you desire rather than manipulating others against their will. For easy reference, the following do's and don'ts are some basic guidelines to follow when doing dream magic for love, romance, and attraction.

DO'S AND DON'TS

Do use love magic to strengthen your relationship.

Do use love magic to spice up your relationship.

Do use love magic to empower your relationship.

Do use love magic to bring more love into the world.

Do use love magic to experience a more expanded sense of love and pleasure.

Do use love magic to experience ecstasy and bliss.

Do use love magic to find the best possible lover and mate.

Do use love magic to keep your faith in love alive.

Do use love magic to protect your relationship.

Don't use love magic to harm others or break up marriages or existing relationships.

Don't use love magic on celebrities, famous personalities, or people you don't know.

Don't use love magic to manipulate people into loving you.

Don't use love magic as a replacement for real love.

Don't use dream love magic to make up for a lack of love in the waking world.

◖ Tonight's Magical Adventure: Bridget's Eve Love Wish

This spell is best done on Bridget's Eve, which is usually February 2 or 3, the perfect time for asking Bridget to grant you one special wish. She is the Celtic Goddess of love, creativity, and healing. Bridget's name means "bright one," for she kindles the need-fire, in this case, the loving fire in your heart and in your lover's heart.

LIST OF ITEMS NEEDED: Lavender incense and censer ★ Fresh flowers ★ 1 white beeswax candle and holder ★ Silver needle or pin ★ Small piece of red cloth

✷ Spinning the Spell

After placing the flowers on your bedroom altar, draw a sacred circle and call in your dream guardians. Then light the incense, dedicating it to Bridget by chanting her name three times. Next bathe the silver needle or pin in the incense smoke for a few moments. Then take the silver needle or pin and pierce the wick of the unlit candle. Now light the candle and chant three times,

> *Goddess Bridget of the sacred fire,*
> *Bring to me my heart's desire.*
> *Sacred Lady, sacred light,*
> *Bring to me this wish tonight!*
> *(Say what your love wish is)*
> *By divine will, so mote it be!*

Sit or lie back comfortably, and merge with the candle flame. Imagine your wish coming true as the candle burns all the way down. As you drift to sleep, keep focusing on your wish coming true.

In the morning, take the silver needle or pin, fasten it to the small piece of red cloth, and put it under or next to your bed, leaving it there until your love wish comes true. Then thank the Goddess Bridget, pull up the circle, and release your dream guardians.

☾ Tonight's Magical Adventure:
Lover Attraction Spell

Perfect for Valentine's Day eve, this spell can be used to really heat
up the passion in your relationship. Love is the most sacred gift we
can give to each other and ourselves. Desire and emotion fuel and
ignite all magical adventure. If you want to draw your lover to you
for a night of romance and passion, use this lover attraction spell.

LIST OF ITEMS NEEDED: Photograph of your lover or
proposed lover ✶ Chocolate candy ✶ Vanilla incense or diffuser
with vanilla oil ✶ 1 red candle ✶ Rose oil ✶ 3 rose petals ✶
Small red pouch or sock

✷ Spinning the Spell

Draw a sacred circle and call in your dream guardians. Then set
the photograph in front of the candle on your altar. Place the
candy and rose petals next to the photograph, and light the
incense. Next dress the candle with rose oil and light it, dedicating
it to a favorite love Goddess or God. Then take the rose petals and
hold them in your hands. Focus on the candle flame, and begin to
see your lover's image in it. As you do this, repeat three times,

> *Sacred petals, sacred fire,*
> *Bring to me my heart's desire.*

Put the rose petals in the red pouch or sock, and tuck it inside
your pillowcase. Now take the chocolate candy in your hands, and
again focus on the candle flame as you say three times,

> *Bring to me love so sweet,*
> *Blessed love, what a treat!*

Unwrap the candy, and begin eating it slowly, savoring each
mouthful just as you savor the sweetness of your lover. Allow the

candle to burn down completely, and as you drift to sleep, visual-ize your lover's image. Within the next twenty-four hours, your lover will come to you.

In the morning, thank deity, pull up the circle, and release your dream guardians.

◖ Tonight's Magical Adventure: Candle Magic Love Spell

The ancient Upanishadic philosophers said that if no desire stirs and no dream is seen, then the human spirit stays in a state of sleep. This points to the importance of desire and dreams as essen-tial elements for awakening your higher self. This Candle Magic Love Spell provides a way to ignite your desires and dreams, resulting in earthly and divine love joining together into One. This spell is best done on a Friday night during the waxing moon. Use it to draw more love into your life.

Candles are fabulous meditative aids, and candle magic works along the same pattern as all other magic, using intention, expec-tation, desire, and merging. When lit, a candle signifies revelation and touches upon the mysterious while its flickering softly illumi-nates the divine connection deep within you. The flame represents your spirit's highest potential, and the smoke carries your wishes and desires to deity.

LIST OF ITEMS NEEDED: 1 red candle ★ 1 white candle ★ Ballpoint pen or quill ★ Vanilla or rose oil ★ 3 clear quartz points ★ 3 bay leaves (fresh or dried) ★ Soft music

✸ Spinning the Spell

Before doing candle magic, take a warm bath with bath salts or essential oil to cleanse your energy field. This also gets you into a more relaxed state of body, mind, and spirit. After washing yourself, begin dressing your candle by immersing it in cool saltwater and drying it. Place the candle and all the other items on your altar.

Next turn on some soft music, draw a sacred circle and call in your dream guardians. Call in one special love God or Goddess to help you with this spell, and also select a power animal to assist you, one that you feel is approachable, not fearful, such as a cat, hare, dove, or deer. Then take the candles, one at a time, and with the ballpoint pen or quill carve the initials of the God or Goddess, the power animal, and your initials on the candle bodies. Next inscribe both candles with interlocking hearts. This symbolizes the linking together of divine and earthly love. Apply the oil to the carved candles, covering them completely with a thin film of oil, and then place the candles back in their holders. Take the three bay leaves and position them in a triangular pattern around the candles. These leaves protect and strengthen your magic. Then place the three crystal points on top of the bay leaves, pointed outward and away from the candles. These stones act as amplifiers for magical energy. Light the red candle with care. Then light the white candle from the red candle. Merge with the two flames and repeat three times,

Fires of passion and desire so true,
Kindle and warm my heart anew.
By silver moon and bright starlight,
Bring to me my love tonight.
Separate flames, joined as one,
As I will, so it is done!

Continue gazing at the candle flames for at least five minutes. You can use a mirror behind the candles to amplify their light, at which point you can gaze into both the flame and its reflection. Moving your eyes between the reflection in the mirror and the actual flame eases eye discomfort. By breathing deeply, you can intensify your focus and, in turn, the depth of your merge. Keep your intention and expectation in mind as you watch the candle flames. You may even see an image of your love in the flames, someone you already know or someone you have yet to meet.

Make a mental note of any images or messages you receive while merging with the flames. After you are finished, anoint your forehead with a drop of oil, lie back, and drift to sleep. Allow the candles to burn down completely. If you need to put out the candles, do so with wetted fingers or, even better, a snuffer. A seashell also works well for this purpose.

In the morning, thank the God or Goddess and the power animal that helped you with the spell. Pull up the circle and release your dream guardians. Place the three quartz points on your altar to draw the love energy to you. Put the three bay leaves under your mattress or in your top bureau drawer to protect and strengthen the spell. Take any remaining candle pieces, put them in a plastic bag, and tuck it into your bureau or desk drawer to bring your lover to you, tonight and every night.

☾ Tonight's Magical Adventure: Linked Souls Dream Charm

People in medieval courts of love speculated about whether romance and love originated in the heart or in the head. They also questioned whether love entered through the eye or through the ear. Using your heart, head, eyes, and ears, this spell promotes a satisfying, romantic, and loving relationship with your current lover. Spin it on a Tuesday or Friday night, on or close to a full moon.

LIST OF ITEMS NEEDED: 1 red candle ⋆ Tube of red lipstick, red crayon, or red felt pen ⋆ Sheet of white paper ⋆ 3 rosebuds (dried)

✳ Spinning the Spell

Draw a sacred circle and light the candle. Use the red crayon, lipstick, or felt pen to draw two interlinking hearts on the paper. Draw the hearts with gusto, tracing them over three times. Afterward, write your name and your lover's name inside each of the two hearts. As you do this, see and feel yourself and your lover experiencing a deeper, more loving relationship than you ever experienced before. Dare to dream for a few moments, experiencing exactly how wonderful your relationship can be and will be in the very near future. Hold the rosebuds between your hands, and charge them with these hopeful and loving energies. As you do this say,

At this hour, on this night,
I seek to find my heart's delight.
I call upon the Ancient Powers,
Link our love with these flowers.
Grant this sacred loving dream,
As I will, so mote it be!

Now sprinkle the rosebuds on the paper, over the interlinked hearts. Wrap the paper around the hearts and flowers, folding it nine times and finally sealing it with red wax from the candle. Place the folded and sealed paper in your bureau drawer or in a special box. Allow the candle to burn down completely as you drift to sleep, thinking about your loving dream. In the morning, write down anything you recall from your dreams. Then pull up the circle. By the next full moon, your relationship will grow more intensely passionate and loving.

C Tonight's Magical Adventure: Beltane Love Spell

Beltane is the "old" pagan name for the May Day festivities still celebrated today. Useful for both drawing a new love interest into your life and deepening the passion in your existing relationship, this Beltane Love Spell provides just the spark to kindle a little romance and old-fashioned passion.

LIST OF ITEMS NEEDED: Red altar cloth ★ 2 pink candles with holders ★ 1 finger-sized clear quartz crystal point ★ Vanilla incense and censer or vanilla oil and diffuser

✳ Spinning the Spell

Draw a sacred circle and set your dream guardians in place. Next put the two pink candles in holders on your altar side by side about four inches apart. Then light the candles. Place the clear quartz crystal point between the candles with the point toward you. Gaze at the crystal, and sense or see the image of your lover (or prospective lover) within the crystal. As you gaze into the crystal, chant these words of power:

> Candle light, lover's fire
> Burn strong, burn bright.
> Crystal fire, lover's desire
> Burn long, burn bright.
> Sacred love, sacred light
> Beloved, be mine tonight.

Leave the circle open while you sleep, allowing the candles and incense to safely burn all the way down. In the early morning, take the crystal outside and wash it in the morning dew and then place it under your mattress. Then pull up the circle and release your dream guardians.

☾ Tonight's Magical Adventure: Finding Your Soul Mate Spell

Your soul mate is that special someone who feels like a divine and essential part of you. Soul mate relationships are sacred relationships and often long lasting. Best spun on a Friday night on a full moon, this spell can be used to find your soul mate by walking through the dream door of Oneness.

LIST OF ITEMS NEEDED: Sheet of paper and pen ★ White votive candle and holder ★ Rose oil ★ Your dream altar stone

✵ Spinning the Spell

Draw a sacred circle and call in your dream guardians. On the piece of paper, write down all the aspects you would like your soul mate to have. Place the paper on your altar where you can see it. Next take the candle and cover it with rose oil, all the while visualizing your soul mate. Place the candle in its holder and light it. While staring into the flame, see each one of the characteristics of your soul mate coming to life in the fire. Say these words:

Who is my soul mate?
Show my soul mate to me,
In this flame, in this dream,
In this life. So mote it be!

Now take your dream altar stone from the altar. Hold it in your receiving hand (left if you are right-handed), and lie back in bed. Close your eyes, get comfortable, and visualize yourself lighting a white candle at your natural stone dream altar. Again stare into the candle flame at the dream altar and imagine your soul mate coming to life in the fire. Repeat the words,

Who is my soul mate?
Show my soul mate to me,
In this flame, in this dream,
In this life. So mote it be!

See yourself enter into the flame as if it is a doorway into another dimension. You see images before you that begin to come into focus. Your senses feel heightened as you see the image of your soul mate before you. Allow the candle to safely burn down on its own. As you drift to sleep, repeat the words "Soul mate dreams."

In the morning, write down your dreams in your dream magic journal. Then pull up the circle and release your dream guardians. By the next full moon, you will meet your soul mate in your waking life.

◖ Tonight's Magical Adventure: Loving Partner Dream Charm

We all yearn for a more loving partner at some point in our lives. This Loving Partner Dream Charm can be used to encourage your lover to be more attentive and amorous in your dreams and in waking life. Ask your lover's permission before doing this spell. Make this charm during the waxing moon in the summer, preferably on a Friday night. I suggest you grow your own sunflowers, drying the seeds to use in this charm. Growing your own herbs, flowers, fruits, and vegetables always gives them a little more magic and power. Plus, it allows you to get in touch with the earth in a more intimate way.

LIST OF ITEMS 36 sunflower seeds ⋆ 1 pinch sweet basil ⋆ 1 pinch cinnamon ⋆ 6-inch by 6-inch piece of pink cloth ⋆ Yard-long pink ribbon, cord, or string ⋆ Red felt pen

✷ Spinning the Spell

Use the felt pen to draw an X on the cloth. Write in your initials and your partner's initials on top of the X. Count out thirty-six sunflower seeds, and place them on the cloth. Next cover the seeds with the pinches of basil and cinnamon. Gather the four corners of the cloth, and tie them firmly with the pink ribbon, winding the ribbon around the bag six times and then tying the knot six times. Six is the number associated with Venus and the home. Hold the charm bag between your hands, merge with the divine, and say,

> *Spice and seeds,*
> *Bring to me,*
> *A more loving partner.*
> *So mote it be!*

Place the charm bag in your lover's bureau drawer to encourage a more loving relationship now and in the future.

◖ Tonight's Magical Adventure:
Lustful Encounters Love Spell

At some point in your life, you have probably wished for a night of intense romance and wild passion, and possibly at times have even had the delightful opportunity to experience this kind of bliss. Now with the Lustful Encounters Love Spell, you can set the stage for a special night of passionate and lustful lovemaking. You can spin this spell with your partner or solo, with the best times being on the eight sabbats, especially Beltane (May Day) and Samhain (Halloween). Fridays and full moons are also good times to cast this spell.

Recent studies have shown that safe sex actually helps to keep your body, mind, and spirit healthier by strengthening your immune system. If making love can keep you healthier, just think what a night of lustful romance and wild passion can do for you! *Lustihood* actually means "robustness" or "vigor of body or spirit," again suggesting lust and sex can be combined to create a powerful healing potion.

As a means of attracting the energies of lust, intense desire, and passion, this spell uses an herb of Venus (apple) with one of Mars (vervain). These herbal energies encourage your natural ability to find joy and pleasure in love. Vervain helps to achieve sexual fulfillment, and lovers or newlyweds sometimes use it to bring extra bliss on their first night together. Known for enhancing the dreaming process, vervain promotes dreams of love and passion. The apple is associated with the qualities of fertility, good luck, and immortality. Also, when cut in half horizontally, the seed cavity of an apple produces a five-pointed star, a sacred magical symbol.

LIST OF ITEMS NEEDED: Soft, sexy music ⋆ Jasmine incense and censer ⋆ 2 red candles ⋆ 1 pinch vervain ⋆ Ylang-ylang oil ⋆ 1 green stone ⋆ 1 clear stone ⋆ 1 red stone ⋆ 1 blue stone ⋆ 1 apple, cut into four sections

✳ Spinning the Spell

I suggest a warm bath or shower with your partner before spinning this spell. This sets the stage, creating a cozy, more relaxed state of body, mind, and spirit.

Begin by drawing the sacred circle of light and calling in your dream guardians. Place everything you will need on the altar, light the incense, and turn on some soft, sexy music. Next rub both candle bodies with ylang-ylang oil, and then anoint your forehead, both wrists, shoulders, hips, knees, ankles, and feet. When doing this spell with another person, you anoint him or her, and vice versa.

Set the candles a few inches apart at the center of the altar, and then build the stone and herbal grid around them. Do this by placing the stones in a cross formation around the candles, with the green stone in the north position (top), the clear stone in the east (right), the red stone at the south (bottom), and the blue stone in the west (left). Next cut the apple in four equal parts, and place a section of apple next to each of the stones. Put a bit of the vervain herb at the base of both candleholders. When working with a partner, take turns placing the objects around the candles.

As you light the candles, dedicate each to a love Goddess and God, honoring the Goddess first: for example, Caer and Angus (Celtic), Shakti and Shiva (Hindu), Freyja and Frey (Norse). Please refer to the appendixes of Goddesses and Gods at the back of this book for specific deities. When working with your partner, you each light a candle and then kiss after lighting the candles. When working solo, blow an etheric kiss to the Goddess or God after lighting the candles.

Next focus all your awareness on the flames of the two candles for a few moments, and say,

> *Candle burning, candle bright,*
> *Show the way to sweet delight.*
> *Candle burning, candle bright,*
> *Your lustful fire heats the night.*

Say the words together when doing this spell with your lover. Next take the apple pieces and eat them one a time, starting with the top (north) piece. Just before eating each apple piece, hold it in your hands and say,

This, a gift so divine
Sends its love for all time.
This, with nectar so sweet
Venus and Mars once again meet.
So be it! So mote it be!

When working with a partner, have him or her feed you the apple, alternating between the two of you. While munching on the apple, visualize a night of intense and pleasurable lovemaking with your lover (or prospective lover). Allow the candles to burn out completely as you enjoy a night of lustful love and erotic dreams.

In the morning, pull up the circle, release the dream guardians, and place the four stones on your dream magic altar as a reminder of your wild, passionate nature. A tip is to use ylang-ylang oil each time you want to have a night of lustful and passionate love-making. In this way, just the scent of the oil will put you in an altered and very sexy state of consciousness.

◖ Tonight's Magical Adventure: Moon Fertility Magic

In Greek mythology, the moon Goddess Selene had influence over the reproductive powers of plants, animals, and people. She was so enchanted by Endymion's beauty that she went to Mount Latmos to kiss him as he slept and to sleep at his side. It was the God Hypnos who allowed Endymion to sleep with one eye open so he could ever gaze upon his beloved. Thus he was placed in eternal sleep, becoming the never-waking but ever-seeing lover of the moon.

This spell taps into the fertile power of the moon. Spin it on a full moon, preferably on a Monday, Tuesday, or Friday night in the spring. Its purpose is to enhance fertility.

LIST OF ITEMS NEEDED: 3 daffodils in a vase filled with water ★ 1 green candle ★ 1 green stone ★ Sheet of paper ★ Green felt pen ★ 6 handfuls of rich soil compost in a bowl ★ Fruit-bearing tree (outdoors)

❋ Spinning the Spell

Draw the sacred circle, set your dream guardians in place, and light the candle. Next put the vase of daffodils next to your bed. Then, on the sheet of paper, write exactly what you expect. For example, "I (name) and my lover (name) want to conceive a strong and healthy child in the next year." Take a handful of the compost and place it on the paper. Then put the green stone on top of the compost. Drip six drops of candle wax on top of the stone. Then fold the compost, stone, and wax up in the paper, folding the paper a total of three times. Hold the paper in your hands and say,

> Soil of fertility, stone of birth,
> Powers of air, fire, water, and earth,
> Make us fertile and help us conceive,
> The healthy and happy child of our dreams.
> So be it! So dream it so! Blessed be!

Place the paper and bowl of soil on the altar overnight, and allow the candle to burn down completely. As you drift to sleep, repeat the words "Fertility grow, dream it so!"

In the morning, pull up the circle and release your dream guardians. Go outside with the paper and bowl of compost. Bury the paper filled with compost, the stone, and wax under a fruit-bearing tree at its easternmost point. Next divide the compost into five mostly equal handfuls, and toss them carefully around the tree, moving clockwise. With each handful say,

Sacred tree, help us conceive
The healthy child of our dreams.

Thank the tree spirit, and take the bowl back inside. Keep the fresh daffodils next to your bedside to increase fertility. When they wither, place them under the same tree and say,

Fertile flowers and sacred tree,
Help us conceive the child of our dreams.

Over the next nine months, tend the tree, touching, watering, and caring for it as you would a child. During this time, you are most likely to become pregnant.

◖ Tonight's Magical Adventure: Dream Lover Charm

The Greeks called the dream lover an incubus. To incubate means "to lie on" and to maintain conditions favorable to optimum growth. The otherworldly incubus or dream lover is symbolic of the mysterious flow of universal awareness, and when the divine dream lover joins his or her light with mortals, sacred knowledge and love can be imparted. The purpose of the Dream Lover Charm is to draw your ideal dream lover to you.

Create this charm on a Tuesday or Friday night during the waxing moon. The red rose, which is a Goddess herb belonging to Venus (the morning and evening star) and the water element, and rose incense and oil are used to conjure up your dream lover. Like other herbs of Venus, the rose has beautiful flowers and red fruits. It attracts devic love energies as well as the highest spiritual vibrations within yourself and the cosmos.

LIST OF ITEMS NEEDED: 1 red rose ⋆ 1 red candle ⋆ Rose oil ⋆ Rose incense and censer ⋆ Small red cloth bag or pouch

✳ Spinning the Spell

Draw a sacred circle and call in your dream guardians. Then rub rose oil on the candle, your wrists, ankles, throat, and forehead. Wipe the oil from your hands, and light the candle and incense. Clear your mind, take a few deep breaths, and then take the rose and hold it gently between your hands. Smell its aroma, taking a few more deep breaths as you inhale the rose's scent. Now hold the rose in front of the candle so that it is illuminated and say,

Candle light, sacred light,
Burn steady, burn bright.
Scent of rose, fill the night.
Dream lover, I do invite.
With this rose as my gift,
Soft asleep I do drift.
In my dreams, make us one,
So be it, this charm is done!

Put the rose by your bed as you sleep, allowing its scent to fill the room. Allow the candle to burn down completely. As you drift to sleep, imagine your dream lover appearing in your dreams.

In the morning, remove the stem of the rose and put the rose flower inside the red cloth bag. Pin the bag under your clothes on the left side of your body. Then pull up the sacred circle and release your dream guardians. Wear the red bag pinned to your clothes during the day. At night before you go to sleep, take the bag and put it inside your pillowcase. You are sure to meet your dream lover as you sleep, perhaps even in a bed of red roses!

☪ Tonight's Magical Adventure: Love Poppets Dream Spell

The purpose of this spell is to promote a stronger bond between you and your lover, bringing you closer together in dream and in waking life. The idea behind the two poppets is that whatever affects the poppets' experience, you and your lover also experience. In this case, you are tied together in a lovers' embrace. Remember to always respect someone else's free will, and only make poppets of other people with their permission.

LIST OF ITEMS NEEDED: 1 green candle ⋆ 1 red candle ⋆ 1 white candle ⋆ Vanilla incense and censer ⋆ Pink fabric or construction paper ⋆ 1 cup dried lavender and rosebuds ⋆ 9-inch piece of green ribbon, yarn, or string ⋆ 8-inch piece of red ribbon, yarn, or string

✴ Spinning the Spell

Draw a sacred circle, and then call in your dream guardians. Invite your favorite love Goddess and God into the circle. Lighting the white candle first, dedicate it to the Goddess by chanting her name three times. Next light the green candle from the white candle, also dedicating this candle to the Goddess. Then light the red candle from the green candle, dedicating it to the God by chanting his name three times. Set the white candle in the center of the other two candles, with the green candle to its left and the red one to its right.

Make your poppets out of two matching pieces of fabric or construction paper. The poppets should resemble you and your lover, but they don't have to be works of art. Cut an outline of a person with rounded edges. You can use thread to stitch up the fabric or paper poppets, or in a pinch you can use a stapler to staple the paper poppets together. While making your poppets, focus on who the two poppets represent, namely you and your lover. Before stuffing the poppets, use colored felt pens to draw facial features and other distinguishing characteristics onto the cloth fronts of the poppets. Afterward, write your names on them. If you are particularly crafty, you can embroider or paint the poppets, give them button eyes, and so forth, to personalize them. Magical symbols such as runes can also be drawn on them to enhance their magical power. Stitch each of the poppets up, leaving their tops open for herbs. Stuff them with the dried lavender and rosebuds, two herbs related to Venus, the Goddess of love. As you stuff each of the poppets, say,

Lavender blue and rose so red,
Bring my love quickly to my bed.
Show me (his or her) face in my dreams,
Glowing with stars and bright moonbeams.
Blessed be the union of these flowers,
Blessed be our union in the dream hours!

After stuffing and chanting over each poppet, sew or staple their tops closed. Next take the nine-inch piece of green ribbon, yarn, or string and the eight-inch piece of red ribbon, yarn, or string, and twist them together. Then tie the braided ribbons firmly around the two poppets, fastening them together in a lovers' embrace. As you wind the ribbon around the poppets, say three times,

Two as one, one as two
You with me, me with you.
Together again, two as one
As I will, the spell is done!

Tie and seal the ribbon around the poppets with a few drops of wax from each of the three altar candles. Thank the Goddess and God you called into the circle as you do so. When you are finished, pull up the circle and release the dream guardians. Keep the poppets in your bedroom, preferably somewhere you will see them nightly, like a bedside table. This reinforces the strength of the bond between you and your lover in both your dream and waking worlds.

◖ Tonight's Magical Adventure: True Love Spell

You can do this spell any night just before going to sleep to draw your true love closer to you, whether you have met this person or not. A fireplace or campfire works great in place of the incense burner for burning the bay leaves. In ancient times, priestesses at the Oracle of Delphi used bay leaves to induce a prophetic trance.

LIST OF ITEMS NEEDED: 1 white candle ★ Incense censer with charcoal block ★ 4 dried bay leaves ★ Romance novel or book of love poems

✳ Spinning the Spell

Draw a sacred circle, set your dream guardians in place, and call in a favorite love Goddess or God. Next light the candle, the incense, and the charcoal block. Then crush three of the four bay leaves one at a time between your fingers, over the charcoal block, so that the pieces fall on the ignited block and burn. Each time you do this, focus on your true love's image if you know what he or she looks like. If you haven't yet found your true love, then focus on the candle flame, and allow whatever images come forth to drift in and out of your mind. Each time you crush and burn a leaf, say,

> *Bay leaves flaming in the fire,*
> *Bring to me my heart's desire.*
> *Blessed Earth, moon, and stars,*
> *Bring my lover, near or far.*
> *So dream it! So mote it be!*

Do this three times with three of the bay leaves. Take the last bay leaf, hold it in your hands, and say,

Sacred scented bay leaf so green
Bring the true love of my dreams.
So dream it! So mote it be!

Do not burn this leaf. Place it inside the pages of a romance novel or book of love poems. Select a page with a favorite passage or poem. Allow the candle to burn down completely. As you drift to sleep, repeat silently to yourself, "Bring the true love of my dreams." In the morning, write down what you recall of your dreams in your dream magic journal, thank your favorite Goddess or God, and then pull up the circle and release your dream guardians. During the next four months, your true love will come to you. He or she may also have a passion for the smell of crushed bay leaves.

☾ Tonight's Magical Adventure: Moon Mate String Magic

Your moon mate is a person who is emotionally in sync with you—someone you feel you can confide in and share your deepest desires with. This may be someone you already know or someone you have yet to meet. By using string magic to harness the energy and power of the full moon, you can draw your moon mate to you. Do this work on a Friday night on or just before a full moon.

As ancient as the Goddess, string magic stems from the Three Fates in Norse mythology, Urd, Verdandi, and Skuld, the Goddesses who weave the strings of birth, life, death, and rebirth. They also appear as the three witches in Shakespeare's *Macbeth*. Urd spins the thread of existence. She passes the spun string to Verdandi, who weaves it into the present pattern of existence, called the "Web of Wyrd." This web is an energetic fabric made of a vast numbers of strings "woven by decrees of fate." Verdandi gives the web to Skuld, who then pulls it apart and throws the untangled threads back into the abyss.

LIST OF ITEMS NEEDED: 1 yard-long piece of white string, yarn, or cord ★ 1 white candle ★ Amber incense and censer ★ A rhythmic, uplifting love song (rock 'n' roll, big band, country)

❋ Spinning the Spell

Draw a circle of light around your bedroom, and then set your dream guardians in place. Light the candle and incense on your altar. Sit or recline for a few minutes, taking a few deep breaths and letting go of all the daily tensions and thoughts. Make an effort to calm your mind as much as possible. Now take the string and tie the ends together in a strong knot. Loop and slide the string in and out of your fingers, cat's-cradle style. Use both hands to cradle the thread, looping it in and out in patterns with your fingers. Slide the string length back and forth, in and out, while you say,

Weaving a web of white,
In the warm candlelight,
Bring my lover tonight.
Threads of the Fates,
Open the bright starry gate,
And bring me my moon mate.
So be it! So mote it be!

Keep working the string, pulling your moon mate to you. Now hold the string in one hand as you put on a favorite love song, or you can just hum or sing a favorite, uplifting tune. Loop the string in both hands again, and begin to work it, in and out, to the rhythm of the song, weaving and knotting the thread in shapes as if you were sculpting a face in clay, the face of your moon mate. Focus all your attention on your task, on bringing your moon mate to you. Allow your fingers, your hands, and the string to tell the story of what you truly desire, threading and knotting your desire into the string and reality. Merge completely with Oneness, with divine light and love, and see and sense yourself tying into this radiant energy, threading this light and love into your life. Feel the movement of your fingers, hands, and thread becoming one with your intention, expectation, and desire, all joined in light. Keep weaving the energy together for a few minutes. When you are finished, put the woven and knotted string under your pillow while you sleep.

In the morning, pull up the circle and release your dream guardians. Take the string outside and plant it beneath a favorite fruit tree or flower bush. This encourages your moon mate's love to grow and blossom.

◖ Tonight's Magical Adventure: Forest Grove Love Adventure

We all know trees are powerful and wise spirits. They provide the oxygen that keeps everything on our planet alive. These are some of the reasons so many of us are working hard to make sure the forests of today will be here for everyone to enjoy in the future. The purpose of this Forest Grove Love Adventure is to show how you can tap into the power of the trees and forest to help bring more love and joy into your life. Again, you don't necessarily need to be in a relationship to do this magical work. A warm spring evening is the best time for going on this journey, but you can also go any night you would like to have a loving adventure in a sacred, old-growth forest.

LIST OF ITEMS NEEDED: 1 green candle ★ Cedar incense and censer ★ Your imagination

✳ Spinning the Spell

Draw the sacred circle and call in your dream guardians. Then light the candle and incense. Read the following three times (or have your lover read it to you), and then lie back and see and sense the following experience.

Begin by listening to the rhythm of your breath. Now slow your breathing down by breathing in to the count of three, holding your breath for three counts, and then exhaling completely. Sense your heart beating like a drum at the core of your being. Allow your eyes to close slowly and completely, relaxing even more as you continue to breathe to the count of three. In your mind's eye, begin to see and sense yourself standing in a thick forest grove on a warm spring evening just before dusk. As you look up, you can see tall and mighty oaks, sinuous ash trees, and huge, old-growth redwoods. As you look down, you see small wild daisies and delicate green ferns covering the forest floor. You can hear birds and the sound of a stream running nearby. You can feel the power in the land all around you, energizing you. The fresh scent of the trees, earth, and water washes over you, carried in the soft breeze.

Suddenly, a thin white fog fills the forest grove, and the mist glows a golden orange as the sun's afternoon rays slice through it. The glistening mist brushes against you like a cat and slowly surrounds and enfolds you. Oddly relaxing and almost warm, it gently swirls over your feet, legs, torso, and limbs and up over your head. The mist rolls in above and below you, before, beside, and behind you. You can feel the moisture on your face and taste the tiny droplets on your lips.

The golden orange fog grows thicker and more cloudlike, and you feel as though you are floating in the forest, being lifted on a golden cloud, sailing through the woods like a boat cutting through the water. You can feel yourself being pulled as if by a current, being carried faster and faster. An opening appears in the forest, and you are pulled through it, traveling to a beautiful Otherworld of experience. In this Otherworld, you experience a tremendous feeling of love and joy. Now begin to see your lover (prospective lover or dream lover), right next to you in this Otherworld, loving you and empowering you. Take a few minutes to enjoy the experience. Feel yourself smiling all over!

When you are done, allow the candle to burn down completely. As you drift to sleep, focus on the candle flame while turning your mind to the forest once again with the intention of dreaming beneath the trees. Repeat over and over, until you close your eyes and fall asleep,

> Forest dreams of love, joy, and light,
> Carry me to the Otherworld tonight.

In the morning, write down everything in your journal that you recall of your dreams. Then pull up the circle and release your dream guardians.

◖ Tonight's Magical Adventure: Mending a Broken Heart

Releasing past hurts and pains is often the first step in mending a broken heart. Leaving the past behind you is essential for personal growth, healing, and happiness. In this work, the chalice symbolizes the well and thus the Goddess. By giving the chalice your past hurt and pain and your broken heart, you allow the Goddess to transform the negative energy into positive energy, making you whole once again. This empowers you to go out and love again. Do this spell on a Monday night during the waning moon.

LIST OF ITEMS NEEDED: 2 orange candles ⋆ Clove oil ⋆ Sheet of paper ⋆ Pen ⋆ Chalice

✳ Spinning the Spell

Smudge your sacred space, and then draw a sacred circle and set your dream guardians in place. Position the candles side by side about eight inches apart. Place the chalice on the altar between the candles. Use the pen to draw a heart in the center of the piece of paper. Then tear the paper in half and think about the pain, sadness, disappointment, and hurt you want to leave behind. Put the paper halves inside the chalice. Hold the chalice in both hands, high in the air, and lower it to your lips as if to take a drink. Whisper into the chalice exactly why you feel brokenhearted, and then state all the negative feelings that you want to be rid of in order to feel better. Do this three times. When you are finished, turn the chalice upside down and place it firmly back on the altar between the candles. Now say,

> *The contents of this cup,*
> *Are no longer mine.*
> *Go, dark memories,*
> *Scatter far and wide,*
> *Into the night,*
> *Be gone forevermore.*
> *Broken heart, mend*
> *And love again,*
> *So mote it be!*

Allow the candles to burn out on their own as you drift to sleep.

When you awaken, turn the chalice right side up, take the paper halves, and fold them together three times. As you do this, feel a burden being lifted from you so that you feel more light-hearted. Pull up your circle, thank the Goddess, and release your dream guardians. Then bury the paper in the ground outside.

◖ Tonight's Magical Adventure: Lover Protection Spell

Best done on Imbolc (February 2), you can use this spell to protect your lover, yourself, your family, and pets. Simply alter a few words in the incantation to fit its purpose.

The main ingredient in this Lover Protection Spell is sweet basil. It protects your lover from fear, no matter how perilous the dangers. Many people grow this herb to provide protection for

loved ones and the home. The scent of sweet basil invokes the elemental creatures of fire called salamanders and also mighty
dragon energies. These powers are called upon for courage,
strength, and fortitude.

LIST OF ITEMS NEEDED: 1 white candle ★ Lavender incense
and censer ★ Wand ★ Chalice filled with sweet basil water

❋ Spinning the Spell

To make the basil water, simply steep a pinch of sweet basil in a
cup of boiling water for about ten minutes. Draw a sacred circle,
sprinkling the basil water around its edges in a clockwise motion.
Then call in your dream guardians. Light the candle and incense.
Next sprinkle the basil water around your bedroom, on your bedcovers and sheets, under your bed, in your hair, and everywhere.
As you do this, say,

> *Sweet water of protection,*
> *Keep this place of love safe.*

Set the chalice back on your altar when you are finished sprinkling the area with basil water. Then face north, and use your
wand to draw a pentacle or five-pointed star in the air, first
upright and then reversed, representing as above, so below. Then
circle the energetic pentacles three times, drawing the circles in a
clockwise direction with your wand. Say these words:

> *By the powers of earth, air, fire, and water*
> *By the power of the boundless One*
> *My lover is divinely protected from all harm*
> *In waking and in dreams*
> *In all times and all spaces.*
> *Everything negative, named or unnamed*
> *Is dissolved and turned positive.*

Protect my lover, now and forevermore.
As above, so below.
So be it! So mote it be!
Blessed be, blessed be, blessed be!

Take a few minutes to gaze at the candlelight, communicating intuitively with the spirit of the flame. When you are finished, pull up the circle, release your dream guardians, and snuff out the candle. As you drift to sleep, see and sense a protective cocoon of white light edged in cobalt blue surrounding your lover and yourself. Each year on Bridget's Day (Imbolc) repeat this protection spell to reinforce its power and reaffirm your intention and expectation to protect those you love.

☾ Tonight's Magical Adventure: Crystal Dream Castle Love Spell

One of my favorites, this spell can be cast any night you like. Its purpose is to help you reach out, touch, and dream about your romantic fantasies, especially in relation to love. Remember, what may begin as a fantasy fast becomes a dream. And dreams, with a little bit of magic, can become very real.

The dream castle is a personal power center that you create with your mind to do magical works. It may resemble a place you have visited in your waking life or a place you have seen in a picture. It can also be a completely original castle, made of crystal, trees, flowers, or gemstones, that doesn't exist anywhere but in your mind. The dream castle stands in the realm between the worlds, a magical place where dreams always come true. You can visit your dream castle right now and create your love life just as you would like it to be.

LIST OF ITEMS NEEDED: 1 clear quartz crystal point ★
2 white candles ★ Soft instrumental music

✴ Spinning the Spell

Wash your crystal in cool saltwater, and then rinse it under cool clear water for at least one minute. Do this with the tip pointed down to wash out any negative energies. Dry the crystal, and place it in the center of your altar with the point toward you.

Draw a sacred circle, call in your dream guardians, and put on some soft instrumental music. I suggest listening to instrumental Celtic music. Place the candles on either side of the crystal point, about four inches apart. Light them slowly, dedicating each candle to a favorite love Goddess and God.

Begin to gaze at the crystal, breathing deeply and allowing your mind to center and focus. Now take the crystal in your hands, look into it, and merge with the stone. Become one with the crystal, and begin to see and sense a beautiful dream castle within its center. In your mind's eye, enter the castle. See, touch, smell, hear, and even taste your surroundings. Be there. Walk through the different rooms or areas of your dream castle, exploring the many hallways and rooms. Just spend a few minutes observing the activity inside your castle, seeing how this has meaning for your life. If there are other people or animals in the castle, they may represent helpers in your life. As you do this, chant these words over and over:

> Magical castle, home of dreams,
> Bring love's inspiration to me.
> As I will, so mote it be!

Now visualize and sense going into the master bedroom of the castle. Remember to use your mind to create the most romantic room you can think of, and then see and sense your lover (waking or dream lover) reclining on the bed, inviting you to join him or her. Watch the best romantic love scene you have ever seen or experienced unfold slowly. Keep in mind that there is no limit to the love, joy, pleasure, and bliss you can experience in the bedroom of your dream castle. Allow the candles to burn all the way down, and as you drift to sleep, visualize yourself exploring the many nooks and crannies of your dream castle hand in hand with your lover.

In the morning, pull up the circle and release your dream guardians. Keep the crystal on your altar, using it each time you enter your dream castle. Every night you visit your dream castle serves to deepen your lovemaking experiences there and in your waking life.

◖ Tonight's Magical Adventure: Love Magic Charm Bags

These three Love Magic Charm Bags can be made over the period of three nights, preferably during the waxing moon. When you make these charm bags in late spring or early summer, you can use fresh ingredients. The magic bags are simple to construct, or you can use colored socks (preferably cotton or wool) knotted at the ends. I encourage you to make your own white, green, and red bags from a washable fabric such as cotton flannel. Then you can reuse them for other spells and charms. In a pinch, you can also used colored pieces of cloth the size of a large handkerchief, fastened together with a piece of colored string or a rubber band.

LIST OF ITEMS NEEDED: *First Night:* 1 pinch mugwort ★ 1 pinch dried lavender flowers ★ 1 pinch dried African violet flowers ★ 1 small piece of rose quartz ★ Small white cloth bag or sock

Second Night: 1 clover leaf (fresh if possible) ★ 1 small piece of tumbled moonstone ★ 3 hairs from your head ★ 3 hairs from your lover's head ★ Small green flannel bag or sock

Third Night: 2 pinches dried rosebuds and petals ★ 7 coriander seeds ★ 3 drops red wine or grape juice ★ Picture of yourself and your love ★ Small red cloth bag or sock

✱ Spinning the Spell

To make a bag, use two six-inch by nine-inch pieces of fabric. Place the squares of fabric together, right sides together, and stitch the sides and bottom together, leaving about one inch at the top for your drawstring. Fold the top edge over about a half inch, and press it with an iron. You can use iron-on fabric tape or fusing to keep this edge down if you prefer. Next fold the ironed edge over another half inch and stitch it into place, leaving the ends open to pull the drawstring through. Use the same color of ribbon or cord for the drawstring as the bag. Pull the ribbon through and then knot both ends. You can get a bit fancier when you knot the drawstrings by threading one bead on each end of the drawstring of the white bag, two beads on each end of the drawstring of the green bag, and three beads on each end on the red bag's drawstring. Fill each bag with the appropriate contents, closing the bags by pulling the drawstrings tight and tying them in a bow. The following are the instructions for the three Love Magic Charm Bags.

FIRST NIGHT

To dream of your lover, put equal parts of mugwort, rosebuds and petals, African violets, and lavender flowers into the white cloth bag or sock. Add a small piece of rose quartz, and say nine times,

> *Magic bag of white,*
> *Bring my love to me tonight.*
> *As I will, so shall it be!*

Place the white bag inside your pillowcase for the next six weeks to encourage dreams of romance and love. Your dreams will be filled with passionate romance and promises of love.

SECOND NIGHT

Place a cloverleaf, a tumbled moonstone, and three hairs from your head and three hairs from your lover's head into a small green flannel bag or sock. Say nine times,

Magic bag of green,
Bring my love to my dreams.
As I will, so shall it be!

Place the bag at the bottom of your bed for as long as you are with your lover, perhaps for all time, to encourage good luck and satisfaction in love, romance, and lovemaking.

THIRD NIGHT
Put dried red rosebuds and petals, seven coriander seeds, three drops of red wine or grape juice, and a picture of yourself with your lover into a small red cloth bag or red sock. As you do this, say nine times,

Magic bag of red,
Bring my lover to my bed.
As I will, so shall it be!

Place the bag under the mattress of your bed to intensify the love and passion in your relationship and to encourage erotic dreams. For the next seven weeks, your nights are bound to heat up from a lot of passionate lovemaking and fun!

☾ Tonight's Magical Adventure: Lovemaking Placket Magic

Made from two colored squares of paper or fabric, plackets are magical pockets made specifically for placing on your altar. The color of the placket matches the kind of magic you are doing. Altar plackets are versatile and simple to create, and they have endless uses. The best time to make this placket is on a Tuesday or Friday night on a new moon. If you prefer, you can substitute felt or fabric squares and a needle and thread for the construction paper and stapler.

LIST OF ITEMS NEEDED: 1 red candle ★ Vanilla incense and censer ★ Photo of yourself ★ Photo of your lover ★ Small slip of paper ★ Pen ★ 2 square 6-inch by 6-inch pieces of red construction paper ★ Stapler

❊ Spinning the Spell

Draw a sacred circle and call in your dream guardians. Next light the candle and incense. Carefully bathe the photos, pen, and paper in the incense smoke for a few minutes to rid them of any unwanted, negative energies. Staple the two squares of red paper together along the sides and bottom edge, leaving the top open. Draw the glyph of Venus (♀), and then draw the glyph of Mars (♂) right on top of it, or visa versa. Do this on both sides of the small slip of paper. Next take the photos and place them face-to-face, and insert the small piece of paper between the two photos. Put the photos and paper inside the placket, and then set it on your dream magic altar for twenty-one nights. Pull up the circle and release the dream guardians. Each night, for the time period stipulated, you need to enhance the power of your Lovemaking Placket with positive thoughts, taking a few moments to focus on the love energy you are drawing to you. Be prepared for some remarkable results, and allow yourself to savor the magical lovemaking that floods into your waking and dream worlds. You deserve it!

◖ Tonight's Magical Adventure: Flying Free Love Adventure

The best nights for doing this work are Monday, Wednesday, and Friday. Inspired by the Celtic tale of Angus Og and Caer, this dream adventure is guaranteed to spark your creative dream imagination, bringing more love and magic into your life for a year and a day.

In Celtic mythology, Angus Og is the God of love and beauty and one of the mighty Tuatha De Danann. He was begotten at the break of day and born by that evening, signifying his magical conception and gestation. Son of the faery queen and river God-dess Boann and the Good God, the Dagda, Angus was fostered by Midir, an elfin God of the Underworld. He was visited by an other-worldly maiden, Caer Ibormeith, in his sleep for a year and a day, and he conceived such a love for her that he fell ill until he found her. Caer was a shapeshifter and sorceress, who alternated between the form of a swan one year and a human shape the next. On Samhain, Angus finally found her at Loch Bel Dracon, also called the Lake of the Dragon's Mouth. She was there with 149 other young women all in swan form, linked together with silver chains. Angus then assumed the form of a swan, and together he and Caer circled the lake three times, singing so sweetly that everyone in the area fell asleep for three days and nights. The lovers then returned to Angus's otherworldly palace, Bruig na Boinne (New Grange, Meath) on the River Boyne.

LIST OF ITEMS NEEDED: 1 white feather ★ Silver chain ★ Your imagination

✖ Spinning the Spell

Put the silver chain around either your left wrist or left ankle. Then lie back in bed and close your eyes, holding the white feather in your left hand. Begin to imagine yourself shapeshifting into a swan and flying freely through the afternoon sky. The ground below you flows by, and you can see a beautiful blue-green lake in the near distance. You fly over to the lake, where another swan joins you in flight. The swan's eyes are exactly the same as the eyes of your lover. You and the other swan circle the beautiful lake clockwise three times, and you can feel the tremendous free-dom and joy from flying through the sky with your love. As you drift to sleep, continue flying in swan form, winging your way toward love. In the morning, write down your dreams, and place the chain and feather on your altar for a year and a day to remind you of the infinite love and pure joy you experienced while flying free. Anytime you would like to fly again, just put on the chain, hold the white feather in your left hand, and repeat the process.

☾ Tonight's Magical Adventure: Romance and Love Pentacle

The purpose of this magical work is to bring romance and love into your life. The best time to do your romance and love pentacle is on a Friday night, preferably while the moon is waxing. By learning successfully to make pentacles, you also learn how to create specific kinds of energetic patterns.

With so many people today wearing the pentacle (five-pointed star), it has become what the peace symbol was in the 1960s. A five-pointed star of elemental and creative thought, the pentacle can be used as a step-by-step method for manifesting your hopes and desires. Just make sure what you are manifesting is something that you really want and that you want it with all your being. Also think about how your pentacle will affect other people. Be realistic as to the probability of the desired outcome. Relationships that have a high probability are easier to manifest than those with only a remote possibility. At the same time, if there is a possibility of romance and love, it may be enough of a foundation to build upon.

LIST OF ITEMS NEEDED: 1 pink candle ★ Citrus incense and censer ★ 2 sheets of white paper ★ Red felt pen ★ Wand

✶ Spinning the Spell

Draw the sacred circle, call in your dream guardians, and also request the guidance and assistance of your favorite Goddess and God. Light the candle and incense. Take one of the sheets of paper, and write down exactly with whom you would like to be in a romantic and loving relationship. Be concise and specific, using as few words as possible and making sure you state everything in the positive. Then draw a large pentacle with the felt pen on the other sheet of paper. The pentacle needs to be large enough to put a symbol or word into each point. Into the topmost point of the pentacle (the head), place a symbol that represents you, and/or write your initials. Make up original symbols, or use ones you already know. A tip for doing pentacles is to keep it simple. In the right arm of the pentacle, place a symbol, such as a heart or flower, that symbolizes romance and love to you. In both of the legs of the pentacle (bottom points), place symbols or words that denote what steps you will take to bring romance and love into your life. For instance, you could write the name of a friend who has been wanting to introduce you to someone. Or you could draw a simple picture of a telephone or computer if you want to receive a call or e-mail from that special someone. Into the left arm of the pentacle, draw a symbol or write the words signifying a successful romantic outcome. You could draw another heart, writing your initials and your prospective love's initials inside it. Chose a bright, colorful, and exciting outcome. After you are done preparing your pentacle, hang the sheet of paper on the wall at eye level.

Now take your wand in your hands, and enter a merged state through emotion or sensation. Chant the names of the Goddess and God you have called into your circle to help you. Do this in triplets, for example, "Anu, Anu, Anu, Dagda, Dagda, Dagda, Ayea, Ayea, Ayea!" Now point your wand tip at each point of your pentacle, beginning at the topmost (head) point and moving clockwise. Allow each symbol, initial, or word to flash into your mind as you do this. Continue to the left arm of the pentacle, which denotes the successful outcome. Then set your wand down on the altar and clap your hands smartly together. Turn away from the pentacle for a few minutes until your mind returns to normal. Your pentacle is done.

Allow the candle to burn down completely. Both as you drift to sleep and just as you awaken, visualize yourself merging with and becoming the head and limbs of your pentacle. Fully transform into a luminous, five-star body, becoming a disk of brilliant red light. Imagine yourself moving like a star on the surface, spinning clockwise below and above the earthly plane, finally soaring out across the universe. Pull up the sacred circle, release your dream guardians, and thank the Goddess and God who guided and assisted you with the work.

Over the next couple of weeks, focus on the pentacle image on your wall frequently, giving it energy and positive reinforcement. Do this every night and morning. This will help you fix a clear image in your mind of exactly the relationship you desire. Remember, the clearer your intention and expectation and the stronger your desire, the more energy you will be able to direct toward the successful romantic and loving outcome. Within the next five months, your pentacle should come to fruition.

☾ Tonight's Magical Adventure: Magical Symbol Love Charm

Symbols are a mainstay of dreaming. They go beyond definition, moving into magical dimensions. We use symbols to communicate on a daily basis, and they are so common that we rarely notice how frequently we use them. All things that exist, whether in waking or dreaming, have some degree of symbolism and association. In this way symbols have a layered quality; many thoughts and feelings coalesce in them.

Magical symbols can focus and intensify the power of every night spell and ritual. Best created on a Tuesday or Friday night, on a full moon, this Magical Symbol Love Charm uses the power of an original magical symbol to charm your lover into being more amorous and attentive. Be sure to ask permission from your lover before making this charm.

LIST OF ITEMS NEEDED: 1 pink candle ⋆ Sandalwood incense and censer ⋆ 1 piece of rose quartz ⋆ Sheet of red paper ⋆ Black felt pen

✳ Spinning the Spell

Light the candle and incense, dedicating each to your favorite love Goddess and God. (Please refer to the appendixes for a listing of deities.) Next take the sheet of paper and draw an original symbol of love on the paper by merging with the divine and then sketching out whatever comes to you. You can also use three symbols you are familiar with, such as the heart, cross, and circle, altering them by connecting them together into one larger symbol. Then write your lover's initials and your initials across your original symbol. Bathe the piece of rose quartz in the incense smoke for at least a minute, and then place it on the paper. Drip three drops of candle wax on the stone. Now fold the paper in half and then in half again and then once more, sealing the stone within the charm. Now seal the folded paper with wax from the candle. Place the charm among your lover's belongings, for example, in a coat pocket in the closet. Allow the candle to burn down completely. As you drift to sleep, repeat these words:

More loving, more caring,
More joy and more sharing.

Leave the charm in place for a year and a day to create a deeper bond of love between you and your lover.

◖ Tonight's Magical Adventure: Dream Knot Marriage Spell

Marriage is also called tying the knot. In this spell you magically tie the knot in your dreams, setting the stage for the live event. String magic may seem simple, but it generates a great deal of magical power toward your desired outcome. This spell is best done on a full moon in May or June. Lavender oil and incense are added to bring a sense of harmony, joy, and peace, qualities that can help make every marriage a more loving and sensual union.

LIST OF ITEMS NEEDED: 1 pink candle ⋆ Ballpoint pen or quill ⋆ Lavender oil ⋆ Lavender incense and censer ⋆ 1 yard-long piece of red string, cord, or ribbon ⋆ Your favorite love song

✺ Spinning the Spell

Draw a sacred circle and call in your dream guardians. Light the incense. Next wash the candle in cool saltwater, and then carve your initials and your beloved's initials on the body of the candle. Rub the candle body with oil, and then anoint your forehead, throat, wrists, and ankles. Afterward, take the red string and rub its length thoroughly with the oil. Wipe your hands completely. Light the candle, dedicating it to your beloved. Put on a favorite love song, and hold the ends of the string in both of your hands. Tie six knots in the string, spacing them evenly apart. Then tie the ends together. As you tie each knot, say,

> *By the light of the stars and the silvery moon,*
> *May my beloved (insert name) and I marry soon.*
> *According to free will and for the good of all*
> *Over the years, in winter, spring, summer, and fall*
> *Our love will endure through eternity*
> *So be it! So mote it be! Blessed be!*

Allow the candle to burn down completely. As you drift to sleep, repeat the words "Dreams of marriage as I sleep." In the morning, write down anything you recall of your dreams in your journal. Then pull up the circle and release the dream guardians. Keep the knot on your dream altar. Within the next six months, you and your beloved will likely reach the decision to marry.

☾ Tonight's Magical Adventure: Samhain Love Magic Spell

On Samhain, the veil between time and space draws to its thinnest point. The portals to Otherworlds of experience open, and the

Goddesses and Gods as well as the elemental spirits interact freely with mortals. On this eve, stretched across a great river, the great sea mother Morrigan made love with the master of life and death, the Dagda. This makes Samhain Eve a particularly auspicious night for any kind of magic, especially Samhain love magic.

Based on a traditional Celtic observance called the "Dumb Supper," this spell taps into the power and passion of the Goddess Morrigan and the God Dagda. The supper is in honor of the Goddess and God and brings the blessings of Morrigan and Dagda to you and your beloved. Customarily, the Dumb Supper consists of generous plates of food and drink placed outside in the dark of night, with lighted red and white candles standing guard. Any morsels or drops that remain the next morning go into the earth and to the Goddess.

LIST OF ITEMS NEEDED: 1 white candle ⋆ 1 red candle ⋆ 6 cloves ⋆ 2 cinnamon sticks ⋆ 2 separate cups of warm apple cider ⋆ 2 cookies ⋆ Large plate

�֍ Spinning the Spell

Place everything on your altar, and then fill two separate cups with warm cider. Next add three cloves to each cup as well as one cinnamon stick. Stir each cup nine times, clockwise, with the cinnamon stick. As you do this, say,

May Dagda and Morrigan bless
This cup of apple and spices,
So mote it be! So be it!

Place one of the cups on a large plate with one of the cookies. Take the plate with the cup of cider and cookie and the white and red candles outside. Set the plate and candles in a place where the candles can safely burn completely down. Make certain you do not set anything but the candles (and your lover) on fire! Now go back inside and drink the cup of cider and eat the remaining cookie. Thank the Goddess and God. As you drift to sleep, see yourself drifting on a slow-moving river or on a moonbeam, making love with that special someone.

In the morning, compost any remaining food and drink in the earth, thanking the Goddess and God for their guidance, blessings, and love. For the next year, the Goddess Morrigan and the God Dagda will bless and protect your union.

◖ Tonight's Magical Adventure: Holiday Mistletoe Ritual

The Druids held nothing more sacred than oak and the all-heal mistletoe that graces it. In Irish, mistletoe is known as "Druidh lus," or Druid's weed. It is considered a sign of happiness and rejoicing, and when you dream of gathering mistletoe you will have your choice of lovers. If you dream of kissing romantically under the mistletoe, often the next person you kiss in waking life becomes very special to you.

This ritual can be used for drawing a lover to you and for heightening passion and sexual expression. It is best done at Yule when mistletoe is readily available, but if you have a year-round source, feel free to do this magical ritual on the summer solstice and full moons. Purchase a sprig, or, better yet, gather some mistletoe on the solstices or the sixth day of the moon cycle by knocking it out of the tree with a rock or stick at dawn or dusk and catching it before it hits the ground.

Sacred to the Goddess of love, mistletoe bestows life and fertility, which is why lovers kiss beneath it. It comprises both male and female plants, which derive water and minerals from the host tree, and ripe berries, green berries, immature leaves, and open flowers can all be found on the same plant.

LIST OF ITEMS NEEDED: Sprig of mistletoe ★ 9-inch length of red ribbon or yarn ★ 1 red candle with holder ★ Ballpoint pen

or quill ★ A few drops of vanilla oil ★ Vanilla incense and censer
★ Bowl with three pinches of salt ★ Chalice or cup filled with
water

✱ Spinning the Spell

Wash the candle in cool saltwater, dry it, and place it on the altar
with the other items listed. Draw a sacred circle, and then say,

> *The circle is bound*
> *With power all around.*
> *In all worlds I stand*
> *Protected in all lands.*

Next set your dream guardians in place. Then decide upon a
favorite Goddess and God to guide and inspire you during this ritual. Carve their initials, together with your initials, in the wax of
the candle with a ballpoint pen or quill. Rub the vanilla oil on the
candle body, and place it back in its holder. Wipe the oil off your
hands, light the candle, and then light the incense from the candle
flame. Take the bowl from the altar, hold it up toward the north
point of your circle, and say,

> *All Mother Goddess and All Father God,*
> *Bless this bowl filled with salt.*
> *I call upon the powers of earth to protect this circle*
> *And to help me discover my true love in waking and in*
>   *dream.*

Set the bowl back on the altar. Then, take the burning incense
from the altar, hold it up toward the east point of the circle and
say,

> *All Mother Goddess and All Father God,*
> *Bless this burning incense.*

I call upon the powers of air to protect this circle
And to help me discover my true love in waking and in
*   dream.*

Set the incense carefully back down upon the altar. Take the candlestick and burning candle from the altar, hold it up toward the south point of your circle, and say,

All Mother Goddess and All Father God,
Bless this burning candle flame.
I call upon the powers of fire to protect this circle
And to help me discover my true love in waking and in
*   dream.*

Place the candle carefully back down on the altar. Take the chalice of water from the altar, hold it upward toward the west point, and say,

All Mother Goddess and All Father God,
Bless this chalice filled with water.
I call upon the powers of water to protect this circle
And to help me discover my true love in waking and in
*   dream.*

Place the chalice back down upon the altar. Take the sprig of mistletoe between your hands. Stand in the center of the circle and face the altar, holding the sprig upward, and begin to chant loudly the names of the Goddess and God you have selected to help you. The Goddess and God names are customarily chanted three or nine times in succession, using alternating female and male deities, for example, "Rosemerta, Rosemerta, Rosemerta, Lugh, Lugh, Lugh, Rosemerta, Rosemerta, Rosemerta!" Merge deeply with these divine energies, and peak the energy in your hands, passing this power into the sprig of mistletoe and thereby consecrating it.

Next tie the ribbon around the mistletoe sprig, winding it around the stem three times and then tying it together with a simple bow or knot. As you do this, say,

> *By the powers of the Goddess and God,*
> *By the sacred Earth, sun, moon, and stars,*
> *I bind the sacred power of divine love*
> *Into this sprig of mistletoe.*
> *May it help me discover my true love*
> *In waking and dream.*
> *So dream it! So mote it be!*

Hang the sprig in your bedroom for the next six months to bring dreams of your true love and dreams of divine happiness, to bring the blessings of the Goddess of love, and to unlock the secrets of immortality. Allow the candle to burn down completely as you drift to sleep.

In the morning, thank the Goddess and God who have helped you, pull up the circle, and release your dream guardians. Use the water in the chalice to water a houseplant. Scatter the salt outside your doorstep or pour it down the drain. Do not reuse it. (Caution: Do not handle mistletoe where small children or pets might swallow fallen stems, leaves, or berries, as it is poisonous.)

◐ Tonight's Magical Adventure: Canceling a Love Spell

As we all know, "to err is human." We all make mistakes, and relationships are no exception. Blindness in love is a human tendency, and at some time or the other you may find you have attracted the "wrong" person. If so, use this spell to cancel out love spells and rid yourself of any unwanted suitors. The best time to do this work is before midnight on the first Saturday night after a full moon.

LIST OF ITEMS NEEDED: Cedar and sage smudge ⋆ 1 black candle ⋆ Large incense burner with charcoal block, or a fireplace, wood stove, or campfire ⋆ Bowl with three large handfuls of dried vervain ⋆ 3 pinches sage

✴ Spinning the Spell

Set the bowl of vervain on the ground just outside your front door. Next smudge your bedroom and then the rest of your home, moving in a clockwise direction and ending back at your bedroom. Extinguish the smudge. Then draw a sacred circle around your entire home, making sure you cut an energetic gate in the circle to your front door so you can go outside without breaking the protective circle of light. When doing this spell outdoors, build a small, safe fire, draw the circle so it includes the fire, and then place the bowl of vervain just outside the circle, again cutting a gate to exit and enter. Call in your dream guardians, and then call in your favorite Goddess and God by speaking their names nine times. Ask them for their guidance, protection, and blessing. Then light the candle and the charcoal block of your incense burner. Next exit your front door through the energetic gate, and take a handful of the dried vervain in your dominant hand. Hold the handful of herbs high above your head, face in the opposite direction as your front door. Then loudly shout the name of the person you want to be free of, and turn widdershins (counterclockwise) three times. Go back into the house, and cast the dried herbs into the lit incense burner, fireplace, or wood stove. As you do so, say with passion,

> *In the past, I cast a love spell*
> *Now, the effect I must quell.*
> *May this spell be undone and (name of person) be gone!*
> *I ask this by earth, water, wind, and light,*
> *By the stroke of midnight tonight,*
> *(Name of person) shall never again return.*
> *Make it so as these leaves burn!*

Repeat the process of going outside and gathering the leaves, shouting the name, turning widdershins (counterclockwise), going inside, casting the leaves into the fire, and chanting a total of three times. Snuff out the candle when you are finished, breaking it into small pieces and then throwing it in the garbage can. Next pull up your circle and release your dream guardians. In the morning, sprinkle the sage into the ashes in the incense burner or from your fire, and then bury the ashes at least nine inches underground, stomping on the ground over the covered ashes three times.

chapter   five

Money and Success Dream Magic

On summer nights when I was a young girl, I would put on my coat and go out to look at the stars. We lived in a small valley nestled high in the Sierra Nevada around 5,500 feet in altitude, and I could clearly see the milk of the Milky Way. I would gaze up at the stars and make a wish, saying, "Star light, star bright, first star I see tonight, I wish I may, I wish I might, have the wish I wish tonight." Then I would say my wish to the stars, sit for a few minutes almost as if waiting for a reply, and then go back inside to get warm.

Singer and songwriter John Butcher writes, "If wishes were horses, then dreamers would ride." In another context, "If wishes were stars, then dreamers would light the night sky." The Milky Way would be like a river of dreamers, spreading out across the celestial realms. Almost universally, ancient civilizations depict the Milky Way as a river of heaven and light. The Concow Maidu tribe of northern California, whose name means "the Garden People," called it Morning Star's Path, representing the sacred shimmering cord between this world and the spirit world, a place where dreams and reality come together as One.

Some ancient cultures saw the Milky Way as a river of the sparkling, life-giving milk of the Goddess, and in Celtic lands it was known as the Track of the White Cow. This parallels the nursery rhyme about the famous white cow who jumped over the moon and in her wake left a trail of star milk across the sky. White cows were thought to be faery cows by the Irish people, and they would guard them suspiciously, suspecting the Sidhe (the faery folk) would try to steal the cows at night.

In Celtic Ireland, cows were the measure of a person's wealth. As such, cattle were honored as being closely associated with the land and as a source of milk, meat, and leather. On Beltane (May 1) cattle were driven between two bonfires in order to purify and invigorate them. Giving milk away on that day was thought to bring bad luck, although spilling some for the Sidhe as an offering was considered wise.

Boann is the Celtic Goddess most often associated with the cow. In Ireland, the River Boyne runs through the Boyne Valley, upon which the ancient ruins of Newgrange rest. Both the river and valley are named after her. In magic, you can call upon Boann's divine power to help you with spells for wealth and prosperity in order to achieve your financial goals.

The value of cattle is echoed in Norse mythology with Fehu, the primary rune in the Elder Futhark, meaning "cattle" and symbolizing a basic form of mobile wealth. Fehu also signifies the pure fire of creativity, from which anything can be manifested in this reality. This creative fire can be used to ignite the power of dream magic!

As dreamers, we are all like the great Milky Way, stretching our spirit light out into the dark night. We bring light to the darkness and in doing so awaken the ancient spirit light, the divine dream, residing in us all. By working together, we can help create a prosperous future for all humankind and not just for a few. We can use our wealth to help heal ourselves and others and to help preserve and honor the flora and fauna on the Earth. Every moment of life is a divine gift for us to enjoy.

The following dream spells and rituals can be used for bringing prosperity, financial success, and abundance into your life. I suggest you use a green altar cloth for these works unless otherwise noted, since green is the color of prosperity and abundance. It's the color of money! In addition, whenever doing these spells, bind yourself to the green harmonic by imagining a brilliant green light surrounding you like a luminous green egg.

◖ Tonight's Magical Adventure: Wildflower Success Spell

Seeds represent beginnings, and the sowing of them cultivates success and personal growth. Within each seed exists the blossoming spirit of Goddess and God and the true self. Flowers symbolize the beauty and stillness of nature, and dreaming about them in full bloom may indicate that happiness and inner healing will soon come your way.

LIST OF ITEMS NEEDED: Package of wildflower seeds ⋆ 1 green candle and holder

✳ Spinning the Spell

Draw a sacred circle of green light around your bedroom. Next light the candle, dedicating it to a Goddess of abundance such as the Great Provider, Rosemerta. After placing the package of seeds in front of the candle, take a few minutes to imagine yourself planting the wildflower seeds, watering them, and watching them grow and flower. Then pick up the package of seeds and, holding it in your hands, empower it by chanting,

Wildflower seeds, free my mind
Let no limits tie or bind.
Wildflower seeds, bring me power
Growing strong with each passing hour.
Bring success and let it grow.
As I will, it shall be so!

Hold the seeds between your hands, chanting these words of power over and over until the seed packet feels warm to the touch. Put the seed packet back upon your altar. Let the candle burn down on its own. As you drift to sleep, imagine the wildflowers blooming and thriving. Repeat silently until you fall asleep, "Wildflowers bring success."

Upon awakening, write down your dreams, thank the Goddess, and then pull up your circle. Take the seed packet from your altar, and plant the seeds in a sunny location, thanking the elemental powers of earth, air, fire, water, and spirit as you do so. Water them regularly, watch them grow, and enjoy your wild success!

◖ Tonight's Magical Adventure: Creating a Dream Magic Money Crystal

The Celtic Goddess Bridget is ideal for stimulating dreams about where to get more money by using magic and by working smarter, not harder. As the beautiful Goddess of creativity and inspiration, Bridget is simply divine! Call on her to help you with this magical work on a Sunday, Thursday, or Saturday night, preferably on a full moon or just before Bridget's Fire.

LIST OF ITEMS NEEDED: Sandalwood incense and censer ⋆ Tumbled piece of clear or rutile quartz ⋆ Your imagination

✳ Spinning the Spell

Draw a sacred circle and then light the incense, dedicating it to Bridget or another favorite Goddess of prosperity. Hold the crystal in your dominant hand, and bathe it in the smoke for a couple of minutes. Next completely clear out any unwanted energies in the stone by placing it in your left hand and covering it with your right. While holding the stone in your hands, merge with the Goddess and imagine a bright full moon in your mind. If weather permits, look at the full moon outside just before visualizing it in your mind. Now breathe in deeply, visualizing the brilliant moonlight filling the stone, and then pulse your breath out sharply through your nose, as if to set the image in place in the stone. To program your Dream Magic Money Crystal, repeat the clearing process, only instead of imagining the moon, imagine a bright green light and lots of money filling the crystal. Visualize the crystal getting larger, and also see and feel your wealth expanding. Repeat the programming process three times. After programming the crystal, place it under your pillow or hold it in your left hand as you sleep, noticing how it affects your dreams. I suggest trying different types of crystals, programming them for money and abundance, while again observing their effects on your dreams. As you drift to sleep, simply repeat to yourself,

Magic money stone, bring to me
Crystal dreams of prosperity.
So be it! So dream it so!

In the morning, write down everything you remember from your dreams. Thank the Goddess and pull up your circle. You can hold the stone as you drift to sleep as often as you like. The more you do so, the more dream messages you will receive regarding how to make more money without working harder.

◖ Tonight's Magical Adventure: Green Underwear Money Spell

Fun, simple, and especially effective, this spell can help bring prosperity and wealth into your life right now.

LIST OF ITEMS NEEDED: 1 pair of green-colored underwear ★ 1 green candle

✴ Spinning the Spell

Draw a sacred circle of light around your bed. Put on the green underwear. The underwear represent the Wearing of the Green, a Celtic tradition in honor of Earth's new green garment in spring. Next carve three dollar signs into the candle body with a ballpoint pen or quill. Place the candle on your altar and light it. Focus on the center of the flame, and begin to see a prosperous new you. As you do this, repeat the following nine times:

Wearing green, sight unseen,
Bring me wealth as I dream.
As I will, so be it!

See and feel yourself having plenty of money. Know that each time you wear your lucky green underwear, you will find more money in your pocket. Concentrate on this as you drift to sleep. Allow the candle to burn down completely. In the morning, pull up the circle.

☾ Tonight's Magical Adventure:
Money Placket Spell

Like the Lovemaking Placket, the Money Placket Spell uses two colored squares of paper—in this case green paper, the color of money. If you prefer, you can use green felt squares sewn with a needle and thread instead of the construction paper and stapler.

LIST OF ITEMS NEEDED: 1 green candle ★ 1 red candle ★ Patchouli incense and censer ★ 1 bay leaf (preferably fresh) ★ Pinch of dill ★ 8 sesame seeds ★ Photo of yourself ★ 1 dollar bill ★ Green felt pen ★ 2 square 4-inch by 4-inch pieces of green construction paper ★ Stapler

✴ Spinning the Spell

Draw a sacred circle and light the incense. Dedicate the candles as you light them to a favorite Goddess and God of prosperity. For example, light the green candle in the name of the Celtic mother Goddess, Anu, and dedicate the red candle to the generous and Good God, the Dagda. Staple the two squares of green paper together along the sides and bottom edge, leaving the top open. Now use the felt pen to write your name on both sides of the bay leaf, and place it in the placket. Next take the photo and slide it into the paper pocket. Add the pinch of dill, eight sesame seeds, and finally the dollar bill. Be sure the photo and currency are face-to-face. Carefully bathe the placket in the incense smoke for a few minutes to strengthen its money-attracting power, and then put the placket on your dream altar. Allow the candle to burn down completely, and as you drift to sleep, repeat these words over and over again:

Placket of green, bring money dreams.

In the morning, thank the Goddess and God and pull up the circle. A few minutes every night, for eighty-four nights, empower your money placket by focusing on the money and prosperity it draws to you. During the next three months, you will have the extra cash to fulfill a few of your dreams!

◖ Tonight's Magical Adventure: Lucky Coin Charm

Everyone can use a little more luck and money. The purpose of this charm is to bring you prosperity using a lucky coin. Make this charm on a full moon.

LIST OF ITEMS NEEDED: Silver altar cloth ⋆ 2 silver candles and holders ⋆ 1 silver dollar ⋆ Sandalwood incense and censer ⋆ Bowl of water

✳ Spinning the Spell

Begin by drawing a sacred circle and setting your dream guardians in place. Next put the bowl of water in the middle of your altar with one candle in front and one candle positioned behind the bowl. Light the incense and candles on your altar, and dedicate them to a favorite Goddess, such as Boann (Celtic), Fortuna (Roman), or Lakshmi (Hindu), and a favorite God, such as Lugh (Celtic), Odin (Norse), or Jupiter (Roman). Ask them to offer their blessings and power to your charm. Now bathe the silver dollar in the incense smoke for a few moments while saying,

> *Silver coin, silver moon,*
> *Bring me luck, bring it soon.*
> *Lucky coin, fortunate moon,*
> *Bring me wealth, bring it soon.*
> *As I will, so mote it be!*

Drop the coin into the bowl of water. Gaze into the water, observing how the candlelight plays upon its surface and the surface of the coin. Visualize the coin multiplying until you see hundreds and thousands of silver coins within the bowl. Use your imagination. Do this for at least fifteen minutes. Allow the candles to safely burn down on their own, and as you go to sleep, visualize both your luck and wealth growing. Delight in your abundance.

In the morning, pull up the circle, take the silver dollar from the bowl of water, and put it in your pocket, wallet, or purse. Pour the water from the bowl on the ground just outside your front door to attract even more luck and wealth. By the next full moon, you will find more money than usual in your pocket, wallet, or purse.

☾ Tonight's Magical Adventure:
I Got the Job! Spell

At one time or another, you have probably found yourself hunting for a new and more rewarding job. One of the most powerful of the huntress Goddesses is the Roman Goddess Diana. Akin to the Greek Artemis, Diana appears lightly clad, with bow and arrows in hand, riding the moon across the open sky. Originally both a moon and sun Goddess, Diana can be called upon to give you both lunar and solar strength and the knowledge of how to hunt down and obtain the job of your dreams. This spell is most powerful when spun on a Sunday or Monday night, during a gibbous moon phase or on a full moon.

LIST OF ITEMS NEEDED: Pine oil ⋆ 8 pecans ⋆ Small glass of orange juice ⋆ Sheet of white paper ⋆ Green felt pen ⋆ Flashlight

✳ Spinning the Spell

Go outside on the full moon. Take all the items you will need outside with you on a tray or in a small box. If you are not able to work outside because of locale or poor weather, do this spell close to a window, in full view of the moon.

Begin by drawing a sacred circle and calling in the Goddess Diana (or other favorite huntress Goddess) to help and guide you. Do this by chanting her name nine times as you gaze at the moon. Merge with the light of the moon for a few minutes, and then say firmly, with great expression, holding the glass of juice upward toward the moon as if giving a toast,

Silvery moon so bright and wise,
Shining in the dark night sky,
I toast to your ever-glowing light,
Many thanks for returning every night.
Please shine on me and bless my dreams,

The job I truly want now bring to me:
(State the job you want three times)
By the stars, sun, land, sky, and sea,
By the light of the moon, so mote it be!

Now drink the juice slowly. After you are done with the juice, blow three kisses to the moon.

Next take the pecans and eat them one at a time. Just before eating each nut, say,

Pecan of prosperity,
Bring success to me.
So be it! Blessed be!

In a comfortable position, gaze at the moon for a few minutes, appreciating its light and beauty. Begin to see and sense yourself already in your new job in the future. If this poses a problem for your logical mind, just allow yourself to pretend for a few minutes. Go ahead and picture yourself exactly where you will be, experiencing what your actions and feelings will be in your new job. See the images of your new job unfolding in a bright, colorful, and exciting light. Merge with Oneness, and then imagine a pathway into the future. Follow that pathway into the future, and stand where the action is, think the thoughts, and feel the feelings. Now amplify the intensity of your desire for the job, creating an even more compelling image in your mind's eye. Really want the job with your heart, body, and soul! Next walk back through time and look at the pathway, allowing your mind to reveal the main steps that led you to getting your new job. Slowly watch yourself methodically carrying out the exact steps and actions needed to get the job. Make an effort to see each action clearly. Make a mental note of the steps you need to take for success. Now allow yourself to savor for a few moments the joy of getting and working at your new job. Delight in seeing the new resources, abilities, and skills you now carry with you as part of your unfolding adventure.

Finally, enter the present moment again, smiling to yourself, knowing that you will be successful in securing the job of your dreams. Use the green felt pen to jot down on the sheet of paper the steps you need to take to get the job. Anoint each of the four corners of the paper with a drop of pine oil. Next fold the paper four times. Thank the Goddess, blow the moon a kiss, pull up the circle, and take everything back inside. Slip the folded paper inside your pillowcase, and leave it in place for three nights. On the fourth night, unfold the paper and tape it to your altar. Read over the steps every night just before you go to sleep until you get the job. By the next full moon, the job will be yours.

◖ Tonight's Magical Adventure: Dream Water Spell

Lugh is the divine presence who has helped me find my calling in life. He is the Celtic God associated with the setting sun and the moon, and his name is pronounced "Loooh," as in "lunar." As the Celtic Mercury and Lord of Light, he was the uncontested master craftsman of all the arts, from which he derived the name Samil-danach, meaning "Many Skills." He was also patron of commerce and business and hence the God of the essence and distribution of skill. As a show of his power, he single-handedly hurled a flagstone that normally would have required eighty yoke of oxen to move. By doing so, he was accepted by the Celtic Gods (Tuatha De Danann) as their deliverer and king. In Celtic tradition, Lugh is well known for his generosity and prowess, always carrying a bag of magical golden coins with him and giving them to those he deems worthy.

By blending this dream water, you can call upon Lugh's solar strength and lunar wisdom to help you find your personal calling. Use the water to gain access to the sacred wisdom within your being and pursue your dreams. Best made during a waxing moon, the water is specially formulated to help you find your calling in your dreams.

LIST OF ITEMS NEEDED: 1 yellow candle ★ Lavender incense and censer ★ Glass jar with lid ★ 1 golden colored coin (such as a Sacajawea dollar coin) ★ 8 bay leaves ★ 8 pinches sweet basil ★ Red ribbon

✳ Spinning the Spell

Draw a sacred circle of light and call in your dream guardians. Dedicate the candle and incense to Lugh as you light them. Next uncap the jar and fill it about halfway to the top with water. Then rub the dollar coin between your hands for a minute until it feels warm. Drop the coin softly into the jar of water, and add the bay leaves and basil. Fill the jar to the top with more water. Then cap the jar and tie the red ribbon around its neck. Hold the dream water in your hands, and empower it by merging with the divine and chanting,

Sacred dream water of dear Lugh,
Ebbing and flowing with the moon,
Reveal my calling in my dreams.
As I will, so shall it be!

Place the jar of dream water in a window that gets plenty of sun and moonlight. Leave it there for three days and nights. On the fourth night, carefully uncap the jar. Dip your fingers into the dream water, and then sprinkle it around your bedroom—on your dream altar, the floor, your bedcovers, sheets, and pillowcases. Rub the water on your body, especially your hands, feet, and hair. Keep about a quarter cup of the water in the jar on your altar for later use. Allow the candle to burn down completely, and as you drift to sleep, repeat the words, "Lugh, reveal my calling to me."

In the morning, write down everything that you recall of your dreams. Remove the coin from the dream water, and put it on your dream altar. Then pull up the circle and release your dream guardians. Finally, add the remaining dream water to your bath just before going to sleep that night to attract more dreams about your true calling. Within the next eight weeks, you will certainly discover your true calling.

◐ Tonight's Magical Adventure: Money Trail Dream Magic

The purpose of this spell is to bring you more cash. Jupiter and his counterpart, Juno, the Queen of Heaven, presided over all human doings. Jupiter's energy is hyperexpansive, which is ideal for bringing more money into your life. A primary aspect of Jupiter's energy is that of prosperity consciousness, which can attract monetary as well as spiritual growth and expansion. Juno's temple on the Capitol contained the Roman mint, and one of her names was Moneta, which came to mean "money." March 1, the month of June, July 7, September 13, or the first night of the new moon—all sacred to the fertility Goddess Juno—are the best times to do this work. Eight dollar bills are used because in numerology eight is the number of money and prosperity.

LIST OF ITEMS NEEDED: 1 green candle ★ 1 blue candle ★ 8 dollar bills ★ 1 green sock ★ 1 peacock feather

✳ Spinning the Spell

Draw a sacred circle around your entire house. Then light the candles, dedicating the green one to Juno and the blue one to Jupiter. Next create a trail of money by placing one of the dollars on the floor just inside your front door. Put the second dollar somewhere in plain sight between the front door and the kitchen, and place the third between the front door and the door to your bedroom. Place the fourth dollar at the threshold of the door to your bedroom, then the fifth on the floor between your bedroom door and your dream altar. Finally, put the other three dollars on your dream altar between the two candles. Each time you put a dollar down, say,

> *Juno and Jupiter, bless me*
> *With plenty of prosperity,*
> *Green money bring to me.*
> *As I will, so shall it be!*

When you are done creating your money trail, start at the beginning of the trail and collect the dollar bills one at a time, putting them in the green sock. As you do this say,

> *Sock of green,*
> *Bring money dreams.*
> *Blessed be!*

Put the sock in your top bureau drawer. Allow the candles to burn down completely, and chant the names Juno and Jupiter silently, over and over again, until you drift to sleep.

In the morning, write down everything you recall of your dreams, and then thank the Goddess and God for their help and pull up the circle. Leave the sock in your top drawer for at least eight days to attract money and prosperity.

◖ Tonight's Magical Adventure: Bindrune Prosperity Charm

This charm uses the ancient runic energies for drawing prosperity into your pocket. The best nights for making the Bindrune Prosperity Charm are Sunday or Thursday, on or close to a full moon.

Bindrunes are two or more upright runes joined together. Their energies are fused into a single shape, thereby creating a powerful magical effect and exhibiting a single runic force. They are widely used for charms.

The most powerful bindrunes consist of three-rune combinations. Clearly demonstrating the union between spirit and science, the number three is locked into your very DNA. The genetic code that tells the cells in your body how to arrange (or bind) amino acids to form protein chains is written in codes that are three bases long, similar to a bindrune. In this way, the pattern of threes is inherently bound within our biochemistry.

LIST OF ITEMS NEEDED: 1 green candle ★ Ballpoint pen or quill ★ Patchouli oil ★ Sandalwood incense and censer ★ Sheet of paper ★ Green felt pen ★ Small piece of pyrite ★ A yard-long piece of green ribbon

✖ Spinning the Spell

Wash the candle in cool saltwater and dry it. Draw a sacred circle and call in your dream guardians. Light the incense. Then use the ballpoint pen or quill to carve the runic symbols of Fehu (ᚠ), Wunjo (ᚹ), and Othala (ᛟ) on the body of the candle, connecting them into one bindrune symbol (ᛟ̷). Fehu represents mobile wealth such as money; Wunjo brings joy and pleasure; and Othala is the rune of reward and inheritance. Next carve your initials directly on top of the runic symbols. Dress the candle with the patchouli oil by rubbing it over the candle body. Wipe your hands, and then light the candle. Take the piece of pyrite and bathe it in the smoke for a couple minutes. Then bathe the pen and paper in the smoke. With the green felt pen, draw the same runes of Fehu (ᚠ), Wunjo (ᚹ), and Othala (ᛟ) in the center of the sheet of paper, and as you do so, again bind the symbols together into one larger bindrune symbol by hooking them together (ᛟ̷). Once again, write your initials over the bindrune. Draw a circle around the whole thing. Next cover the pyrite with patchouli oil, and place the stone in the center of the paper, on top of the bindrune. Then take the candle and drip eight drops of green wax on the pyrite. Fold the paper in half, and then in half again, and again, and again, for a total of four folds. Wind the ribbon around the charm eight times and knot the end eight times. To empower your charm, hold it in your hands and chant these words:

Prosperity, come to me from near and far,
Speeding faster than a shooting star.
Fu, Fa, Fi, Fe, Fo
Wu, Wa, Wi, We, Wo
Othul, Othal, Othil, Othel, Othol
Hu, Ha, Hi, He, Ho
Hu, Ha, Hi, He, Ho
So be it! Dream it so!

Put the charm on the altar overnight, and allow the candle to burn down completely. As you drift to sleep, repeat silently, "Hu, Ha, Hi, He, Ho."

In the morning, pull up the circle and release the dream guardians. Put the charm in a pants or coat pocket of a green garment, and leave it there for at least eight months to draw more prosperity into your life. During that time, you will most definitely see your financial resources grow.

◖ Tonight's Magical Adventure: Apple Abundance Spell

In Greek mythology, at the edge of night far to the west lived the evening stars, the sweet-singing maiden daughters of the night Goddess Nyx. They were called the Hesperides, and they numbered three, four, or seven and were most likely originally Arcadian. Stewards of many otherworldly treasures, the maidens and a majestic dragon named Ladon, who never slept, guarded a tree of magical golden apples. The apple tree grew in the western Gardens of Ocean (where the fabled Hyperboreans lived) and was given to the Sky Queen Hera as a wedding present by the Earth Goddess Gaia when Hera married Zeus.

This simple and delicious spell can be used to bring luck and long-lasting opportunity into your life. Apples are symbols of life, fertility, renewal, and immortality. Sweet and juicy, they represent something that tastes good. For best results, do this spell on a sabbat or full moon.

LIST OF ITEMS NEEDED: Golden apple ★ Athame or knife ★ Plate

�֍ Spinning the Spell

About an hour before going to bed, draw a sacred circle of golden light around your bedroom and call in your dream guardians. Hold the apple in your hands and say three times,

> *Sweet fruit of luck and abundance*
> *Sweet fruit of opportunity*
> *Blessed be, Blessed be, Blessed be.*

Now carefully cut the apple with your athame in half horizontally. You will see the shape of a five-pointed star in the seed cavity. Now cut it in half again, making four pieces. Then cut each piece in half for a total of eight apple pieces. Eat the pieces one at a time. Before eating each piece, empower it by saying,

> *Apple so abundantly sweet,*
> *Bring opportunity and luck to me.*
> *So dream it! So mote it be!*

Pull up the circle and release the dream guardians. You can repeat this spell as often as you like to bring extra luck and fresh and sweet opportunities into your life.

☾ Tonight's Magical Adventure: New Moon Dream List

The Gypsies say that when you dream of a partially clouded moon, it indicates you will be lucky in love. A full moon means you will be blessed, while dreaming of a new moon means your wishes will be granted. You can use the untapped potential of the new moon to help make your wishes and dreams come true, especially when you keep turning your mind toward a successful outcome. By writing your New Moon Dream List out on a sheet of paper, you can refer to it nightly, thus building your expectation and desire for your dreams to come to fruition. Do this work on a new moon, preferably in the spring or early summer.

LIST OF ITEMS NEEDED: 1 white candle ⋆ Rosemary oil ⋆ Sheet of paper ⋆ Green bow ⋆ Green felt pen

✳ Spinning the Spell

Draw a sacred circle and call in your dream guardians. Rub the candle with a thin film of rosemary oil, and wipe your hands completely. As you light the candle, dedicate it to one of your favorite Goddesses of prosperity (see appendix 1). Next use the green pen to write down your most cherished dreams on the sheet of paper. Leave a couple of lines or some space between dreams to write a few words. In this space, write down three actions or steps that you can take right now to make your dreams come true. Use as few words as possible. For example, if one of your dreams is to become a famous painter, your actions or steps might read: paint every day, obtain an art gallery contact, and find a studio with lots of natural light. After you have finished writing your action steps, place a drop of rosemary oil on each of the four corners of the paper. Be careful not to smear the green ink. Place the paper on your altar for the time being. Then drip eight drops of the oil onto the surface of the green bow. As you apply the oil to the bow, with each drop repeat,

Bow of wishes so green,
Remind me of my dreams.
As I will, so mote it be!

Allow the candle to burn down completely, and as you drift to sleep, visualize your dreams coming true. Feel the feelings of happiness and joy that come from your dreams being actualized in real life.

In the morning, thank the Goddess, pull up the circle, and release your dream guardians. Now take your New Moon Dream List and tape or tack it somewhere where you will read it several times a day. Be sure to take the actions or steps you wrote on the list. Then place the green bow on your dream altar in a prominent position to remind you that your dreams can and will come true.

◖ Tonight's Magical Adventure: Success Story Charm Bag

The Buddha was a remarkable man who discovered that success in life was not based on wealth and riches but rather was gained through faith in the divine and the enlightenment of the spirit. His mother, Maya, is said to have conceived him after a dream. In her dream, she saw him descend from the heavens and enter her womb in the shape of a white elephant. When the Buddha was born, earthquakes and miracles occurred and the ocean water became sweet. At birth, he bore thirty-two primary marks on his body and, being the extraordinary baby that he was, uttered a shout of victory and took seven steps forward. At the same moment of his birth, his future wife, his horse, elephant, charioteer, and the bo tree were also born.

By invoking the Buddha to help you make this charm, you gain both the material riches of his childhood and the spiritual wealth of his adult life. He reminds you that success reflects the wellness of your body, mind, and spirit. Do this charm on a Thursday or Sunday, on a full moon at midnight.

LIST OF ITEMS NEEDED: 1 green candle ★ Cinnamon oil ★ Sandalwood incense and censer ★ Fresh flowers ★ 1 pinch dried ginger ★ 1 pinch sweet basil ★ 1 pinch dried rosemary ★ 32 tiny bits of orange peel ★ Green drawstring bag or pouch ★ Small Buddha figurine

❋ Spinning the Spell

Place the fresh flowers on your altar. Next draw a sacred circle of light around your bedroom. Rub cinnamon oil on the candle, and then anoint your wrists and ankles with the oil. Wipe your hands thoroughly, and then light the candle and incense, dedicating them both to the Buddha. Bathe the green bag or pouch in the incense smoke for a couple of minutes. Then open it up, and add the pinches of basil and rosemary. These herbs help you to savor your success. Next add the pinch of ginger and eight drops of cinnamon oil to the mixture in the charm bag. The ginger and cinnamon increase and strengthen your ability to focus on the powers of success. All the herbs used in the charm bag are considered green herbs because they are used to flavor food and also have known magical properties. Now drop in the bits of orange peel. The orange is a fertility symbol and is used to help your success grow and prosper. Then close the bag, pulling the drawstring tight. To empower your Success Story Charm Bag, hold it in your hands and say three times,

> *The story is, the story goes,*
> *Prosperity, come to me and grow,*
> *Success, come to me and flow.*
> *The story is, the story goes,*
> *So be it! Make it so!*

Now place three drops of oil on the belly of the Buddha figurine. Rub each drop into his belly three times, and as you do, say,

The story is, the story goes,
Prosperity, come to me and grow,
Success, come to me and flow.
The story is, the story goes,
So be it! Buddha, make it so!

Place the Buddha back on your dream altar, next to your charm bag. Allow the candle to burn down completely as you drift to sleep.

In the morning, thank the God of abundance and pull up the circle. Put the charm bag inside one of your favorite books. Leave the Buddha on your altar to remind you that success is not only material but also spiritual. Finally, within the next eight days, take the flower petals and scatter them into a body of water like a nearby creek, pond, lake, or sea, once again thanking the God of abundance as you do so. Within the next thirty-two nights you will begin to feel the benefits of this magical work both financially and spiritually.

C Tonight's Magical Adventure: Money Mantra Spell

A mantra is a spoken or written prayer, charm, spell, incantation, or magic word. If spoken, the mantra is often repeated over and over. This Money Mantra Spell can be used to bring you good luck and plenty of money. The best time to spin it is on a rainy Sunday or Thursday night, during a waxing moon.

This spell invokes the Hindu Goddess Lakshmi. She represents all forms of wealth, including money. Goddess of the wealth of the Earth and mother of the world, Lakshmi is a symbol of the delights of material and spiritual prosperity. Considered the greatest power of the Orient, she is Goddess of growing rice, since rice is associated with money, rain, and fertility. As the bestower of good luck, fortune, and health as well as wealth, gold, and fame, Lakshmi lives in everything: jewels, coins, shells, animals, plants, and in every child. She existed for all time, floating before creation on a lotus, and she emerged from the ocean covered with necklaces, bracelets, and pearls, crowned and golden, bearing a lotus. She is often accompanied by her magical symbols, two elephants.

I have had the great fortune of riding an elephant, feeling the power under me. Indeed, it is said that when you dream of elephants, you are realizing your own power and overcoming all obstacles in your life. Whether or not you have ridden an elephant, you tap into their enormous power as well as the Goddess Lakshmi's wealth to bring riches and happiness into your life.

LIST OF ITEMS NEEDED: 1 green candle ⋆ Patchouli incense ⋆ Lotus oil ⋆ Bowl of uncooked rice ⋆ Small toy elephant or elephant statue

✳ Spinning the Spell

Draw the sacred circle and call in your dream guardians. Sprinkle your altar with the rice. As you do this, say nine times,

Lakshmi, please come to me.

Rub the candle with lotus oil, and then anoint your forehead, wrists, and ankles. Place the candle in its holder on the altar. Wipe the oil off your hands, and then light the candle, dedicating it to the Goddess Lakshmi by saying,

I dedicate this candle to the beautiful Lakshmi.

Light the incense, dedicating it to the Goddess by saying,

I dedicate this incense to Lakshmi of the lotus flower.

Then take the elephant in your hands, and rub nine drops of lotus oil over it. As you do this, say,

Ommmmm, Ommmmm, Ommmmm

Dear Goddess of wealth, beautiful Lakshmi,
Please grant me dreams of prosperity,
May money and wealth now rain down on me.
By the lotus-gem Goddess, Blessed be!
Ommmmm, Ommmmm, Ommmmm

Place the elephant next to your pillow. Allow the candle to burn down all the way, and as you drift to sleep, repeat the ancient mantra "Om mani padme hum" over and over.

In the morning, write down everything you remember of your dreams. Put the elephant on your dream altar, and repeat the money mantra,

Ommmmm, Ommmmm, Ommmmm
Dear Goddess of wealth, beautiful Lakshmi,
Please grant me dreams of prosperity,
May money and wealth now rain down on me.
By the lotus-gem Goddess, Blessed be!
Ommmmm, Ommmmm, Ommmmm

Then pull up your circle and release your dream guardians. Leave the elephant on your altar to remind you of the constant protection and presence of Goddess of wealth and abundance, Lakshmi. Whenever you find you need more money in your life, repeat the money mantra over and over as you drift to sleep, bringing you sweet dreams of prosperity. You will discover that the Goddess can be very generous, sharing her great wealth with you when you have a genuine need or desire.

◑ Tonight's Magical Adventure: Mojo Money Dream Bags

Mojo or gris-gris bags are magical charms. These Money Mojo Dream Bags can be used to really "get your mojo working" for you, doubling your money for paying bills and enjoying yourself.

Make these two bags on a Thursday night, on or close to a full moon. Bag #1 is designed to bring you silver and Bag #2 to bring you gold.

LIST OF ITEMS NEEDED: 1 silver candle ★ 1 gold (not yellow) candle ★ Sage and cedar smudge

Bag #1: 8 cashews ★ 8 almonds ★ 3 pinches dried mint ★ 1 silver coin ★ 1 dollar bill ★ Piece of green jade ★ Green flannel drawstring bag, pouch, or sock ★ 16-inch piece of green ribbon or string

Bag #2: Piece of green moss from a tree (preferably a fruit- or cone-bearing one) ★ 8 sesame seeds ★ 8 cloves ★ 3 pinches rolled oats ★ 3 pinches allspice ★ Gold (plated or colored) chain ★ 1 dollar bill ★ Piece of green malachite ★ Green flannel drawstring bag, pouch, or sock ★ 16-inch piece of green ribbon or string

✦ Spinning the Spell

Thoroughly smudge your bedroom, altar, yourself, and everything you will be putting into the mojo bags, including the bags themselves. If you are allergic to smudge, use a room diffuser with cedar and sage oil instead.

Place everything you will need on your altar, and then light the silver candle, dedicating it to a favorite Goddess or God. Assemble Bag #1, adding the ingredients to the bag one at a time in the order listed. Wrap the silver coin inside the dollar bill before inserting it into the mojo bag. Close the bag, and then wind the green ribbon around it eight times in a clockwise motion and knot the ends of the ribbon eight times. Hold the Mojo Money Dream Bag in your hands, and empower it by merging with the divine energy to whom you dedicated the silver candle and saying three times,

Money grow, double, and thrive,
Generous spirits, come alive.

Silver and green, come to me,
Hoodoo, bring me prosperity.
As I will, so shall it be!

Place Bag #1 on the altar, in front of the silver candle.

Next light the gold candle, dedicating it to another Goddess or God of prosperity. Put everything in Bag #2 in the order listed. Wrap the gold chain in the dollar bill before putting it in the bag. Then close the bag. Wind the green ribbon around the bag eight times clockwise, and knot the end eight times. Hold the bag in your hands, merge with the Goddess or God you dedicated the gold candle to, and say three times,

Money grow, double, and thrive,
Generous spirits, come alive.
Gold and green, come to me,
Hoodoo, wrap me in money.
As I will, so shall it be!

Place Bag #2 on the altar in front of the gold candle.

Allow the candles to burn completely down, and as you drift to sleep, repeat these words silently: "Money grow, double, and thrive."

In the morning, write down everything you remember from your dreams. Place the Money Mojo Dream Bags next to your checkbook, in your purse, pocket, or safe, in your mailbox if you receive money through the mail, or in a cash box with other coins and dollar bills. The idea is to put the gris-gris bags in two different places where they make physical contact with sources of money so that your income will double and thrive. Leave both bags in place for at least eight months. During this time, your money will grow and multiply. When you disassemble the bag, return the organic materials to the Earth and put the two stones on your altar for future use. Take out the dollar bills, and place them (with the gold and silver items folded inside of them) in a special pocket in your wallet or purse. Do not unfold them or spend them, but carry them with you as a reminder of your ever-growing source of silver, gold, and green. This will ensure your financial prosperity.

☾ Tonight's Magical Adventure: Candle and Coin Abundance Spell

The purpose of this spell is to strengthen and solidify your financial outlook over the next year, using a candle and coin.

Cast this spell on a Sunday or Thursday night, on or close to the full moon.

LIST OF ITEMS NEEDED: 1 green candle in a silver holder ★ Frankincense incense and censer ★ Patchouli oil ★ Ballpoint pen or quill ★ 1 Sacajawea dollar coin or a silver dollar ★ A recent photo of yourself (one that can be creased) ★ Glue ★ 1 green sock

✴ Spinning the Spell

Wash the candle in cool saltwater and dry it. Then draw a sacred circle and call in your dream guardians. Light the incense, dedicating it to a favorite Goddess of creation and prosperity such as Bridget (Celtic), Felicitas (Roman), or Sarah (Hebrew). Ask the Goddess to offer her blessings and power to your spell. Next carve the name of the Goddess into the candle body with the pen or quill. Inscribe your name next to hers. Join the names together with a large dollar sign, and then inscribe a circle around the names and symbol. Rub a thin film of patchouli oil on the candle body, and use the oil on your hands to anoint the top of your head, your forehead, and the bottoms of your feet. Wipe the oil from your hands, and then light the candle, once again dedicating it to the Goddess, while saying,

Candle of abundance and plenty,
Let your fire flame fill me.

By the will of (name of the Goddess).
So shall it be! Blessed be!

Now hold the coin in your dominant hand, and bathe it in the incense smoke for a couple of minutes. Place three generous drops of glue on the face of the coin, and then fold it into the photo. Be sure the face of the photo and the face of the coin are glued together, face-to-face, when you do this. Seal the photo with the candle wax. This may take a few minutes, as you will need to let the first coat of wax dry and then apply another, repeating the process many times until the photo stays closed around the coin. Hold the photo with the coin lightly in your dominant hand, merge with the Goddess, and say three times,

Coin of abundance and plenty,
Into the moon and stars I see.
With leaps that generously bound,
My money grows all year round.
So be it! So dream it so!

Place the folded photo and coin in front of the candle. Allow the candle to burn down completely, and as you drift to sleep visualize yourself being surrounded by vibrant, warm green light.

When you wake in the morning, pull up the circle and release your dream guardians. Put the photo with coin in the green sock, and put the sock in your sock drawer. Leave it there for a year, taking it out once a month on the full moon and placing it on your altar to reinforce its abundance-drawing power. Each time you reinforce its power, you will find extra cash coming into your life.

☾ Tonight's Magical Adventure: Dragon Riches Dream Spell

Dreaming about a dragon signifies good luck, great potency, and personal power as well as wisdom and wealth. The mythical dragons often guarded treasures of precious gems and metals, secretly hidden in deep caverns beneath the wildest forests. Even today there are people who firmly believe in their existence.

The Anglo-Saxon word *drakan,* a Greek derivative, is either from *draco,* meaning a dragon or large snake, or from the verb *derkein,* which means "to see clearly." Accordingly, dragons had clear sight and the ability to foretell the future. Found at sulfur springs, wells, lakes, and inside mountains, and living for thousands of years, the dragon is synonymous with the Ouroboros or Earth Serpent, an ever-continuing symbol of power and wisdom. The dragon exemplifies elemental power, especially of the Earth. These dragon energies figure predominantly in the practice of feng shui. In fact, experts in feng shui are also called Dragon Masters.

In Celtic mythology, there is an isolated wooded hill called Dinas Emrys in Wales, where it is said that Merlin dealt with two dragons, one red and one white, who were fighting in an underground lake beneath the rock. He eventually built his own fortress on the legendary hilltop. The official emblem of Wales is the red dragon, derived from the Great Red Serpent, which was associated with the Welsh God Dewi. The Celtic dragon represents sovereignty such as Pendragon, the Celtic word meaning "chief," and thus the Red Dragon was emblazoned on King Arthur's helmet in battle.

The Mester Stoorworm of Scottish faerytales was the largest, the first, and the father of all the Stoorworms. The gargantuan creature had venomous breath and one eye that glowed and flamed like a ward fire. His body stretched halfway across the world, and his tongue was thousands of miles long. Upon his death, his teeth became the Orkneys, the Faroes, and the Shetland Islands, his forked tongue entangled itself on one horn of the moon, and his curled-up body hardened and became Iceland.

The best time to do this spell is on one of the eight sabbats, preferably on Beltane or Samhain. To add more power to the spell, spin it during a thunderstorm.

LIST OF ITEMS NEEDED: 1 gold (not yellow) candle ⋆
Dragon's blood oil ⋆ 8 pinches sweet basil ⋆ Gold-colored cup or
chalice filled with water ⋆ Golden string or ribbon ⋆ Music that
stirs your blood

✷ Spinning the Spell

Wash the candle in cool saltwater and dry it. Place the candle and
other ingredients on your altar. Turn on the music, and then draw
a sacred circle of golden light and set your dream guardians in
place. Next call in your favorite Goddess of prosperity. Use the pen
or quill to inscribe the word *Treasure* into the candle body. Next
carve your initials just above this word. Rub a thin film of
dragon's blood oil over the candle body. Next put the pinches of
basil on a cutting board or similar surface, and roll the candle in
the powdered herbs. The sweet basil is used to tame the dragon
and was considered the antidote for the dragon's or basilisk's poisonous breath. After you are finished rolling the candle in the
basil, place it in its holder on the altar and light it, saying three
times,

> *O great dragon, let your golden fire enter my dream.*
> *O great dragon, bring me golden treasures of prosperity.*
> *By the light of the stars and moon, so shall it be!*

Now anoint the top of your head, forehead, wrists, and ankles
with the oil. As you do this, say three times,

> *Dragon's blood, grace my body,*
> *I am the dragon as the dragon is me.*
> *So it is! So shall it be!*

Drop eight drops of oil into the cup or chalice of water. With
each drop say,

Into the water goes the dragon's power,
Let my prosperity begin to flower.
So be it! So shall it be!

Saturate the string with oil, and wind it around the cup or chalice eight times without tying it. Then knot each of the ends eight times. Merge with the Goddess and say,

With each wind, I bind myself to wealth,
Until the number does equal eight,
With each knot, I ride the golden string,
That leads me up to Draco's Gate.
I wind it round the stars and pull
Till my treasure trove is full.
So be it! So shall it be! So be it!

Allow the candle to burn down on its own, and as you drift to sleep, repeat silently, "I am the dragon as the dragon is me."

In the morning, thank deity, pull up the circle, and release your dream guardians. Keep the knotted string next to your money to attract your dragon's share of wealth and prosperity. Within the next eight months, you will attract an unexpected boon.

☾ Tonight's Magical Adventure: Wendrune Money Spell

Considered powerful magic, wendrunes are a coded form of runes that are written backward, from right to left, with their shapes reversed or upside down. This spell uses magical wendrunes to help you get your finances turned around—out of the red and into the green! Select a Monday, Thursday, or Saturday night to spin this spell, close to or on a new moon.

LIST OF ITEMS NEEDED: 1 green candle ⋆ Ballpoint pen or quill ⋆ 1 teaspoon honey

✱ Spinning the Spell

Wash the candle in cool saltwater and dry it. Next draw a sacred circle of bright green light around your bedroom, and call in your favorite Goddess and God of abundance. Use the pen or quill to inscribe the word *Money* three times in the candle body, using runic symbols but writing them backward, like this:

ᛃᛖᚾᛟᛗ

Then spread a very thin film of honey over the body of the candle and put it in its holder on the altar. Merge with the Goddess and God of abundance, light the candle, and say three times,

Magic wendrunes of money,
As sweet as wild honey,
Turn my finances from red to green.
So be it! So mote it be!

Warm both of your hands in the candle flame for a couple of minutes, being careful not to burn your skin, and say,

Money sticks to me like honey.
Money sticks to me like honey.
Money sticks to me like honey.
So be it! So mote it be!

Allow the candle to burn down completely, and as you drift to sleep, silently repeat the words "Red into green."

In the morning, thank the Goddess and God of abundance and pull up the circle. In the next five weeks you will find more money than usual in your pocket and bank account. Your financial resources should grow and blossom.

☾

chapter six

Self-Empowerment
Dream Magic

The first time I had this dream I awoke screaming. I had broken out
in a cold sweat, and the room was pulsating with a strange, unset-
tling energy. It took me a moment to regain my sense of balance,
and then I started reconstructing what had happened in the dream:

*It's late at night, and I'm in a house that is well lit. It seems
familiar but not really. There are antiques and old rugs here and
there, and the air smells old but not stale. Suddenly the lights start
going out, one at a time. I keep trying the light switches, but they
don't work. I am walking down the hallway to what seems to be
my room, and I get inside and turn on the light and shut the door
most of the way. The light suddenly flickers off, and I can see this
wave of strangely bright, greenish light begin coming through the
doorway. I rush over to slam the door, and it takes all my strength
to close it. I finally do close the door, but I feel terrified and wake
up screaming, "No!"*

This same dream continued to recur at intervals of once or twice a month, and when I woke up from the dream I would feel completely drained of energy and personal power. In the back of my mind I knew the light represented all my fears and insecurities. Knowing this only made me push the door closed even harder every time the greenish light tried to enter my room in the dream. It was getting tiresome!

Then I gave myself the suggestion to wake up immediately upon finding myself in the house in the dream but while the lights were still on. This worked for a while, but I knew I would eventually have to face my fears if I was ever to regain my personal power. Finally one night as I was having this same dream, I felt myself finally coming to grips with the dream. Instead of using all my strength to push the door closed against the light, I flung the door wide open, daring the light to come into the room. Suddenly all the lights in the house came back on, and everything returned to normal. The all-pervasive greenish light was gone, and I felt full of energy when I woke up. Since that night the dream has not recurred.

The spells in this chapter can help you in your personal quest toward self-empowerment. Ultimately, no one else can empower you. This is something you must do yourself, just as I did when I faced my fears in the recurring dream. Traditionally, it was the individual dream that empowered a person and provided meaning within the whole of Oneness. Dream magic restores this individual dream by providing spells that can enrich and empower your life.

◖ Tonight's Magical Adventure: Happy Home Ritual

Use this ritual to make your home happier and to promote peace, happiness, and protection as well as good health, prosperity, and longevity in your life. It is best done on a gibbous or full moon. By invoking the elementals in this home blessing, you not only clear out any unwanted energies, you also charge your home with elemental and divine power. The potted fern sets this Happy Home Ritual in place, allowing it to grow and thrive along with the plant. Traditionally considered a powerful protective plant, ferns are grown in and around the home for protection from negativity and harm.

LIST OF ITEMS NEEDED: 1 white candle ★ Frankincense incense and censer ★ Chalice or cup filled with water ★ Bowl ★ 6 pinches loose chamomile flowers (from tea bags) ★ 6 pinches rosemary ★ 36 coriander seeds ★ Potted fern

✳ Spinning the Spell

Begin in your bedroom, setting up your altar and putting all the items on it. Place the fern a safe distance from the candle and incense. Next combine the chamomile, rosemary, and coriander together in the bowl. Draw a sacred circle, but this time as you visualize the circle of light, imagine it surrounding your entire home, not just your bedroom. Then light the candle and incense, dedicating them to your favorite divine energies.

Face east, take the burning incense from the altar, and hold it in your hands. Wave it carefully three times side to side toward the east point, merge with the powers of air, and say,

> *Powers of the east, masters of air,*
> *I greet, honor, and welcome you here!*
> *Powers of the east, masters of wind,*
> *Come protect my home and forever be my friend.*

Set the incense back down on the altar, and take the candle-holder in your hands. Face south, and wave the candle from side to side three times toward the south point, being careful not to get hot wax on your skin or furnishings. Merge with powers of fire and say,

Powers of the south, masters of fire,
I greet, honor, and welcome you here!
Powers of the south, masters of light,
Come bless my home and light my nights.

Set the candle back on the altar, and hold the chalice of water in your hands. Face west, dip your fingers into the water, and sprinkle the west point with the drops of water. Do this three times while merging with the powers of water, and then say,

Powers of the west, masters of water,
I greet, honor, and welcome you here!
Powers of the west, masters of mist,
Come protect my home and grant my wish.

Set the chalice on the altar, and take the bowl of herbs in your hands. Sprinkle three tiny pinches of herbs into the north corner of the room, merge with the powers of earth, and say,

Powers of the north, masters of earth,
I greet, honor, and welcome you here!
Powers of the north, masters of ground,
Come bless my home and remain around.

Place the bowl back on the altar. Facing your altar, hold your arms upward in the Goddess position, merge with Oneness, and say,

Helpful divine powers of all elements,
I greet, honor, and welcome you here!
Come and stay, I pray you, helpful divine powers.
Please bless and protect my happy home.
By air, fire, water, earth, and spirit, So be it!

Next take a few minutes to scatter tiny bits of the herbs in the bowl throughout the corners of your house. Start just inside your front door, and move clockwise through your home, covering the four corners of each room with a tiny sprinkle of the protective herbal mixture. When you are done, lie back and gaze at the candle flame on the altar for a few minutes. Imagine the candle flame being a bright spirit light. Close your eyes, and begin to see and feel the white spirit light growing larger and filling you, your bedroom, and your entire home with positive, happy, and loving energy. Allow the candle to burn down completely.

When you wake in the morning, thank the elemental powers and the Goddesses and Gods who assisted you, and pull up the circle. Finally, place the potted fern in a sunny location where it will thrive, and water it with the water in the altar chalice. This will guarantee your home stays happy and safe.

☾ Tonight's Magical Adventure: Chakra Sevenfold Empowerment Spell

Chakras are actual points in the body where psychic energies and bodily functions merge and interact. Eighty-eight thousand chakras exist within the human body. Out of these many thousand, there are seven primary chakras or major energy centers. These are the crown chakra (top of head), third eye (between and above eyebrows), throat chakra (center of base of neck), heart chakra (over your heart), solar plexus (below breastbone), sacral areas (just below navel), and root chakra (base of spine and genitals).

Treating yourself to a chakra cleansing bath both clears out any negativity in these energy centers and charges your magical field of intention. To take a chakra cleansing shower, follow the basic guidelines below, but put the rosemary oil and sea salt inside a washcloth or glove. As you shower, rub the cloth over your chakras, starting at the root chakra and moving upward to the top of your head.

LIST OF ITEMS NEEDED: Smudge or diffuser with sage and cedar oil ★ Warm bath (or shower) ★ 4 drops rosemary oil ★ ½ cup sea salt ★ Soft robe

✖ Spinning the Spell

After smudging your bathroom and bedroom, draw your bath and put the rosemary oil and sea salt into the tub. Now place your hands, palms down, over the bathwater and visualize and sense the bath cleansing and energizing you. Immerse your hands in the water, and sense yourself charging the water with energy. Next slip into the tub, sit back, and relax. After a few minutes of soaking, begin to chant the following:

Salt and rosemary, balance and clear
Wheels of energy, front and rear.
Water, restore me from head to toe.
Blessed be, now make it so!

Next take a washcloth and, using small clockwise spiral motions, rub the cloth softly over your chakras, one at a time, along the front of your body. Start at your root chakra, and move upward to the top of your head. Stay in the bath as long as you like, immersing yourself at least three times while visualizing and feeling all your tensions floating away. Towel off using clockwise spiral motions from your head to your toes. Sense a strong golden cord moving from your spine into the Earth below you. Put on your robe and go to bed. As you drift off to sleep, visualize yourself being completely enveloped by a warm, egg-shaped, golden light. Repeat silently, "Wheels of light spinning in harmony."

In the morning, record your dreams. As you start your day, once again visualize the golden cord of light moving from your spine into the Earth below you. By doing so, you will remain more grounded and energized.

C Tonight's Magical Adventure: Creating a Dream Magic Garden

Gardens are naturally magical places, and every gardener is a magician. The aroma of a budding rose, the crispness of fresh snow peas, and the cooling shade of a fruiting apple tree are all unforgettable. Creating a dream magic garden is a way for you to bring these experiences into your dream world. Like your astral dream altar, your dream magic garden does not have to conform to the laws of nature. No need to water, weed, or mulch this garden. Instead, lie back and watch as it magically grows.

LIST OF ITEMS NEEDED: 1 white candle ★ Rose incense and censer ★ Picture of a favorite garden ★ Your imagination

✳ Spinning the Spell

Light the candle and incense, and place the garden picture on your altar so you can see it easily. Focus all your attention on the picture, feeling almost as if you could step inside the picture and enter the garden. Now close your eyes and gradually begin to imagine your dream garden. What kind of garden space appears in your mind's eye? Is it untamed or orderly, sunny or partly in the shade? What kinds of plants, flowers, and trees are in your dream garden? Is there a pond or stream? Are there birds, insects, and animals? Any special colors, a garden bench, or trellis? What otherworldly qualities appear in your garden?

Allow the candle and incense to burn out on their own, and as you drift to sleep, see and feel yourself in the middle of your dream garden. You feel peaceful and at one with everything as the beauty of the garden envelops you in its vibrant energy. Visit this garden any night to revitalize yourself. Its healing energies can help relieve daily stress, ensuring more personal energy and a better night's sleep.

◖ Tonight's Magical Adventure: Flying Without a Broomstick

Flying in your dreams creates a kind of euphoria. Flying dreams can also have life-altering consequences because they allow you to see the overall direction of your life. Through the ages, flying dreams have been connected to ecstatic love because the soul of the dreamer can sprout wings and be released from all earthly burdens, finding ways out of difficult situations. Samhain or Halloween often conjures up the stereotype of a witch flying on a broomstick, but face it, most modern witches use their broomstick (besom) to clean their ritual circle, not to fly on, and I, personally, wouldn't be seen dead wearing a pointed hat! The following is a form of flying you can do without your broomstick. The best time to do this magical work is on Samhain Eve or on a full moon.

LIST OF ITEMS NEEDED: White candle and holder ★ Picture of your favorite bird ★ 2 sheets of paper and pen ★ 1 white envelope

✳ Spinning the Spell

Draw a sacred circle and call in your dream guardians. On the first sheet of paper write down all the things you feel you have accomplished in the past year. Fold this paper in half eight times, and place it in a bottom bureau drawer. On the second piece of paper, write down the things you want to do in the upcoming year. Where do you want to find yourself a year from now? Put this sheet of paper on your bedside altar where you can read it easily, and place the picture of your favorite bird next to it. Light the candle and focus your attention completely on the paper and picture while you chant or sing these words:

> *Let dreams and visions surface with my flight,*
> *Let them wing and soar unto new heights.*
> *My wishes will come true, this I know.*
> *So mote it be, it shall be so!*

As you focus on the picture and paper, breathe deeply and begin to sense your arms becoming the wings of the bird in the picture. After the transformation is complete, spread your feathered wings, and within an instant sense yourself flying high in the sky. Imagine looking down below you, noticing how everything seems small as you soar ever higher. Behind you, see the past year. Before you, the upcoming year shines brightly with all its potential, like a brilliant full moon. From your vantage point in the sky, everything has an added clarity because you see the entire picture, both where you have been and where you are going. You are winging your way to personal empowerment. Now nothing can stop you from discovering the magical person you truly are. Spend a few minutes looking at the upcoming year.

Next place the picture and the sheet of paper together, facing each other. Fold them in half nine times and place them inside the envelope. Seal the envelope with candle wax from the altar candle and put it in your top bureau drawer. Allow the candle to burn down on its own. As you drift to sleep, imagine yourself as a magnificent bird flying to new heights.

In the morning, write down your dreams in your journal, pull up the circle, and release your dream guardians. Over the next year, you will begin winging toward where you would like to find yourself.

☾ Tonight's Magical Adventure: Castle Light Dream Adventure

Like the Crystal Dream Castle Love Spell earlier in this book, this adventure uses your dream castle crystal as a magical focal point. Fashioned from your imagination, your dream castle is a personal power place where dreams always come true. It's a place where you can do just about anything, including raise your drawbridge and recharge your batteries. My castle looks sort of like the Taj Mahal in the front, with huge water gardens and enormous spires of clear quartz crystal jutting out behind it. When the moonlight hits the crystals, it's literally out of this world!

This dream adventure expands your awareness and vitalizes your entire being. The best time for taking this adventure is on the sabbats or a full moon. Remember to use your dream castle crystal every time you step between worlds and visit your dream castle. Your crystal amplifies your magical field of intent, allowing you to merge more fully with the experience.

LIST OF ITEMS NEEDED: 2 white candles ⋆ Sandalwood oil ⋆ Dream castle crystal ⋆ Soft instrumental music ⋆ Your imagination

�֍ Spinning the Spell

Rinse the candles off, dry them, and then rub them with sandalwood oil. Anoint yourself with the oil on the third eye (forehead) and behind each ear, and then dab three drops on both wrists and ankles. Next draw a sacred circle, call in your dream guardians, and put on some soft instrumental music. Place your dream castle crystal in the center of your altar with the point toward you, and put the candles on either side of it, about four inches apart. Light the candles, and dedicate each to a favorite Goddess and God such as Kerridwen and Kernunnos or Odin and Frigga.

Next gaze at the crystal, breathing rhythmically and calming your mind. Let go of the tensions and worries of the day as you exhale. Now focus all your attention on the stone while holding it in your hands and gazing into it. Merge with the crystal and become one with it, imagining a magnificent dream castle, your dream castle, within its center. The moonlight shines brilliantly on its walls and towers as you enter. Imagine touching, hearing, smelling, and even tasting this castle. As you begin to walk through the different rooms of your castle, select a room with lots of windows and filled with moonlight. Now imagine a thick golden cord of energy connecting you to your castle, and as you take a deep breath, sense all the magical energy of your castle flowing through the cord into your body, mind, and spirit. Take several deep breaths, and fill yourself with pure golden energy. Afterward, imagine a strong silver cord of light connecting you to the moon. Breathe in the lunar energy, and draw its power through the silver cord, filling yourself to the brim with moonlight. Ask the moon for divine guidance, blessing, inspiration, and protection. Next imagine a sphere of bright silver-gold light radiating from your heart, and feel as it pulses outward into the heavens with your every breath. Use rhythmic breathing to amplify your silver-gold radiance, seeing and sensing it increase with each breath you take. Feel yourself becoming a star of vibrant light. Allow this starlight to fill your castle, and then let your spirit fly out into the night sky as a whirling star of light. There is no limit to the energy, power, and vitality you can absorb through the gold and silver cords, so keep drinking in the energy until you feel completely full. Allow the candles to burn all the way down, and as you drift to sleep visualize your energy field becoming so bright that you illuminate your entire castle. Breathe in this sense of power and vitality, and repeat silently, "I am Oneness, I am light."

Record your dreams when you wake up, and then pull up the circle and release your dream guardians. Keep your dream castle crystal on your altar for more castle adventures later in this book.

☾ Tonight's Magical Adventure: Secret Name Dream Spell

Every seafarer knows the value of a safe harbor from storms. By employing the traditional Druid secret name work, you can find a safe harbor no matter where you are when things start getting stormy.

Names are sacred and can be used as magical tools for personal empowerment as well as for protection from harm and attack. To discover the name of a person or a supernatural being such as an elf or faery is to gain power over that being. Tales and legends abound with individuals who needed to discover a true name of someone to be saved, and many of the ancient deities had secret names, which they only revealed to mortals at certain times. From these beginnings arose the use of hidden or secret names.

Your secret name arises out of the Eternal Now, from that point between worlds where you can see and find everything. When you discover and begin using your secret name you become, in essence, a new person with a new name. The optimum time for doing this spell is on a Monday, on or just before a full moon.

LIST OF ITEMS NEEDED: 1 silver candle ⋆ Bowl of sea salt ⋆ Seashell

✳ Spinning the Spell

Draw a sacred circle of white light around your bedroom, and then take the bowl and sprinkle a circle of sea salt around your altar and yourself, always moving clockwise. Next call in your dream guardians and then light the candle, dedicating it to a Goddess and God of the sea for protection and power. Good choices are the Celtic Sea God and king of the oceans, Llyr, and the Great Sea Mother, the wise and powerful Morrigan. These divine powers of the sea can help awaken psychic abilities and provide insights, prophetic dreams, and lunar wisdom.

Hold the seashell in your hands, merge with the ocean energy, and say three times,

Helpful powers of the sea,
Bring my secret name to me.

Still holding the shell, speak aloud to yourself, repeating this question over and over again:

What is my secret name?

Many names will come to mind, but make an effort to hone in on the one name that keeps popping up in your mind. It may be a name (or word) you are familiar with, or it might be a name (or word) you have never heard before. Once you know your secret name, perform the following steps to strengthen your name's protective power as a safe harbor:

1. State aloud that you are now known by your secret name (say the name) and that all the previous names you have been known by are not really your true names. Only one name represents the true you, and that is your secret name (say the name).
2. State aloud that you are safe from harm and from any negative thoughts from anyone unless that person knows your true name. Say your secret name once again.
3. Create an eternity clause in your secret name by setting up impossible tasks that would have to be performed by any person who discovered your secret name and wanted to use it against you. For example, you might say aloud, "Before anyone can use my secret name against me, they would have to count the atoms, one by one, of all the celestial bodies of the cosmos over and over again, backward and forward, forever and a night."
4. Repeat steps 1 to 3 a minimum of three times to reinforce a pattern or shield of strength, providing you with a safe harbor whenever and wherever you may need one. Also remember, *never* write down or tell your secret name to another person, even your mate or best friend. Allow the candle to burn down completely. As you drift to sleep, silently repeat your secret name over and over again.

In the morning, place the shell on your altar to remind you of your safe and protective harbor. Thank the divine energies who helped you with the spell, pull up the circle, and release the dream guardians. Leave the salt circle in place for three nights, and then vacuum or sweep it up, tossing the salt outside your front door for added protection. Use your secret name whenever you need protection.

◖ Tonight's Magical Adventure: Warm, Fuzzy Feeling Spell

This spell helps you attract your most treasured desires by identifying your wants, getting that warm, fuzzy feeling in place, and letting the energy flow, flow, flow! Most of us have an amazing inventory of hidden desires and long-forgotten fantasies that are just waiting to be taken out of the closet and dusted off. Take some time to give each one of your deepest desires another long, hard look. Choose those desires that make you happy, and you'll vibrate them into your life. Using this spell, you can also learn to discern positive vibrations from negative ones and to immediately flip the switch from feeling bad to feeling good. The waxing or gibbous moon is the best time to do this spell.

LIST OF ITEMS NEEDED: 1 purple candle ∗ Lavender oil ∗ Warm, fuzzy blanket

✳ Spinning the Spell

Apply lavender oil to the candle body, and place it in its holder on the altar. Anoint yourself with lavender oil for peaceful sleep and protection by rubbing three drops on the top of your head and three drops on your wrists and ankles. Draw the sacred circle, call in your dream guardians, and light the candle, dedicating it to one of your favorite deities. Gaze at the candle flame for a few minutes while you think about your deepest desires, particularly those that make you feel all warm and fuzzy inside. Make certain your desire comes, not out of fear-based need, but out of want, which derives from desire and breeds excitement. Now phrase your desire in a positive way to make it so. Stay tuned in to how you feel when you say your phrase. If what you are saying makes you feel warm and fuzzy all over, like sailing into the heavens in sheer delight, you are on the right track. For example,

> *I want the happiness in my life to expand into ongoing and boundless joy.*

Or,

> *I want my creative talents to expand and grow a hundred-fold.*

When you find the desire and positive statement that makes you feel all warm and fuzzy inside and out, you have plugged into your power source. Now rethink, rephrase, and refeel your desire until it feels terrific. Then take your warm, fuzzy blanket and snuggle into it. Envelop yourself in its softness, and feel its warm, cushy texture next to your skin. Cuddle into your blanket as if you are cuddling your warm, fuzzy desire until you feel completely safe and sound there. As you snuggle into your blanket, feel your desire getting stronger and stronger. Feel it, and keep feeling it, until it's completely warm and fuzzy. If you can feel it, you can make it so. Snuggle into the blanket and drift to sleep, allowing the candle to burn down on its own.

In the morning, thank your favorite deity, pull up the circle, and release your dream guardians. Keep the blanket on your bed, and use it to get that warm, fuzzy feeling whenever you want. Remember to take at least five minutes every evening, and dare to desire, dream, want, and intend. Take a few minutes to flow energy toward your most treasured desires. Realize that they are forming, happening, and on their way. Get that warm and fuzzy feeling, and know it, with your body, mind, and soul!

◖ Tonight's Magical Adventure: Brain Child Spell

Whether you are cramming for a final exam or learning a new job, this Brain Child Spell will help you tap into the knowledge and wisdom to make you a success at whatever you do. This spell is particularly effective when cast on a Wednesday night during a waxing, gibbous, or full moon.

LIST OF ITEMS NEEDED: 1 yellow candle ★ Rosemary oil ★ 13 whole cloves ★ Tumbled piece of citrine ★ Small glass ★ Dictionary

✶ Spinning the Spell

Wash the candle in cool saltwater, dry it, and then rub a thin film of rosemary oil on the candle and set it in its holder. Anoint yourself with the oil at your wrists and ankles. Next put the candle in a window where the moon shines in on it, and then light it, dedicating it to a God or Goddess of knowledge such as Odin (Norse), Ogma (Celtic), or Bridget (Celtic). Drop the cloves into the glass, one at a time, and then rub seven drops of rosemary oil on the piece of citrine and carefully put it also in the glass. Set the glass on top of the dictionary. Place your hands on either side of the glass, making contact with both the glass and the dictionary, and say three times,

> *Essence of clove, let all knowledge flow,*
> *Essence of rosemary, let my wisdom grow,*
> *Let my connection to the whole be One,*
> *So that I may know all that I desire.*
> *By the light of the moon, so be it!*

Before you retire, take the candle out of the window and place it in front of the dictionary and glass at a safe distance. Allow the candle to burn down completely as you drift to sleep. Keep the glass and dictionary next to you whenever you are studying to remind

you of your natural ability to tap into the wisdom of the universe.
You will find you are more alert and your mind more agile.

◖ Tonight's Magical Adventure:
   Creating a Dream Amulet

People traditionally wore amulets as protective charms, usually in
the form of a necklace or ring. Amulets were also hung in the
house and used to repel or drive away harmful energies. Traditionally made of metal or stone, amulets are similar to talismans but
differ in that amulets contain specific protective powers. Throughout history, amulets have been made by alchemists, witches,
shamans, and priests and sold to people wanting to protect themselves against violence, illness, thieves, and bad luck. Worn by
queens and kings, popes, diplomats, merchants, and nearly everyone else, amulets appeal to the part of human nature that puts
trust in certain lucky objects. You probably already have some
kind of amulet or little object in your car, at home, or on your person that has a special meaning to you.

You can create your own amethyst dream amulet to use for
protection while you sleep and dream. Amulets made of gemstones, such as amethyst, have always been valued more highly
than those made from other materials. Amethyst has a reputation
for its protective, healing, and spiritual powers. When worn during
sleep or placed under your pillow, it will protect you with its magical powers and bring meaningful dreams. The best time for creating this dream amulet is on Midsummer's Eve or on a full moon.

LIST OF ITEMS NEEDED: Small piece of tumbled amethyst ⋆
Cedar incense and censer ⋆ 1 purple candle ⋆ 1 white candle ⋆
1 blue candle ⋆ Quill or ballpoint pen ⋆ Lavender oil

✳ Spinning the Spell

Wash the candles in cool saltwater, dry them, and then place them
on the altar with the other items. Now draw a sacred circle of

lavender or purple light and call in your dream guardians. Light the incense, dedicating it to Nodens, the Celtic God of healing sleep and dreams. Dating from the third century C.E., his temple at Lydney Park in Gloucestershire contained an *abaton,* or dormitory for healing sleep. Use the quill or pen to inscribe the words *Dream Protection* on each of the candles, and then dress them by rubbing a thin film of lavender oil on their bodies. Place the candles in their holders on the altar in a triangular configuration. Rub three drops of oil over the amethyst, and then position the stone in the middle of the triangle. Wipe the oil off your hands and light the candles, dedicating each one to the cloudlike and protector God Nodens. Next face the altar, and focus all your attention on the amethyst stone. Merge with Oneness, and fill your mind with protective power. Imagine everything that means protection to you, for example, a locked door, a favorite God or Goddess, your family, or a large dog. Now pick up the stone and, holding it between your palms, use deep rhythmic breathing to breathe your feelings and thoughts of protection directly into the amethyst. See and sense your mind energy being absorbed by the stone. Merge with the stone and say three times,

> *Nodens, bestow upon this stone,*
> *The power to repel all negativity,*
> *Protect my dreams so they may be free.*
> *Hear me now, so mote it be!*

Place the stone back on the altar, in the middle of the candle triangle, and then clap your hands three times. Put the amethyst inside your pillowcase, and allow the candles to burn down completely as you drift to sleep.

In the morning, pull up the circle and release your dream guardians. Keep your dream amulet in your pillowcase, putting three drops of lavender oil on it once a week to reinforce its protective powers.

◐ Tonight's Magical Adventure: Cone of Dream Power

Use this ritual to empower your dream experiences. Each time you do a cone of power, you are actually handling a large mass of merged energy and then directing it to a preselected destination, in this case your dreams. When your merging with Oneness is deep and your expectation is clear, you have a better probability of achieving the results you desire. The best time for raising the cone of dream power is on a full moon.

LIST OF ITEMS NEEDED: Wand ★ 1 purple candle ★ Honeysuckle oil ★ Pinch of ginger ★ Pinch of nutmeg ★ Pinch of cinnamon

✦ Spinning the Spell

Dip the candle in cool saltwater, dry it, and place it on your altar. Next draw a sacred circle and call in your dream guardians. Rub honeysuckle oil all over the candle, and then sprinkle it with the herbs before placing it in the candleholder on the altar. While lighting the candle, give homage to a favorite Goddess or God. Now hold your wand in your dominant hand, and draw a magical circle of white light approximately one foot in diameter on the floor in front of you. This circle of energy is not for standing in. Merge with Oneness, and let it be as if you have no body but are just floating freely. Then fill your mind with a brilliant violet light. Turn to the north point, then to the east point, then to the south point and west point, turning in a clockwise circle, holding your wand high in the air, building the intensity and density of the brilliant violet light. Each movement builds the energy. Do this in a circular pattern at least three times. After spinning around, face the white circle of light you have drawn on the floor in front of you, and say,

Ayea, Ayea, Ayea!

Lower your wand, pointing to the center of the circle of white light. In your mind's eye see a shaft of white light descending from your wand into and filling the circle. See it growing stronger and brighter until it is a cone of vibrant power. Take a moment to see and sense this swirling cone of dream power picking up speed and gathering energy. Feel the energy spiral up and become more intensely powerful, and then draw up the cone, lifting it in your mind, higher and higher. Allow the cone to fill the entire room and beyond. It's similar to the tension that builds when pulling an arrow back in a bow, the moment before letting it go. When you are ready, release the cone of dream power with the intention of sending it into your dreams tonight. With a great shout say,

Go!

Breathe deeply for a few minutes, stretch your body completely, and lie back in bed. Allow the candle to burn down completely, and as you drift to sleep visualize yourself sleeping in a vibrant cone of white light.

When you awaken, write your dreams in your journal. Then thank deity, pull up the circle, and release your dream guardians.

◖ Tonight's Magical Adventure: Charming the Bad Guys Away

Using St. John's wort, a traditional herb used for banishing negativity, this protective dream charm is great for warding off illness while in the process increasing your courage and willpower. You can hang St. John's wort in your bedroom to prevent nightmares and to protect you during your dreams from negative powers. Make this charm on a waning moon, preferably on a Sunday or Tuesday night.

LIST OF ITEMS NEEDED: Large bowl ★ 1 oz. ground cumin ★ 1 lb. sea salt ★ 9 bay leaves ★ 9 pinches St. John's wort ★

9 pinches dried anise ★ 9 pinches dried rosemary ★ 9 whole cloves ★ 9-inch by 9-inch white cotton cloth ★ 18-inch length of purple ribbon or yarn

❋ Spinning the Spell

At dusk just before it gets dark, mix the sea salt and ground cumin together in the large bowl and take it outside. Begin at the end of your driveway (or the entryway to your home such as a stairwell or walkway), turn to the east, and walk completely around your property, sprinkling the herbal mixture in the bowl along the edges of your property, ending at the same point you began. Imagine a protective border of white light coming from the herbs. The salt and cumin keep unwanted energies from entering your property. The cumin can be irritating to your eyes, nose, lips, and so forth, so handle it carefully.

Next go back inside, wash the cumin off your hands, and then mix the other herbs together. Pile them in the center of the white cloth, and then bring each corner of the cloth up to the center, one at a time, in a clockwise motion, beginning with the topmost (north) corner. When all the corners are together, four folds will be sticking out. In a clockwise motion, bring the corners of these folds into the center as well. Use the purple ribbon or yarn to wrap around the cloth nine times, just above the herbs, holding them in place. Each time you wrap the ribbon around, say,

Three and three and three is nine.
Each wrap makes this charm divine.

Then knot each of the ends nine times. With each knot you tie, say,

Three and three and three is nine.
Each knot makes this charm divine.

Lie back and hold the charm in your hands. Close your eyes and imagine a warm white light completely surrounding you like a brilliant white egg. See and sense this white light moving through your arms and hands and into the charm bag. Feel the warmth, the safety, the protection of this bright white light. Imagine the charm bag radiating this brilliant light, and then merge completely with the light. Hold the sachet in your hands as you sleep, or place it in your pillowcase for the night. Empower the charm every week or so, and make a new charm bag once a month, until you feel you have charmed the bad guys away.

◑ Tonight's Magical Adventure: Dark Moon Craft Name Magic

Names are magical, as shown by the belief in the extraordinary significance of names through the centuries. For example, which name conjures up the image of a beautiful Goddess in your mind, Venus or Frankie? In the past, Chinese societies invented names for every baby by giving each name a mixture of sounds and symbols with secret significance. Even now African–American names are often created and given because of the significance of their sounds.

Magical names are often chosen for the distinction they carry, for example the Celtic names of Herne or Rhiannon. Most of those who follow the Mystery Traditions such as Wicca and Druidism select a magical or "craft" name upon initiation that they use when doing magic and ritual. The magical name you select represents the new, reborn you. It expresses your power and energies in this incarnation on the earthly plane. As you become more aware of the meaning of the name you select, its creative potential begins to unfold within you.

The following Dark Moon Name Magic is best done on the new moon and is designed to help you discover a magical name of power. Read it over a few times, and then do it. If you prefer, you can tape-record the work and play it back while you recline.

LIST OF ITEMS NEEDED: 1 white candle ★ Pine oil ★ Hand-kerchief, scarf, or small piece of fabric ★ Piece of paper and pen

✳ Spinning the Spell

Wash the candle in cool saltwater and dry it. Rub it with the pine oil and place it in its holder on the altar. Anoint a handkerchief, scarf, or other small piece of fabric with the oil, and hold it in your hands as you do this work. Light the candle.

Recline comfortably and breathe deeply. Inhale to the count of three, holding your breath for three counts and then exhaling completely. Just let go of all the daily tensions and worries as you exhale. Do this a few times until you feel centered, relaxed, and calm. Now as you breathe in, imagine you are breathing in a protective white light into your body. Feel the light inside you, and as you breathe out, feel the light surrounding you in all directions. Now begin to imagine yourself walking barefoot along a forest path just before dusk. The patches of new grass along the path feel soft and spongy on your feet as you walk along. You can smell the grass, the earth, the trees, and water nearby. The songs of birds echo in the trees, filling the forest with a natural symphony. Green and purple violets dot the forest floor here and there, and you can smell their sweet scent mixed with the damp scent of the forest. As you near a grove of pine trees, you see many paths leading off in different directions. You take a few moments to study the paths, selecting the one that seems the brightest. Follow the path as it winds deeper into the pine forest. You reach a clearing, and in it is an ancient library, completely made of stone. You move up the stone steps of the library and enter the building through a large open door. Once inside, you are amazed as how bright everything is and how easily you can see the titles to the volumes of books that cover every wall. Take some time to browse through the books, selecting a particular volume. Study the book's cover, and then open it and slowly look through its pages. What do you see? Make a mental note of what you read and see. Is there a particular name that pops into view or draws your attention? Take a few minutes to completely look through the book, and then replace the book and exit the ancient library. Take the same path that led you to the library, walking back through the forest. Smell the fresh coolness of the evening air as you walk along, and hear the crickets in the distance. Take your time, sauntering to the edge of the forest and out into the grassy meadow beyond, noticing the lush sounds, scents, and sights of nature all around you.

Now come back to the present moment and place, moving your toes and fingers and finally slowly opening your eyes. Use the pen and paper to note all the details from your experience, listing the specifics of the book you looked through and any name or names that you were drawn to. Put the paper on your altar in front of the candle. Allow the candle to burn down naturally, and as you drift to sleep imagine yourself, once again, in the ancient library, picking up the book and leafing through it one page at a time.

In the morning, record your dreams. Use the name you received from your experience in the library as your magical name. If you haven't received a specific name, take a few nights to allow the information to soak in, and then repeat the process. You will certainly discover a name of power in the process. Use this name to protect and empower you when dreaming and doing magic.

◖ Tonight's Magical Adventure: Words of Power Dowsing Magic

This work not only empowers you with words of power, it also demonstrates the power of both words and thoughts using dowsing rods. You can do this work on any night, and you can even have fun with your family and friends by showing them how to use the rods. Keep in mind that it does take a little bit of practice to learn how to work the rods properly. Be patient and have fun!

LIST OF ITEMS NEEDED: 2 wire coat hangers ⋆ 2 plastic straws ⋆ Wire cutter or pliers

✴ Spinning the Spell

Cut the wire hangers into L shapes, with the main extending arm measuring twelve inches and the handle five inches long. Cut the plastic straws to fit over the handles in such a way that the rod arm swings freely. Bend the ends of the handles slightly to keep the straws securely in place. To make extremely responsive rods, use two seventeen-inch pieces of copper wire in place of the coat hangers and two five-inch pieces of hollow copper tubing instead of the straws.

Once you have assembled your rods, hold the handles about waist high, one in each hand, with the rod arms extended straight out in front of you. Take a few deep breaths to calm your mind. Now focus on one of the best experiences you have ever had, something that delighted and filled you with joy and happiness. The arms of the rods will open outward, demonstrating the power of your positive thoughts and feelings. Next focus on someone you don't like, someone who has hurt you in the past. Watch how the rods swing inward and even touch, showing how your energy field contracts and diminishes with negative thoughts and feelings.

Next select a favorite Goddess or God and say the name aloud three times. Merge with the divine energy, and watch how the rods swing wide apart as your energy field expands in response to your positive energy flow.

Then say a word such as *hate* or *pain,* and focus on the word, watching how the rods swing inward and almost touch as your energy field diminishes.

You have now actually seen just how much your thoughts and words affect yourself and others, so make an effort to talk tenderly to yourself and others, using positive, uplifting words and thinking loving thoughts. The rods are also a handy gauge when meeting new people and entering new situations. Just find a quiet moment, take a few deep breaths, hold the rods, say the person's name or state the situation, and watch how the rods respond. You can also use your rods to dowse your dreams by holding them in your hands, thinking and talking about a dream you have had and noticing their response.

◐ Tonight's Magical Adventure: World Peace Placket Spell

People, animals, trees, and spirits all dream together upon the Earth. Dreaming permeates all life on this planet. Best spun on a Sunday night during a gibbous or full moon, this World Peace Placket Spell uses the power of dreams to promote harmony, peace, and healing throughout the world. It uses the color blue, which both clears out negativity and soothes the soul. Also, the Earth looks mostly blue from space. If desired, you can substitute blue felt squares and a needle and thread for the paper and stapler.

LIST OF ITEMS NEEDED: 1 blue candle ⋆ Sandalwood incense and censer ⋆ Lavender oil ⋆ Picture of the Earth from space ⋆ 7 bay leaves ⋆ Blue felt pen ⋆ 7 coriander seeds ⋆ 2 square 4-inch by 4-inch pieces of blue construction paper ⋆ Stapler

✴ Spinning the Spell

Draw a sacred circle and light the incense. Rub the candle with lavender oil, wipe the oil from your hands, and then light the candle, dedicating it to an Earth Goddess such as Anu (Celtic), Gaia (Greek), or Flora (Roman). Anoint yourself with the oil as well, placing three drops on the insides of both your wrists and ankles. Then staple the two squares of blue paper together along the sides and bottom, leaving the top open. Next use the blue felt pen to write the words *World Peace* on the picture of the Earth and on both sides of the seven bay leaves. Let the ink dry, and then fold the picture and slip it and the bay leaves into the paper placket. Add the seven coriander seeds. These seeds represent the seven continents of the world. Next put a drop of lavender oil on the four corners of the placket, and then bathe it in the incense smoke for a few minutes to strengthen its protective and healing powers. Hold the placket in your hands, merge with the powers of Earth, and say three times,

> *Let the powers that be*
> *Bring peace and harmony.*
> *Blessed be the Earth!*

Put the placket on your dream altar. Allow the candle to burn down on its own. As you drift to sleep, imagine putting your arms around the entire Earth in a loving and compassionate embrace. This signifies all-embracing knowledge, the highest degree of wisdom that a dream can symbolize. Then repeat the words "Healing dreams of world peace" until you fall asleep.

Record your dreams in the morning, thank the Earth Goddess, and pull up the circle. For a few minutes each night, through an entire moon phase (twenty-eight nights), empower the placket by visualizing more peace and harmony in the world and sending out positive, healing, and protective prayers to people around the world and to all of Earth's plants and creatures. By doing so, you help create a more positive reality.

☾ Tonight's Magical Adventure:
New Moon Creativity Spell

Best spun during a new moon, this spell sends out creative sparks intended to get your creativity flowing. Your own divine nature is expressed in your creative efforts, so what better way to increase your creativity than to call upon divine assistance? I suggest you do this spell on thirteen consecutive new moons, beginning with the first new moon after the winter solstice. The more you practice this spell, the more creative you will be.

LIST OF ITEMS NEEDED: 1 red candle ★ 1 green candle ★ Pine oil ★ Rose oil ★ 2 bowls of warm water ★ Music that inspires you

✳ Spinning the Spell

Begin by selecting a Goddess and God to work with you in this spell. I like to call upon Kerridwen, the Celtic All-Mother of inspiration and knowledge, and Kernunnos, the Celtic All-Father of the forests and animals. You can choose this Goddess and God, or select deities from another spiritual pantheon such as Isis and Osiris (Egyptian) or Shiva and Shakti (Hindu). Please refer to the appendixes for more selections.

Next wash the candles in cool saltwater, dry them, and then rub the red one in pine oil and the green one in rose oil. Place them in their holders on the altar, the green one on the left and the red on the right. Then draw a sacred circle and call in your dream guardians. Light the green candle, dedicating it to the Goddess, and then light the red candle, dedicating it to the God. Turn on music that inspires you, something that plays for at least a half hour. Next place the bowls of warm water in front of each of the candles so you can easily rest both your hands in the bowls of water as you face the altar. Then put nine drops of rose oil into the bowl in front of the green candle on the left and nine drops of pine oil into the other on the right.

Now immerse your left hand in the bowl of water on the left and your right hand in the bowl of water on the right. Take a few deep breaths, imagining the bright light from the candles filling and energizing you. Begin to see and sense roots sprouting from your root chakra at the base of your spine, shooting down into the Earth. With each breath you take, see and sense the roots burrowing deeper into the Earth. Now imagine a bright sphere of light at the center, and see your roots penetrate it completely. Breathing deeply, begin drawing this light up through your imaginary roots, into your being. Do this for a couple of minutes.

Now imagine two brilliant streams of light coming down from the night sky and filling the two bowls of water. See and sense the creative power of the Goddess filling the bowl of water on the left. Merge with this creative energy, drawing it up through your left hand and into the very core of your being. Do this for a couple of minutes. Next see and sense the creative power of the God filling the bowl of water on the right. Merge with this creative power, drawing the energy up through your right hand and into your body, again for a couple of minutes. Now draw the creative power from both bowls through your hands and into your heart. Imagine this creative energy becoming brighter and brighter, and sense its power building to a peak. Then allow the creative energy of the Goddess and God in your heart to spread out and flood your entire being. As you do, loudly shout the words,

Creativity Spark!!! Creativity Flow!!!

Keep imagining the divine creative power flooding your being for a few minutes, and enjoy the sensations, making a mental note of any creative ideas that come to mind. After a few minutes, draw your imaginary roots back into the base of your spine, take your hands out of the water, and wipe them off. Clap your hands three times. Allow the candles to burn down completely as you drift to sleep.

In the morning, thank the Goddess and God, pull up the circle, and release the dream guardians. Take the bowls of water outside, and pour them on the ground at the base of a favorite tree. In the future, care for this tree in some way, for it is an expression of Oneness that has been blessed by divine creativity. Each time you do this magical work, your creativity will increase proportionally.

C Tonight's Magical Adventure: Forgiveness Dream Spell

When anger comes between family members and friends, everyone involved often finds it difficult to get past their negative feelings and resolve their differences. Even after an apology, a certain amount of residual anger and distrust may linger. The Forgiveness Dream Spell helps you rid yourself of these negative feelings. Cast it during the waning moon.

LIST OF ITEMS NEEDED: 1 blue taper candle ⋆ Lavender incense and censer ⋆ Honeysuckle oil ⋆ Ballpoint pen or quill ⋆ Cup or chalice filled with water

✳ Spinning the Spell

Wash the candle in cool saltwater, dry it, and place it on your altar together with the chalice of water. Next draw a sacred circle of blue light, call in your dream guardians, and light the incense. Use the pen or quill to inscribe the word *Forgiveness* on the candle body three times, and then dress the candle with the honeysuckle oil. Wipe your hands and light the candle. Hold the chalice of water between your hands, and then pour out all your negative feelings into the water. Let the water absorb all your painful and hurt thoughts and feelings. Say the word *forgiveness* nine times aloud, and then take the water and flush it down the toilet. Pull up the circle and release your dream guardians. Allow the candle to burn down naturally as you drift to sleep. Within the next nine nights, you will feel relief and release.

◖ Tonight's Magical Adventure: Power Animal Dream Message

Meeting and communicating with power animals, especially in dreams, can open up your magical gifts. Your divination, healing, and prophetic abilities increase from this experience, and often your magical states of awareness deepen and become more powerful. An incredible source of inspiration, power animals can help you expand your perception of the many dimensions of existence.

LIST OF ITEMS NEEDED: 1 white candle ⋆ Sage and cedar smudge ⋆ Your imagination

✳ Spinning the Spell

Smudge your bedroom, altar, and yourself, and then draw a sacred circle of blue-white light and call in your dream guardians. Light the candle, taking a few deep breaths while focusing your attention on the candle flame. Next ask yourself the following questions to determine your power animals. Which animals do you dream about, either while you are sleeping or while daydreaming? One of the best ways to meet and communicate with power animals is through dreaming. Has the memory of any animal dream ever stuck with you for a more than a year? Which animals keep coming into your environment? Which animal or animals do you most resemble? For example, are your movements more like a cat, wolf, lizard, or bird? Which animals are attracted to you and come up to you? Which animals attract and draw you to them? When visiting an aquarium, zoo, animal reserve, or farm, which animals take up your focus? Which animals are you most interested in right now as you read this sentence? Don't so much think about your answer, but feel it. Write down your first response.

Next read over the following meditation a few times and then try it. If you prefer, you can tape-record the meditation and play it back. Be sure to turn on about thirty minutes of soft, instrumental music and then recline comfortably, taking a few deep breaths and closing your eyes. Allow the music and your breathing to merge into one. When you are completely relaxed, surround yourself with a bright white light. Allow the white light to swirl energetically around you in a clockwise motion. Make sure the white light is above, below, beside, in front of, and behind you, in all directions.

Now imagine you are in a peaceful place in nature, a favorite place that you have been to before or somewhere that comes into focus just for this meditation. Focus all your attention on this peaceful place. Notice how the details of this place in nature become more vivid and alive with each breath you take. Flow into this natural place, walking around, taking in the beauty around you, feeling calm and serene.

Stand still for a few moments and look around. You see an animal approaching you. As the animal comes closer, you communicate with it, noticing as many details about the animal and its behavior as you can. Make an effort to trust your instincts and connect with the animal spirit's energy. Listen to it or feel what it has to share. Power animals may speak as softly as the breeze or as loudly as ocean waves crashing against the shoreline cliffs. At first you may think or feel that you are talking with yourself, but after a few moments you realize that the messages and ideas that are being described to you are not your own. They are a flow of universal information that you can tap into for beneficial purposes. After listening to the power animal for a time, be sure to take time to share your feelings and thoughts with the animal as well. Ideally you will experience a two-way exchange.

You will know when the communication is complete because the energy will recognizably shift. You may feel a coolness or the animal will begin to fade or move away from you. Thank your power animal, knowing you can return to this place and communicate with it, tapping into its natural power, whenever you choose.

Stretch your body, and then write down any messages or other information that you received from your power animal in your journal. Allow the candle to burn down completely, and as you lie back and close your eyes, sense yourself becoming one with your power animal. Repeat to yourself, "I am the (name of power animal), the (name of power animal) is me, we are one." An example would be, "I am the swan, the swan is me, we are one." Keep repeating this phrase over and over again until you drift to sleep.

In the morning, record your dreams, pull up the circle, and release your dream guardians. Keep in mind that your power animal is always with you and can be asked for help whenever it is needed.

◖ Tonight's Magical Adventure: Runic Triads Dream Magic

You can use the following simple runic triads to gain access to and amplify the universal runic energies and to empower your dreams. Some of the most effective rune triads are key words or names in the Norse tradition. Do this work on a Wednesday night, three nights before the full moon.

LIST OF ITEMS NEEDED: 1 blue candle ⋆ 1 white candle ⋆ 1 green candle ⋆ Quill or ballpoint pen ⋆ Pine oil

✷ Spinning the Spell

Wash the candles in cool saltwater, dry them, and place them on your altar. Draw a sacred circle of blue light, and then inscribe the blue candle with these runes:

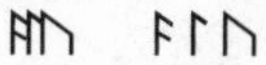

Ansuz, Laguz, and Uruz spell the word *ALU*, symbolizing the water of life, literally translated as "ale." This runic triad changes things for the better, protects, and promotes divine inspiration. Next inscribe the white candle with these runes:

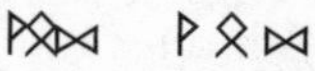

Wunjo, Othala, Dagaz make *WOD*, the runic triad of divine inspiration, spelling the name of Woden or Odin, which invokes the powers of the Norse God of wisdom. Then inscribe the green candle with these runes:

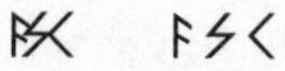

Ansuz, Sowilo, and Kenaz make *ASC*, the name of Yggdrasil, the World Tree. This is the runic triad of pure power, survival, and longevity.

Now rub each of the candles with the pine oil, and place them in their holders, side by side on the altar. Light them one at a time and say,

Runes of three, empower me.
So be it, So shall it be!

Allow the candles to burn down completely as you drift to sleep. In the morning, record your dreams in your journal, and pull up the circle of blue light. Within three months, your life will be empowered and enriched by the runic energies employed in this magical work. Get ready for a real blast of power!

◖ Tonight's Magical Adventure: Triple Knot Power Spell

Best cast on the full moon, this spell can help you tie three positive qualities into your life. The knot is a spiritual bond much like the ring, with the triple knot being a symbol of the threefold Goddess. Wise women would tie up the power of the wind by knotting rope, scarves, cord, or thread. Seafarers would buy the knotted item from these women. When they were at sea and untied a knot, the wind would fill their sails. In addition, knotted fishermen's nets were one of the first forms of string magic. These nets were made not only to catch fish, but also to honor and attract the helpful fishing spirits.

LIST OF ITEMS NEEDED: A yard-long piece of green string, yarn, or cord ★ 1 green votive candle ★ Patchouli incense and censer

✱ Spinning the Spell

Draw a sacred circle, and then light the candle and incense. Call in your favorite deities to guide you. Next take the string and hold an end in each hand. Think about the three qualities you most admire in others. They might be a loving heart, open mind, optimistic spirit, patience, courage, generosity, common sense, compassion, tolerance, creativity, and wisdom. Begin to tie three knots in the string, one at a time, thinking about tying in those three positive qualities into your being as you do so. Say,

The first knot for (name the first positive quality).
The second knot for (name the second positive quality).
The third knot for (name the third positive quality).
By the light of the moon, so be it! Blessed be!

With each knot you tie, you tie these three qualities into your-self. Now take the knotted string and tie it to the leg of your bed. Snuff the candle or allow it to burn down completely. Thank any Gods and Goddesses who are present, and ask them to watch over you as you dream. Think about the three qualities you tied into yourself as you drift to sleep. In the morning, pull up the circle. Within three weeks, the positive qualities you selected will make themselves known in your life.

◖ Tonight's Magical Adventure: Slipknot Mistake-Proof Magic

Also known as "the stupid human spell," because "to err is human," this is a form of string magic that helps you undo mis-takes by untying them.

LIST OF ITEMS NEEDED: 1 black votive candle ★ Sage and cedar smudge ★ 13-inch length of black string, yarn, or cord ★ Scissors ★ Bowl

✳ Spinning the Spell

Thoroughly smudge the area with the sage and cedar. (If you are allergic to smudge, use sage oil in a diffuser or on a cotton ball.) Next draw a sacred circle and call in your dream guardians and also any favorite Gods and Goddesses. Light the candle. Now think about one mistake you have made that you really want to let go of and forgive yourself for. Next take the black string from the altar and make a slipknot in the middle of it, the knot representing the mistake. Hold an end in each hand, but don't pull the knot out yet. Focus all your awareness on detaching from the mistake and releasing it and all the feelings surrounding it into the universe. Transfer all the energy of the mistake into the slipknot, and then suddenly yank the knot out, knowing that as you pull out the knot, the mistake is released and forgiven. Know this with all your being. Really let go of it once and for all. Use your scissors to cut the black string into tiny pieces. Do this over the bowl, catching all the pieces. Then carefully burn all the pieces, a couple at a time, in the flame of the candle. Smudge the area briefly once more to get rid of any residual negative energies. Pull up the circle and release the dream guardians before you go to sleep. Allow the candle to burn down completely on its own, throwing it in the garbage in the morning.

◖ Tonight's Magical Adventure: Dream Knight Protection Spell

All of us at one time or another could use our very own knight-errant to keep us from harm and attack. This spell helps you establish communication with your dream knight for purposes of protection and guidance. Spin this spell on a Sunday, Tuesday, or Thursday night, on or just before the full moon. Allow about one hour for completing this three-part spell, which blends into one spell a ritual bath, candle magic, and the ancient magical art of scrying.

LIST OF ITEMS NEEDED: A warm bath ★ 3 pinches thyme ★ 3 lemon slices ★ Jasmine oil ★ 3 white candles and holders ★ 3 blue candles and holders ★ Sandalwood incense and censer ★ Ballpoint pen or quill ★ Clear glass of water

✳ Spinning the Spell

First take a warm bath, adding the three pinches of thyme, lemon slices, and three drops of jasmine oil to your bath. Soak for at least ten minutes. As you bathe, breathe deeply by inhaling for three counts, holding your breath to the count of three, and then exhaling completely. As you do this, visualize and sense a protective egg of white light surrounding you. Now take a few minutes as you soak in your magical bath to decide what you would like to ask your dream knight when you meet him or her. Is there something you would like your dream knight to help you with? Is there someone or something you need your dream knight to protect you from? Make a mental note of the things you would like to say when you meet. I also suggest you jot down a few questions or ideas for your dream knight as soon as you get out of the bath, and put the paper on your altar where you can refer to it easily. Also, take the six candles and dip them in the bathwater before draining it. Dry the candles and place them on your altar, along with the pen or quill and a clear glass of water.

Next draw a sacred circle of blue-white light around your bedroom, and light the incense. Focus on the purpose of the spell, and state your intent and expectation:

I am here tonight to make contact with and gain protection and guidance from my dream knight.

Then use the pen or quill to inscribe the words *Dream Knight* on the first blue candle. Next apply a thin film of jasmine oil on the candle body, and put it in its holder on the altar. Light the candle, merging with the candle flame, and say,

May this candlelight stretch beyond,
Across the celestial realms to all worlds,
Creating a path of light for my dream knight
To come and merge with me tonight.

Use the pen or quill to inscribe the words *Dream Knight* on the second blue candle, and then apply jasmine oil to the candle body. Place the candle back in its holder and, merging with the candle flame, say,

May this spirit light reach beyond,
Across the celestial realms to all worlds,
Building a bridge of light for my dream knight
To cross and merge with me tonight.

Inscribe the same words, *Dream Knight,* on the third blue candle, once again applying oil to the candle body and putting the candle in its holder on the altar. Light the candle and, merging with the flame, say,

May these three lights shine beyond,
Across the celestial realms to all worlds,
Weaving a thread of light for my dream knight
To follow and merge with me tonight.

Next inscribe the word *Protection* on the three white candles, and dress them with jasmine oil. Place them in their holders, positioning them in front of the three blue candles. Then light the white candles one at a time. As you do, merge with each flame and say,

May this spirit flame burn true,
Dream knight, now let me see you!

Position the clear glass of water in the middle of the candles, and sit or recline comfortably. Gaze into the glass of water while chanting the word *merge* over and over again. After a few minutes, allow your chanting to fade out, all the while continuing to gaze at the water. Just allow images or sensations to occur in the water. As you gaze into the water, blink naturally, remaining focused on the water. Eventually a shadow, figure, or face will appear in the water. The image usually appears within five to twenty-five minutes. When a shape appears, ask the image if he or she is your dream knight. You will sense an answer. If the answer is yes, proceed with your request or questions. Ask your dream knight to return when you call him or her. When you are finished communicating, thank your dream knight and make a note of any answers or messages you received. Allow the candles to burn down completely, and as you drift to sleep, know that your dream knight is always there to protect and guide you, especially in your sleep.

In the morning, drink the glass of water, write down what you recall of your dreams, and pull up the circle.

☾

chapter seven

Health, Beauty, and Wellness Dream Magic

One evening as I drifted between consciousness and subconsciousness, I had a dream of a woman who looked like me but was not me.

She moves clockwise around a timeworn circle, three times, as she hums and chants. Around her, the green wood clearing comes alive. Peering from the thickness of the fir trees, a group of deer watch the woman do her healing work. She holds a large censer, suspended by a silver chain, filled with smoldering cedar and sage. In her left hand is a bunch of fresh rosebuds, and she sprinkles them along the circular path she treads. Around her neck are several necklaces made of nuts, acorns, vines, and flowers, and they move and sway in rhythm to her slow and deliberate footsteps. The woman stops at the north point and merges deeply. She sees the image of her mate, herself, and her children. Chanting a blessing of health, she seals the image in her mind. Calling in the four ele-

ments of earth, air, fire, and water, she casts the pattern upon the wind.

Much like the woman in the dream, each one of us is a conduit of the healing light of the Goddess and God. We are all channels for divine healing energy. When you do healing spells and rituals in tune with solar, lunar, planetary, and stellar cycles, you act as a catalyst in the healing process, directing this healing energy where it is needed.

Many physical diseases are related to unresolved emotional pain and are the result of inhibited soul life—in other words, something you still haven't worked out. Often illness is connected to negative relationships, either with yourself or others. Suppressed emotional pain can transform into physical pain or sickness. Your perceptions also relate directly to your state of health, for your body can heal or remain unhealthy depending upon your mental patterns and interpretations. It is truly amazing how effortlessly the body's hard mask can melt with a shift of awareness, especially magical awareness.

As human beings, we are teleological, meaning that that we move toward what we picture. We shape ourselves into patterns according to the images that fill our minds. Images color our emotions. Thinking of positive images creates a positive self-image, while dwelling on self-destructive images creates a negative self-image. The images we hold of self, others, and the world produce behaviors and feelings as well as sensations, thoughts, perceptions, and problem-solving strategies. In other words, we are our images. They are our reality, for they influence our response to the world.

In healing dream magic, you can use positive images to promote healing and well-being. There is a predictable transfer from imagery to reality in all magic, and healing magic is no exception. Imagery influences your response to your world even though it's a mental picture or symbol of something not actually present. Through your imagination, it is possible to reach out in dreams to images that are not physically present. By doing so, you can use these images and symbols to transform, heal, and enrich your life. When you picture yourself healthy and beautiful, the image begins to overlap with your reality. A strong imagination can generate the actual event, particularly when you apply your magical skills and merge deeply. If you wish to accomplish something in reality, first see or sense yourself achieving it in your mind, and then dream it into reality!

The bedroom is the perfect place to do healing work, since it is a place of relaxation and renewal. It is removed from ordinary reality, a place of dreams. The following spells and rituals can be used to promote personal healing and improve the way you look and feel.

◖ Tonight's Magical Adventure: Creating a Healing Dream Crystal

In Irish mythology, the goddess Creide placed Art, son of King Conn, in a crystal chamber where all the healing rays of the sun and moon converged into one. After a month he had acquired a new strength and energy, enabling him to face the worst of perils. This myth shows the great power that the ancients attributed to crystals, from healing to energy balancing. The best time for doing this work is on a full moon.

LIST OF ITEMS NEEDED: Cedar and sage smudge ⋆ Piece of tumbled clear quartz ⋆ 1 white candle ⋆ Your imagination

✷ Spinning the Spell

Light the smudge and bathe the stone in the smoke for a few minutes. Next smudge the altar and yourself to get rid of any unwanted energies. Extinguish the smudge, and then draw a sacred circle and light the candle, dedicating it to your favorite Goddess or God of healing, such as Bridget or Belenus (Celtic). Now put the crystal in your left palm, covering it with your right palm and imagining a clear pool of water in your mind. Breathe in deeply, visualizing the clear water washing out your dream crystal, and then pulse your breath out sharply through your nose three times, as if to set the image in place in the stone. To program your crystal for healing, repeat the clearing process, only instead of clear water, imagine whatever means healing to you. For example, in your mind's eye imagine soaking in natural hot springs or lying on a warm sandy beach, and then pulse that image into the crystal by taking a deep breath and sharply pulsing your exhale through your nose. After programming the stone, place your healing dream crystal under your pillow or hold it in your left hand as you sleep, noticing how it influences your dreams. You can also intentionally bring your healing dream crystal into your dreams and use it for energizing, restoring, and healing. Allow the candle to burn down completely, and as you drift to sleep hold the stone in your hand and silently repeat,

> *Healing dream crystal of divine light,*
> *Share your healing power with me tonight.*

In the morning, record your dreams in your journal, thank the Goddess or God whom you invoked, and pull up the circle. Carry your healing dream crystal with you during the day or place it on your altar, using it when you sleep. Reprogram it using the pulse breath method every three nights to strengthen its healing power. You will feel an improvement in your health and state of mind almost immediately.

◖ Tonight's Magical Adventure: Inner Message Dream Spell

This spell can be used to find an answer to a personal question. It taps directly into the power of the Goddess and the divine wisdom of Oneness. For best results, spin this spell on a Saturday night on a new moon.

LIST OF ITEMS NEEDED: 1 silver candle ⋆ 1 cauldron ⋆ 1 chalice or cup filled with juice (to put inside the cauldron) ⋆ Patchouli incense and censer

✴ Spinning the Spell

Draw a sacred circle and call in your dream guardians. Light the incense and candle, dedicating them your favorite Goddess. Facing west, say,

> *Guardians and ancient ones come tonight,*
> *Protect and bless and clear my sight.*
> *Guardians of north, east, south, and west,*
> *Generous dream spirits of the inner quest,*
> *Assist me now, this sacred night,*
> *As I seek the inner message of light.*
> *O blessed Lady of wisdom (state the Goddess's name),*
> *I, (state your name), seek the answer to*
> *(State your question or concern).*
> *Please share your wisdom with me now!*

Take a few minutes and listen for the answer from the Goddess. It may come as a silent voice or a sensation, or an image of the Goddess may appear in front of you and speak with you. Hold the cup of juice in front of you in both hands and say,

> *Blessed be this cup of wisdom.*

Put the cup of juice inside the cauldron, hold your hands over it, and say three times,

> *Great Lady, fill this cup*
> *With the wisdom I desire!*

Now drink the juice, and as you do, imagine the answers you seek flowing through your being. See and sense the power of the Goddess filling you. Say these words:

Knowledge and wisdom
About and around.
Reasons and answers
Everywhere abound.
Within and without,
Green, red, and white,
Circle front and center,
Goddess, dream with me tonight.

Allow the candle to burn down on its own, and as you drift to sleep, repeat silently, "More answers in my dreams."

In the morning, write down any answers that you recall in your dreams. Then thank the Goddess, pull up the circle, and release your dream guardians. You will most likely discover the answer to your question within three nights.

☾ Tonight's Magical Adventure: Candle Magic Healing Ritual

The time to do this ritual is when you have been sick but are beginning to feel better. It will energize you and help you feel completely well much faster than you thought possible. The best night for performing this ritual is on one of the eight sabbats or on a full moon, whenever you are in need of extra healing energy.

LIST OF ITEMS NEEDED: 1 blue candle ★ Jasmine incense and censer ★ Sandalwood oil ★ Quill or ballpoint pen ★ Pinch of dried rosemary ★ 3 almonds (shelled) ★ Warm cup of chamomile tea

✴ Spinning the Spell

Wash the candle in cool saltwater, and then dry and place it on the altar. Next draw a sacred circle around your bedroom and call in your dream guardians. Use the quill or pen to inscribe your name on the body of the candle. Dress the candle with sandalwood oil, sprinkle the dried rosemary on it, and then place the candle in its holder on the altar. Next anoint yourself with the oil, putting three drops on the top of your head, a drop on your third eye, and three drops on each on the insides of your wrists and ankles. Wash and wipe your hands thoroughly. Hold the almonds in your dominant hand, face north, and merge with the powers of earth. Focus on a sense of well-being and say,

> *Welcome, healing spirits of the north,*
> *I ask that you now come forth.*
> *Earth, air, fire, and water,*
> *Peace, health, love, and laughter.*
> *Earth grow, wind blow!*
> *Fire warm, water flow!*
> *Natural rhythms that be,*
> *Bring healing energy to me!*

Then eat the almonds one at a time.

Next light the incense. Hold it upward while facing east, and wave it three times back and forth. Set the incense back on the altar, and then merge with the powers of air while focusing on a sense of well-being and say,

> *Welcome, healing spirits of the east,*
> *I ask that you now come forth.*
> *Earth, air, fire, and water,*
> *Peace, health, love, and laughter.*
> *Earth grow, wind blow!*
> *Fire warm, water flow!*

Natural rhythms that be,
Bring healing energy to me!

Place the incense back on the altar, and then light the candle. Face south, holding the candle, and wave it carefully back and forth three times before setting it back down upon the altar. Merge with the powers of fire while focusing on a sense of well-being and say,

Welcome, healing spirits of the south,
I ask that you now come forth.
Earth, air, fire, and water,
Peace, health, love, and laughter.
Earth grow, wind blow!
Fire warm, water flow!
Natural rhythms that be,
Bring healing energy to me!

Then face west and, holding the cup of tea, dip your fingers into the tea three times. Sprinkle a few drops of water toward the west as you do so. Put the cup of tea back upon the altar, and then merge with the powers of water while focusing on a sense of well-being and say,

Welcome, healing spirits of the west,
I ask that you now come forth.
Earth, air, fire, and water,
Peace, health, love, and laughter.
Earth grow, wind blow!
Fire warm, water flow!
Natural rhythms that be,
Bring healing energy to me!

Drink the tea slowly, and as you do, imagine that you are drinking in a sense of well-being. Let the candle burn out on its own as you drift to sleep.

In the morning, give thanks to the healing spirits of the four directions, pull up the circle, and release your dream guardians. Within the next three nights, you will experience a marked improvement in your health.

☾ Tonight's Magical Adventure: Healing Spirit Placket

Best done during a gibbous to full moon phase, on a Sunday or Monday night, this healing placket can be used to heal your spirit, bringing new hope to your most cherished dreams. If desired, you can substitute purple felt squares and a needle and thread for the paper and stapler.

LIST OF ITEMS NEEDED: 1 purple candle ⋆ Sandalwood incense and censer ⋆ 3 pinches chamomile flowers (from tea bags) ⋆ 3 pinches powdered cinnamon ⋆ 3 pinches dried mint leaves ⋆ 3 pinches powdered ginger ⋆ 3 pinches rose petals ⋆ 3 bay leaves ⋆ 2 square 7-inch by 7-inch pieces of purple paper ⋆ Stapler ⋆ Tape ⋆ Purple felt pen

✳ Spinning the Spell

Draw a sacred circle and then light the candle, dedicating it to a Goddess or God of healing, such as Bridget or Diancecht (Celtic). Next light the incense, dedicating it to the same deity. Then staple and tape the two squares of paper together along the sides and bottom edge, leaving the top open. Use the purple felt pen to write the word *Heal* on both sides of the placket in large letters. Then write the same word on both sides of each of the three bay leaves. Once the ink is dry, insert the three leaves into the placket. Add the other ingredients in the order they are listed, and then bathe the placket in the incense smoke for a few minutes to reinforce its healing power. To further empower the placket, hold it in your hands, merge with the divine, and say three times,

Energies with the power to renew,
Hear me now as I call to you.
Heal my spirit and heal my soul,
Cherished dreams, make me whole.
So be it! So mote it be!

Then put the placket next to your bed. Allow the candle to burn down, and as you drift to sleep, repeat the words "Heal my spirit and heal my soul."

In the morning, thank the Goddess or God who helped you with the work, and then pull up the circle. Leave the placket next to your bedside for twenty-one nights to gain the maximum value of its healing power.

◖ Tonight's Magical Adventure: Dream Castle Healing Spring

Traditionally, water relates to the Goddess, spiritual alignment, and attunement and accordingly possesses a sense of sanctity. People throughout the world consider bodies of water, from oceans and rivers to wells and springs, to be sacred, and each water source is thought to possess its own divine spirit. It is said that when we die our spirits flow back into the sacred waters of dream.

With properties of purity and heat, and often containing curative minerals, healing springs were especially valued by the ancient Celts. Welling up from deep below the ground, springs were considered to be supernatural in origin, and the Celtic people tossed coins into them as offerings to the divine resident spirit. They also tied pieces of white cloth onto bushes and trees that surrounded healing springs. At the healing springs, those visiting the sanctuaries slept in special rooms where they dreamed with the intention of seeing a vision of the Goddess or God who resided there and thus were cured by her or his visitation.

Tonight's adventure leads you into the heart of your dream castle to a curative sanctuary with a magical healing spring.

This spring represents the waters of life, which are the source of your vitality. By bathing in this magical spring, it is possible to imagine what it would be like to be healthy and feeling completely well. By first imagining yourself in splendid health in your castle sanctuary, you will become healthier. Thought image transfers into reality with a little magical power behind it. The optimum time to do this healing work is on a Sunday or Monday night just before or on a full moon. I suggest you read it over a few times and then do it.

LIST OF ITEMS NEEDED: Dream Castle Crystal ★ 2 green candles ★ Lavender incense and censer ★ Chalice or glass filled with water ★ Soft healing music ★ Your imagination

✖ Spinning the Spell

Place the chalice or glass of water next to your bed so it will be close to your head as you sleep. Then hold your dream castle crystal, with the tip pointed downward, under cold running water for at least one minute to wash out any negative energies. After drying the stone, place it in the center of your altar with the tip pointed toward you. Now draw a sacred circle, and then draw a second circle of healing green light around your bedroom. Next call in your dream guardians. Turn on some soft healing music and light the incense. Then place the two green candles on each side of the crystal, about four inches apart. Light them slowly, dedicating each candle to a favorite Goddess and God of healing springs, such as Sirona and Borvo (Celtic).

Begin to gaze at the crystal, breathing deeply and allowing your mind to center and focus. Then hold the crystal in your hands, looking into it and merging with the stone. Become one with it, and imagine your beautiful dream castle within the crystal's center. Now in your mind's eye, slowly enter the castle. Allow all your senses to come alive as you see, touch, smell, hear, and even taste your surroundings. You notice that with each deep breath you take, you find yourself in another fascinating room of the castle. As you take another deep breath, you suddenly find yourself in a large room, much larger than any of the others, with a magical healing spring spilling out of the floor in the center of the room and into a immense pool made of solid crystal. You move over to the spring and take off your clothes. You sit or lie back in the spring, noticing how warm and silky the crystal clear water feels as it flows over your skin. Allow the soft bubbling water of the thermal spring to absorb all your pain, hurt, and illness. Imagine yourself releasing your emotional, physical, and spiritual pain into the healing waters. Keep doing this until you feel a sense of relief, and then allow the warm healing water to recharge your batteries and refresh you for several minutes. When you are done, come back to the present time and place and take three deep breaths.

Place your dream castle crystal back on the altar between the candles, and allow the candles to burn down naturally. As you drift to sleep, imagine bathing in the warm healing waters of the castle spring, and once again see and sense the water absorbing your illness, pain, or disease. Imagine all your ills flowing into the glass overnight.

In the morning, pull up the circle, thank the Goddess and God, and release your dream guardians. Keep the crystal on your altar, using it whenever you want to imagine yourself bathing in the healing spring of the castle. Take the glass of water by your bed and, using your nondominant hand, empty it into the toilet. Rinse the glass three times, emptying that water into the toilet as well. As you flush the toilet, imagine flushing away all the negative, unhealthy energy in the glass. In the next few days, make an effort to visit a body of water such as a natural spring, lake, the sea, or even a fountain, and take some time to energetically drink in the healing powers of the water. By the next full moon or sooner, you will feel the benefits of the healing spring.

◖ Tonight's Magical Adventure: Druid Blessing of Health

A sign of healing potential, wholesomeness, health, and vitality, apples are traditionally associated with good health and longevity. In Celtic mythology, Avalon is the island of the apples, the Celtic paradise where the apple trees are always in full fruit. Nine sister priestesses live there and are able to shapeshift, divine the future, and heal the incurable. King Arthur was taken there after his last battle to be healed by the nine sisters.

This magical work is derived from a modern Druid tradition and draws upon the old adage "An apple a day keeps the doctor away." It can be used for healing just about any ailment or disease. The deeper you merge, the stronger the healing power of this Druid Blessing of Health. The best time to do this magical work is the night of a full moon. There needs to be enough light outdoors for you to go out and dig a small hole.

LIST OF ITEMS NEEDED: 1 green candle ★ Athame or knife ★ Cutting board ★ Wand ★ Chalice filled with water ★ Bowl of salt ★ Large incense burner or cauldron ★ 1 sheet of white paper ★ 1 sheet of green paper ★ Blue felt pen ★ Green felt pen ★ 1 envelope ★ 1 red apple ★ A plate

✴ Spinning the Spell

Put all the items needed for the spell on your altar. Be sure your incense burner or cauldron is large enough to accommodate a burning sheet of paper. Make certain the blade of your athame will not damage the surface where you excise the disease. I suggest you use a cutting board for this purpose. Then draw a sacred circle of light around your bedroom and light the candle, dedicating it to a Celtic Goddess or God of healing, such as Bridget and Belenus or Coventina and Diancecht. Next use the blue pen to draw a picture of yourself, and clearly outline the problem area. It doesn't have to be work of art; just show your head and limbs. Then write all the particulars of the problem or illness next the problem area, and highlight the area by circling it. If there is more than one problem or disease, I suggest you do a separate healing work for each one. Then take a deep breath, merge deeply with Oneness, and use your athame to excise the problem or illness, first cutting and scraping the problem area in your mind and then carefully using the tip of your athame to cut and scrape the problem area on the paper in front of you. Burn the paper in your incense burner or cauldron, keeping all the ashes in the burner for now.

For the Blessing of Health, take the green sheet of paper, and use the green pen to draw another picture of yourself, this time without the problem or illness, making the drawing a little larger. All around and across your image, write down all of the qualities of good health that you desire.

Focus on the picture, merge again with Oneness, and chant this blessing of health three times:

May I now be filled with the healing power of Oneness.
By the stars, moon, sun, earth, and sea, So mote it be!

Merge with your picture of health in front of you, and become one with it. See and sense the completed healing, as if you were moving into the future for a few minutes and feeling a tremendous sense of well-being and splendid health. Return to the present moment, and then say,

So be it! So be it! So be it!

Next fold the green paper a total of nine times, into a small square, and seal it with wax from the candle. Do this over something, such as a plate, to catch any drops of wax, being careful to avoid burning yourself or dripping wax on the furniture and rug. Place the sealed paper in the envelope. On the outside of the envelope, use the green pen to draw three symbols of the Goddess. Examples are a circle with a dot in the center, a star, a crescent moon, and a spiral. Tuck the envelope under your mattress, or put it in your top bureau drawer.

Next pour the water from the chalice into the bowl of salt, and then pour the bowl of saltwater over the ashes in the censer or cauldron. The salt purifies, removing all energetic record of the disease from the ashes. Use your athame to stir the ashes counterclockwise three times, being careful not to spill any of the mixture. Take the censer or cauldron outside, dig a small hole with your athame, and then pour the contents of the censer or cauldron into the hole. Cover it over and put a large rock on top. Make an effort to leave the area looking as undisturbed as possible.

Go back inside, face your altar, and clap your hands loudly three times. Thank deity and pull up the circle. Wash all your tools with saltwater, rinse them in cool water, and then dry them.

Finally, use your athame to cut the apple crosswise so you can see the five-pointed star inside and say,

> *Sacred apple of the sisters nine,*
> *Heal me with your sacred sign.*
> *Blessed be! Blessed be! Blessed be!*

Eat the two halves, and as you do, imagine the apple imparting the healing power of the Goddess and God to your being. Allow the candle to burn down on its own. For the next nine nights, eat an apple in the evening before going to sleep. Within the next nine weeks, you will become healthier and stronger.

☾ Tonight's Magical Adventure: Sleeping Beauty Placket

Often beauty lies dormant within you, waiting to be awakened by a divine kiss. This Sleeping Beauty Placket encourages the beautiful you to emerge, like a butterfly from its cocoon, allowing your bright face to shine! The best time to make this placket is on a Friday night on or just before a full moon. If you prefer, rose-colored felt squares and a needle and thread can be substituted for the paper and stapler.

LIST OF ITEMS NEEDED: 1 rose-colored candle ★ Amber incense and censer ★ A recent photo of yourself ★ 3 pinches of dried rose petals ★ 2 square 6-inch by 6-inch pieces of rose-colored paper ★ Stapler ★ Tape ★ Pen

✳ Spinning the Spell

Draw a sacred circle around your bedroom and then a second circle of rose-colored light on top of the first circle. Light the candle, dedicating it to a Goddess of beauty such as Rosemerta (Celtic), Freyja (Norse), Venus (Roman), or Oshun (African). Then staple and tape the two squares of paper together along the sides and bottom edge, leaving the top open. On the front and back of your photo, write the sentence "I am becoming more and more beautiful every night." Insert the photo into the placket and then add the rose petals. Bathe the placket in the incense smoke for at least six minutes to strengthen its powers. Then hold the placket in your hands, merge with the Goddess to whom you dedicated the candle, and say six times,

Beauty sleeping in me, arise and awaken!

Place the placket next to your bed. Allow the candle to burn down, and as you go to sleep, repeat the words "I am beautiful." In the morning, thank the Goddess of beauty and then pull up the double circle of light. Leave the Sleeping Beauty Placket next to your bed for thirty nights to awaken the beautiful you within.

◖ Tonight's Magical Adventure: Willpower Wonder Spell

You may not think of a belt as magical, but in Celtic mythology Kernunnos's serpent belt was his companion and symbol of magical power. You can use a belt in this Willpower Wonder Spell to help you strengthen your willpower in all areas of your life and also to cinch up your craft robe. The best time to spin this spell is on a Friday or Sunday night during the gibbous moon phase.

LIST OF ITEMS NEEDED: Sandalwood incense and censer ★ A belt with a buckle that can be tightened ★ 9-inch length of green ribbon or cord ★ 9-inch length of red ribbon or cord ★ 9-inch length of white ribbon or cord

✳ Spinning the Spell

Light the incense, dedicating it to a favorite deity, and then bathe the belt and ribbons in the smoke for a few minutes to cleanse them of any unwanted energies. Section the belt into three sections, and then, moving clockwise around the belt (from the perspective of wearing it), tie the green ribbon around the central point of the first section. Knot the ends of the green ribbon nine times, merge with Oneness, and then say,

> Belt of power and will,
> With these ninefold knots of green,
> Bring the willpower that I need.
> By the light of the moon, so be it!

Next tie the red ribbon around the central point of the second section of the belt, knotting the ends of the red ribbon nine times. Merge with Oneness and then say,

Belt of power and will,
With these ninefold knots of red,
Bring the willpower that I need.
By the light of the moon, so be it!

Then tie the white ribbon around the central point of the third and final section of the belt. Knot the ends of the white ribbon nine time, merge with Oneness, and say,

Belt of power and will,
With these ninefold knots of white,
Bring the willpower that I need.
By the light of the moon, so be it!

Put the belt on, merge again with Oneness, and say,

Nine times more willpower,
Every moment, every hour.
So be it! So shall it be!

Spin nine times clockwise, and then wear the belt to bed. As you drift to sleep, repeat the words "Willpower wonder times nine." Whenever you need to strengthen your willpower, just put on your magical belt! It will help you to buckle down.

☾ Tonight's Magical Adventure: Mirror, Mirror, on the Wall Spell

In ancient times, Celtic women considered their personal mirrors soul carriers and were buried with them. In more recent times, famous mediums used mirrors to interact with angels and other spirit guides. Both folklore and faerytales talk of how the mirror acts as a magical entryway or portal between this world and other realms, as described in Lewis Carroll's wonderful story *Through the Looking Glass*. In the folktale "Sleeping Beauty," the spirit who resides in the mirror that hangs on the wall actually speaks, divining who's the fairest of them all.

In this spell, you will use a mirror to gain personal perspective and reflect on who you really are as a person. After all, mirrors reflect the world of form around you. This spell is spun on three consecutive nights, beginning on a Friday night in spring or early summer just before a full moon. You can also do this spell with your children, partner, and friends.

LIST OF ITEMS NEEDED: 8-inch by 10-inch mirror (or larger) ⋆ 1 pink taper candle ⋆ Patchouli oil ⋆ Jasmine incense and censer ⋆ Bowl of potting soil ⋆ Flower pot ⋆ Packet of flower seeds

✷ Spinning the Spell

Begin by drawing a sacred circle and calling in your dream guardians. Next dress the candle with the oil and set it in the center of the bowl of soil. Prop the mirror up on your altar so you can see your reflection when you are standing in front of it. Then position the bowl of earth so that the candle sits in between the mirror and your body. Light the candle, and then gaze into the mirror, focusing on your reflection while saying three times,

> *Inside out, outside in,*
> *Looking out, looking in.*

Ask yourself about your outer and inner beauty. What are the most beautiful qualities of your body, mind, and soul? Address the mirror, and ask three times,

> *Mirror, mirror, on the wall,*
> *What are my fairest qualities of all?*

Keep gazing at your reflection, fully concentrating on your beautiful aspects for about ten minutes. Feel good about yourself, realizing you have a lot to offer. Then snuff out the candle, pull up the circle, and release your dream guardians. Do this spell for three consecutive nights, and on the last night allow the candle to burn down on its own as you drift to sleep.

In the morning, remove any remaining wax from the bowl of soil, and put the soil in the flowerpot. Plant the flower seeds in the soil according to the directions on the package, and then water and care for the potted seeds so they germinate and thrive. As their beauty grows, your inner and outer beauty will also grow and flourish. Keep the mirror in a place where you will look into it now and again.

☾ Tonight's Magical Adventure: Letting Go of Grief Dream Magic

Sometimes it seems impossible to let go of painful feelings of grief, especially when you have lost someone dear to you. This magical work will help you separate yourself from painful feelings, freeing up and releasing the blocked energy within your being. Do this work during a waning moon phase on a Saturday night.

LIST OF ITEMS NEEDED: Sage and cedar smudge ⋆ 3 black candles ⋆ Dragon's blood oil ⋆ Silver bell ⋆ 18-inch length of black ribbon or string ⋆ Censer or cauldron ⋆ Scissors

✳ Spinning the Spell

Smudge yourself and all the items you will be using for this spell. Next draw a triple sacred circle, laying down white light first, cobalt blue light second, and white light third. Then call in your dream guardians. Rub a fine film of the dragon's blood oil over the three candles, and as you do, imagine yourself letting go of your grief. Then light the candles one at a time. Next hold the silver bell over the altar, ring it three times, and say,

I call upon the powers of the Goddess this night.

Ring the bell three more times and say,

I call upon the powers of the God this night.

Ring the bell three more times and say,

I call upon the ancient powers that be.

Place the bell back on the altar, and then pick up the ribbon, holding an end in each hand. Imagine that the right end represents you while the left end represents your grief. Name the ends as such by holding up the right end and saying your name three times, and then holding up the left end and naming your grief three times. Set the ribbon back upon the altar. Take a few minutes to center yourself completely, aligning your being with the energies of peace, love, and harmony. Pick up the bell, ring it three times, and say,

Below and above, earth and sea,
I awaken these energies in me.
Witness tonight that I now release
My grief and painful feelings about (name grief).
By the will of the Ancient Ones,
By the will of the One,
As I will, it is done!

Now saturate the ribbon or string in the dragon's blood oil and cut it in half. Light the ribbon in the candle flame, and then burn both pieces in your censer or cauldron. As the ribbon burns, chant these words:

Sacred flame, take my pain!
Sacred fire, consume my grief!

Once the smoke has cleared, take a few deep breaths. See and sense yourself breathing in bright white light and breathing out your feelings of grief into a cobalt blue balloon. This balloon can be filled more and more without ever popping. Now keep filling the balloon with any painful feelings, imagining it expanding more and more. Do this for as long as it takes to exhale all your grief into the balloon, and then release the balloon into the sky, watching it disappear into the night.

Next pick up the bell and ring it nine times. Snuff out the candles, and thank the divine powers that have helped you with your work. Pull up the triple circle of light in the order that you laid it down, and then release your dream guardians. Next smudge yourself for a few minutes, and then smudge your tools, altar, and bedroom. Complete the work by taking a warm saltwater bath, using one-half cup of sea salt in your bathwater. As you soak, imagine any residue feelings of grief being absorbed by the water. Within the next three days, you will be able to release a good deal of your grief. This will lighten your load and energize you.

◖ Tonight's Magical Adventure: Living Long Dream Spell

Living longer is a reality in the twenty-first century, and living to be two hundred or even three hundred years old may not be that far-fetched in the near future. This spell shows you how to tap into the divine power of Oneness to promote a healthy, prosperous, and very long life. It combines candle magic, meditation, and a traditional toast to the Goddess and God. The three candles represent the three stages of life: maiden, mother, and crone or son, father, and wise man. The optimal night to cast this spell is the sixth full moon after the Winter Solstice, when the moon is at its highest point in the sky. I suggest you read it over a few times before attempting the spell or, better yet, tape-record it and play it back.

LIST OF ITEMS NEEDED: 3 white candles ★ Chalice filled
with sparkling cider or white wine ★ Soft music

✳ Spinning the Spell

Turn on some soft music, and then draw a sacred circle and call in
your dream guardians. Next invoke a favorite Goddess or God by
chanting her or his name nine times aloud. Place the candles side by
side, and light the leftmost candle. Then use the lit candle to light
the middle candle, and finally use the middle candle to light the
rightmost candle. As you do this, dedicate each candle to the stage
of life it represents: left (youth), middle (adulthood), and right (old
age). Place the filled chalice in front of the burning candles.

Next sit or recline comfortably and center your mind by taking
a few deep breaths. Breathe in to the count of three, hold your
breath for three counts, and then exhale completely, allowing all
the tension and worry to flow out of you. Now close your eyes
and slowly begin imagining the beautiful, white light of the full
moon all around you, like a radiant crystal sphere that sparkles
and shimmers. Use your deep breathing to make the bright moon
sphere shine even brighter. Imagine the white sphere of light radiating outward and filling your entire bedroom and home. Use your
field of intention to fill the sphere with the power of longevity,
love, good health, and happiness. Know that this bright sphere of
moonlight can be used to add years onto your normal life span.
Take a few minutes to make the shimmering crystal sphere of light
all around you even brighter and then brighter still, until you feel
as bright as the full moon in the night sky. Imagine this bright
light sparkling all around you, and then step into the future and
imagine yourself growing older, then older still. Then, depending
upon your level of curiosity or tenacity, continue to move forward
through the years, and see your death. Rather than being a negative experience, seeing your own death can often expand your
perspective. It reminds you that it's later than you think and time
to set those dreams in motion. It also gives you an opportunity to

pattern your life so that you can extend the time you have, enjoying it to its fullest. Most of all, keep in mind that fate is changeable, much like the weather, so if you don't like what you see, you can change the image in your mind to a happier ending. By doing so, you plant the energetic intent for change, making it more likely to occur.

Now come back to the present moment, and once again fill yourself with the bright white light of the full moon. Face the altar, and pick up the filled chalice. Holding it up in your hands, toast your long life by saying,

> *To the Goddess (state name) and the God (state name),*
> *May you never thirst and always thrive.*
> *By your divine power, love, and protection,*
> *I ask that you grant me splendid health and long life!*
> *Blessed be the Goddess and God! So be it! Make it so!*

Now drink the liquid, and as you do, imagine drinking in the pure white light of the moon. Set the chalice back on the altar, and let the candles burn down on their own. As you drift to sleep, imagine snuggling into the crystal sphere of white light.

In the morning, pull up the circle and release your dream guardians. Each night as you drift to sleep, snuggle into the bright crystal sphere of moonlight to add years to your life. Also consider adding traditional herbs for longevity to your diet, such as gotakola, ginkgo, rosehips, and ginseng.

☾ Tonight's Magical Adventure: Bathing Beauty Aromatherapy Spell

Using the magic of aromatherapy, this spell can help you look and feel more beautiful, both outside and inside. It works by combining the natural beautifying powers of aloe and rose with the divine beauty of the Goddess (or God) to encourage your inner beauty to surface and become more visible outwardly. You are bound to feel more confident, and you will find people begin noticing and complimenting you on your growing beauty. If you prefer showering, just put the aloe vera, rose, and chamomile into a shower mitt and softly rub your skin with the beautifying herbal blend. If you want to draw upon the powers of beauty of the God, you can easily alter the gender accordingly. Feel free to do this spell anytime you want to feel and look more beautiful.

LIST OF ITEMS NEEDED: 1 rose-colored candle ⋆ 1 orange candle ⋆ A warm bath ⋆ 3 cups aloe vera juice ⋆ 3 chamomile tea bags ⋆ Rose oil ⋆ 1 rose

✸ Spinning the Spell

You will most likely be doing this spell in the bathroom, so set up a temporary altar on a surface that will accommodate the two candles and holders. Draw a sacred circle of rose-colored light around the bathroom, and then light the candles. Next draw a warm bath and add the aloe vera juice, chamomile tea bags, and three drops of rose oil. Place the rose next to the tub, and then get into the water. After you get settled in, hold the rose in both hands and then pull the petals off, one at a time, dropping them into the bathwater. With each petal you pull, say,

> *Flower of beauty and delight,*
> *Share your loveliness with me tonight!*

Now sit back in the tub, close your eyes, and focus all your attention on your best features. Make your best features even better, and allow everything else to diminish. Continue to concentrate only on your best features as you say,

> *O beautiful Lady of the night,*
> *Bright Goddess of jeweled starlight,*
> *Generous mother of the Earth,*

Swift sister of the wind,
Passionate lover of the sea,
Weaver of the elemental spirit,
Grant me your love and beauty,
Beauty within, shining without.
May I become One with you
And reflect your divine beauty.
Great Lady, please make me brighter,
Beauty be drawn, and beauty come.
O beautiful Lady of the night,
I thank you and give you love.
Remain with me, now and forevermore.
So be it! So mote it be!

Soak for a few more minutes, and then get out of the tub and dry off with a fluffy towel. Snuff out the candles, and use them when you do this spell again. Next pull up the circle. Then anoint yourself with the rose oil by putting three drops on each wrist and on the inside of both ankles. Snuggle into bed, and as you drift to sleep imagine your inner beauty blossoming like a beautiful rose.

◖ Tonight's Magical Adventure: The Sandman Sleep Spell

In European nursery stories and lullabies, the sandman comes gliding in when the sun sets at night. He brings his bag filled with the sands of sleep and puts yawning sleepyheads to sleep by sprinkling sand in their eyes. This Sandman Sleep Spell will help you go to sleep, even when you are troubled by problems and stress.

LIST OF ITEMS NEEDED: Small bowl of sand ★ Three small pebbles ★ Sandalwood incense and censer ★ 1 brown candle ★ Soft, soothing music

✪ Spinning the Spell

Draw a sacred circle of light around your bedroom. Put on soft music, light the candle and incense, and place the bowl of sand and pebbles on your dream altar. Dim the lights, and use your fingers to create a hole in the middle of the bowl of sand. Do this slowly, sifting the sand with your fingers a bit and thinking about the things in your life that are most troubling you right now. Imagine putting all your problems and worries into the hole in the sand, and actually toss them energetically into the bowl. Cover the hole over, and level out the surface of the bowl of sand, placing the three pebbles on its surface. As you do this, repeat these words three times:

> *Peaceful sands of sleep*
> *Troubles buried so deep*
> *The sandman sings*
> *Sleep awhile*
> *Sleep awhile.*
> *Peaceful sea of dreams*
> *Worries washed away*
> *The sandman sings*
> *Sleep awhile*
> *Sleep awhile.*
> *So be it!*

Put the bowl back on your altar, and then lie back in bed and begin visualizing yourself on a sandy beach on a warm sunny afternoon. See and sense yourself digging a deep hole in the soft sand with your hands. You can feel the warmth of the sand on your fingers, hands, and arms as you dig, and you can smell the salt in the air, water, and earth. All these sensations help you feel more and more relaxed and peaceful. The hole you have been digging is now deep enough. You begin to energetically put all your problems and worries in the hole, tossing them in one by one, letting go of any negative or burdening feelings. Once all your problems and worries are in the hole, use your hands to completely fill it in. Pat the sand down on the top of the hole, and place three small pebbles on its surface. See and sense yourself lying back in the warm sand. Slowly allow the evening sun and rhythmic surf to lull you to sleep, feeling peaceful and calm, warm and sleepy.

In the morning, pull up the circle. Keep the three pebbles on your dream altar to remind you of your natural ability to let go of problems and worries. Bury the sand in a hole outside, preferably in the garden.

◖ Tonight's Magical Adventure: Sleep, Perchance to Dream, Spell

Taking off from Hamlet's famous "To be or not to be" soliloquy in Shakespeare's play, this spell shows you how to encourage divine dreams to be and nightmares not to be. The "mare" in *nightmare* is not a female horse but a *mara,* a spirit from Anglo-Saxon and Old Norse traditions that sat on the chests of sleeping people, causing them to have bad dreams. This spell uses your hands, since by learning in your dreams to focus on your hands you can become adept at stopping unpleasant nightmares for good. For best results, do this spell on a new moon.

LIST OF ITEMS NEEDED: A pair of shoes ⋆ Lavender oil ⋆ Sprig of rosemary

✳ Spinning the Spell

Draw a triple circle of white light around your bedroom and call in your dream guardians. Next anoint yourself with the lavender oil, applying three drops to the top of your head, inside both wrists, and on the bottoms of your feet. As you do, say,

As I now dream and sleep,
No nightmares shall plague me,

Until they swim all the waters
That flow upon the earth,
And count all the stars
That appear in the firmament,
Over and over, forever and a night!
Help me, divine and ancient Ones,
Protect me now and forevermore!
So be it! Ayea! Ayea! Ayea!

Then put three drops of the oil inside each of the shoes and place them next to your bed, pointing them toward the door. Put the sprig of rosemary under your bed to induce sound sleep and for added protection. Then get into bed backward, and sit comfortably. Begin to stare at your hands, and continue doing so for at least fifteen minutes. Focus all your attention on your hands, and really get to know their every nuance. After focusing on your hands, close your eyes and take a few deep breaths. Next open your eyes and clap your hands three times. Then say three times,

Hands, help me, hands, wake me.
As I will, so shall it be!

As you lie back to sleep, cross your hands over your chest or stomach. In your mind's eye, imagine your hands, and keep imagining them until you fall asleep. In the morning, pull up the circle and release your dream guardians. Keep the rosemary under your bed, and repeat this spell as often as you like. You will discover that if you find yourself in an unpleasant dream, all you have to do is simply imagine your hands and you will immediately wake up.

c

chapter   eight

Practical Dream Magic

Dreams are not generally considered practical. This chapter proves that dreams can be applied to everyday life in useful and practical ways. My dreams have often revealed answers to questions.

Several years ago, before my son was born, my husband and I purchased property in the woods of northern California with the dream of building a home and living in the country. The night we signed the contracts, I had a dream:

I am inside a beautiful home. There is a warm fire burning in a wood stove, and outside it is snowing. The snow is soft and fluffy and swirls around in the gentle wind outside a large picture window. I am sitting on a dark green overstuffed chair that faces the large picture window. There is a little boy sitting next to me. He's about eight years old, and we are reading a book. It feels so warm and comfortable inside the house. We read for several minutes, first me reading to him, and then him reading to me. We both look out at the snow, now and again. I feel very happy and then wake up.

This dream stayed with me for several years, just as vivid as the night I originally dreamed it. Over the years I found myself designing our home much like the home I saw in my dream. Just recently, I found myself sitting in the dark green overstuffed chair in the great room, reading a book with my eight-year-old son and watching the snow fall outside the large picture window. I suddenly realized that I was living my dream!

The term *déjà vu,* which in French means "already seen," refers in one sense to the reoccurrence of events in waking life, but on another more mystical level it refers to events happening in waking life that replicate what has already been seen in dream. Like two cameras moving just out of sync, dream and waking reality often move in parallel, and since dream is often one step ahead, it can be extremely useful for staying ahead of things in a practical sense.

In a more directed way, I have often gone over anticipated events in dream, such as job interviews and social events. I usually see myself going through the steps in my dream, which makes me better prepared and more self-confident during the actual event. Also, if something unusual or negative occurs in the dream, it acts as a forewarning about the actual event. This has saved me a lot of grief over the years.

Dreams offer a means for role playing and thus prepare you for what's to come in practical reality. By adding magic to your dreams, you make them even more useful in a practical sense. They become vehicles not only for your personal and social development, but also for your overall spiritual development. In turn, you become not only a master of your dreams, but also a master of life itself. In this sense, dream magic awakens the magician within you.

Magic is about setting goals through expectation and desire and then attaining these goals by merging with the divine whole of Oneness. It is also about taking the necessary steps toward making your dreams come true. For example, a well-prepared résumé never hurts when looking for the perfect job. Magic is what happens when you turn your mind toward a specific goal, and then, through effort and practice, everything falls into place, giving the experience a mystical and synchronistic feeling. Magic is about doing everything in your power to make the dream come true without destroying the sense of wonder or mystery. As with anything, the balance is important.

The following spells use the concept of dream magic in the practical realms of solving a problem, buying and selling real estate, and protecting your home from harm. They show you how to tap into the practical power of dreams, helping you to cope with day-to-day life and making your world a little more magical.

◖ Tonight's Magical Adventure: Solving a Problem in Your Dreams

Dreams tap into your subconscious, often showing clarity and vision not apparent in waking reality. Because of this, dreams provide an excellent medium for solving problems. This technique uses your dream altar to solve a problem. The best time to do this work is on a Monday or Wednesday night on or just before a gibbous moon phase.

LIST OF ITEMS NEEDED: Your dream stone ★ Yellow votive candle and fireproof holder ★ Quill or ballpoint pen ★ Patchouli oil

✴ Spinning the Spell

Pick a problem that you want to solve. In your mind, begin examining all sides of the problem. Do this for a few minutes. Now keep thinking about the problem while you wash the candle with cool saltwater, dry it, and set it on the altar. Take a few minutes to become familiar with the objects by observing and touching the candle, holder, and quill or pen and smelling the oil. Now draw a sacred circle and call in your dream guardians. Use the quill or pen to write the word *Problem* on the body of the candle. On the other side of the candle, write the word *Solution*. Rub a thin film of oil over the candle before lighting it. Next, gazing into the candle, repeat these words three times:

> *As I dream I discover and remember*
> *The solution to my problem.*
> *(State the problem aloud)*
> *In my dreams, I discover and remember.*
> *So be it! So dream it! Blessed be!*

Focus on the flame of the candle for a few minutes. Either snuff out the candle or allow it to burn out on its own in a fire-proof container. Lie back in bed, holding your dream stone in your left hand. Close your eyes and move your mind to your astral dream altar. (See chapter 2 for constructing your astral dream altar.) See yourself repeating all the steps of the ritual at your dream altar as you drift off to sleep.

Upon waking, write down what you remember of your dreams. Then pull up the circle and release your dream guardians. Repeat the process every night until you receive a solution. You may find a solution the first night, within a week, or in a month. Most find some solution within a few days.

◖ Tonight's Magical Adventure: You've Got Mail Cyber Ritual

The Internet has changed the face of communication. Now you can e-mail someone almost anywhere on the planet at the fraction of the cost of a phone call. This cyber ritual can be used to attract more great e-mail and less spam. All you need is a candle, a computer, e-mail service, and your imagination. You will be seeing or hearing the "You've Got Mail" message on your computer much more often. The best time to do this cyber ritual is on a Wednesday night at midnight, just after a new moon.

LIST OF ITEMS NEEDED: 1 white votive candle ⋆ Computer ⋆
E-mail service ⋆ Your imagination

✴ Spinning the Spell

Draw a sacred circle around your computer, and then place the votive
candle in front of your screen a safe distance away. Light the candle
and turn on your computer. Click on your e-mail program, and then
sit back and merge with the candle flame and screen. Take a few
deep breaths to center your body, mind, and spirit, and then say,

By moonshine the animals sing
By starlight the owl does wing
Across the window of the Web
Gliding into the timeless ebb.

O computer, cyber cauldron of creation,
Weave a brilliant Web for my navigation.
In Internet server and user circles tonight,
Filter out the spam and bring e-mail bright.

I call upon all of my cyber friends
And invite them to click on now!
I call upon the cyber spirits of earth
And invite them to click on now!
I call upon the cyber spirits of air
And invite them to click on now!
I call upon the cyber spirits of fire
And invite them to click on now!
I call upon the cyber spirits of water
And invite them to click on now!

O Great Cyber Mother, keep us whole,
Let your power and love fill our souls.
O Great Cyber Father, keep us whole,

Let your power and love fill our souls.
We are the flow, we are the ebb,
We are the weavers of the Internet Web.

Blessed be the Cyber God and Goddess,
Blessed be the providers, servers, and users!
Blessed be all the weavers of the Web.
Blessed be! Blessed be! Blessed be!

Now e-mail three people you know. You can use e-cards to add some visuals to your communication. Just use a search engine and type in the keyword *ecards,* and you will find a large list to choose from. Next surf the Internet for some of your favorite pagan and environmental organizations. Get on their e-mailing lists so you can keep abreast of the latest news and happenings. I also suggest subscribing to daily news, weather, or joke services. These services automatically send you e-mail every day, keeping you current and helping you keep your sense of humor. When you are done surfing, retrieve your e-mail and reply to it. Next thank the cyber Goddess and God, turn off your computer, and pull up your circle. Take the candle into your bedroom and place it on your altar. Allow it to burn down completely, and as you drift to sleep, repeat silently, "E-mail me in my dreams." In the morning, record your dreams in your journal, and retrieve your e-mail again.

☾ Tonight's Magical Adventure: Blissful Dream Vacation Magic

Most people could use a vacation from the daily grind but often don't have enough time off from work or the financial where-withal to go on a really blissful vacation. Tonight's adventure takes you on the vacation of your dreams, and all you need for the trip is your dream stone and imagination. You don't even need to bring your toothbrush!

LIST OF ITEMS NEEDED: Dream stone ⋆ Your imagination

✱ Spinning the Spell

Begin by drawing a sacred circle around your bedroom. Next lie back in bed, holding your dream stone in your left hand. Your dream stone can be created using the directions in chapter 3. Close your eyes and take several deep breaths, relaxing the muscles in your body by flexing them as tight as you can and then letting them go limp. Imagine breathing in white light and exhaling all the tensions and worries of the day. Do this as long as it takes you to feel more relaxed and calm.

Once you feel more centered, start imagining the ideal spot for a blissful dream vacation. This can be anywhere, any planet, or any dimension. You might find yourself on a warm sandy beach under a palm tree at dusk, feeling the warm breeze against your face and the warmth of the sand on your skin as you lie back. Or you might find yourself in a old-growth redwood forest, sitting underneath an ancient majestic tree, gazing at the full moon and taking in the beauty of the woods while breathing in the fresh, moist air. Or perhaps you find yourself in a flower garden, surrounded with blooming flowers of every kind, their fragrance filling your senses. Or perhaps you decide to travel to another realm altogether, for example, to a world made of crystal or pure light. The main idea is to set your imagination free and then see where it takes you. If you have a problem staying focused on your ideal vacation spot because of distracting thoughts, one trick is to first pretend to walk into an entirely different life where none of those worries, problems, or responsibilities exist, and then allow your mind to find the ideal vacation spot. Once there, engage your senses and see, feel, hear, touch, taste, and intuit your surroundings. For example, if you are lying on a sandy beach at dusk, dig your feet into the warm sand and feel it between your toes, or dip your toes into the ocean water. Smell the air, and then taste the salt on your lips from the mist off the waves. Take a few moments to listen to the hypnotic rhythm of the rolling waves and to the Sea Queen's divine song. Remain in this ideal vacation spot as you drift to sleep, absorbing all the pleasant sights and sensations.

In the morning, write down your dreams and also a description of your dream vacation spot. Then pull up the circle and place your dream stone on your altar. Anytime you want to take another blissful dream vacation, just lie back in bed, holding your dream stone, and let your mind travel to your ideal spot. I suggest that you also take blissful mini-vacations during your waking hours, especially if you have a stressful occupation. For example, you can take mini-vacations for a few minutes during breaks at work, when traveling on airplanes, trains, or buses, or while waiting in line. Just carry your dream stone with you, hold it in your left hand, close your eyes, and no matter where you are, there you go!

☾ Tonight's Magical Adventure: Planes, Trains, and Automobiles Travel Spell

An ancient and powerful amulet that ensures safe travel, the fouled anchor, emblem for naval groups, is also used in magic rituals. In hoodoo it stands for fidelity, and in Freemasonry it is used as a symbol of hope. This spell uses the protective powers of the fouled anchor, plus lavender oil, to keep you and your luggage on course when you're traveling, night or day, and to ensure your safe return home. I suggest you use a silver-colored fouled anchor charm made of sterling silver or pewter. Bracelet charms, anchor key rings, or anchor pendants all will work, but I recommend using a key ring charm. It makes an especially nice safe travel charm because you can keep your house and car keys on it, carrying them with you wherever you go, whether in a plane, train, or automobile. The best time to spin this spell is on a full moon, preferably on a Wednesday night.

LIST OF ITEMS NEEDED: 1 white candle ★ 1 brown and/or blue candle ★ Quill or ballpoint pen ★ Lavender oil ★ Sandalwood incense and censer ★ Silver anchor charm ★ 1 handkerchief or small scarf for each of your pieces of luggage, plus an extra one to carry with you ★ 9-inch length of blue ribbon for each handkerchief or scarf

✳ Spinning the Spell

Choose a blue candle if your journey will be over water, and use the brown candle if you will be traveling over land. If your journey will be over water and land, use both the blue and brown candles. First wash the candles with cool saltwater, dry them, and place them on the altar. Then draw a sacred circle and call in your dream guardians. Next light the incense, dedicating it to the Roman God of travel, Mercury. Also chant his name nine times, and ask him to come into your circle. Use the quill or pen to inscribe the name *Mercury* three times on the white candle body. Also inscribe your initials on the candle. Repeat this procedure with the other candle(s), and then dress them with a fine film of oil. Next bathe the anchor charm in the incense smoke for a couple of minutes, and anoint the charm with the oil. Hold the charm in your hands, and empower it by saying,

> *Powers of the stars and moon,*
> *Great God Mercury, hear me tonight.*
> *With this anchor charm of travel,*
> *Work your magic and keep me safe,*
> *Whenever, wherever, and however I go,*
> *In all worlds, both dream and waking,*
> *Mercury, always bring me safely home.*
> *So be it! Make it so!*

Then put the anchor back on the altar, and bathe the handkerchiefs in the incense smoke for a couple of minutes. Next apply nine drops of lavender oil on each of the handkerchiefs, and fold each of them three times. Tie the blue lengths of ribbon around each of the handkerchiefs, knotting the ribbon five times as you do so. Place the anchor on top of the stack of folded and tied handkerchiefs, hold the bundle in your hands, and say three times,

> *Sacred lavender purple*
> *And ribbons of blue,*
> *Protect and watch over me*
> *And all my bags, too!*
> *Keep us right on course*
> *Wherever we may roam,*
> *May we travel safely*
> *To and from our home.*
> *Wherever water may flow,*
> *This magic spell is cast*
> *Wherever we may roam,*
> *This spell will always last!*
> *So be it! Make it so!*

Set the handkerchiefs and anchor charm on the altar overnight to charge them with the divine powers of the stars, moon, and the Great God Mercury. Allow the candles to burn out on their own.

In the morning, thank Mercury and then pull up the circle and release your dream guardians. Tuck a handkerchief into each one of your bags, and carry one with you while you are traveling. This will ensure that your bags go where you go. Always carry the fouled anchor charm with you for safe travel.

☾ Tonight's Magical Adventure: Real Estate Dream Ritual

In ancient times, the priests in the sacred sanctuary of Zeus at Dodona said that the first prophetic words came from an oak tree.

The wise women and men of that time listened to the oak and the stone to discover the past and future. Designed to help you both buy and sell real estate, this ritual draws its power from the helpful tree and stone spirits of nature. A tree spirit, called a dryad, is bonded with a certain tree and needs the tree in order to survive, as the tree provides the spirit with energy, power, and knowledge.

At dusk one winter's evening, I met the dryad in our large oak. It had been raining all day, and I was taking advantage of a break in the storm to step outside and get a breath of fresh air. Suddenly a beautiful woman literally flowed out of the thick trunk of the old oak. She was luminous, with delicate features, and her long, flowing, green hair streamed freely about her, seeming to have a life of its own. I wasn't so much frightened as awestruck because she was over eight feet tall. I realized that she was the spirit who lived in the tree. You, too, can merge with the tree and stone spirits. They can help you buy and sell property. The best time to do this ritual is on a Saturday night on a new moon.

LIST OF ITEMS NEEDED: A tree on the property you want to buy or sell ★ 1 brown candle ★ 1 yellow candle ★ 1 red candle ★ 1 blue candle ★ Quill or ballpoint pen ★ Amber oil ★ 4 pinches powdered echinacea ★ 5 thumb-sized pieces of tumbled clear quartz ★ 4 envelopes ★ Brown felt pen

✺ Spinning the Spell

A preliminary to setting up the charm involves visiting the property you intend to buy at dusk for a few minutes by yourself. When you get there, determine the dominant tree, and then place both hands on its trunk, take a few deep breaths, and become one with the tree. Imagine yourself merging with the spirit of the tree, called the dryad, who often looks like a beautiful luminous woman with long flowing hair, clad only in green and white light. Listen for any messages, and then state directly to the dryad your intentions with regard to the property. For example, say aloud, "Tree spirit, I intend to buy this property within three months. Please help me in this endeavor. I thank you. So be it!" If you are selling your property, simply step outside, place your hands on the dominant tree, and substitute the word *sell* for *buy*.

That evening, set up your altar with the items listed. Wash the candles, dry them, and set them on your altar. Then draw a sacred circle and call in your dream guardians. If you are buying property, inscribe the words *Buying Property* on each of the candles. If you are selling property, inscribe the words *Selling Property*. Dress the candles in the amber oil, and then roll them in the powdered echinacea to strengthen their magical power. Next set the candles in their holders, and place them in a four-quarter cross formation, with the brown candle at the top point, the yellow candle at the east point, the red one at the south point, and the blue candle at the west point. Place a piece of quartz in front of each candle and one in the center of the candles. Light the brown candle, and use it to light the other candles, moving in a clockwise pattern. Merge with the candle flames and say,

> *Powers of the north, east, south, and west,*
> *Come here now, at my bequest.*

Next take each of the pieces of quartz, one at a time, starting with the piece in front of the brown candle. Hold it in your dominant hand, and empower the stone by saying,

> *Crystal marker of the north,*
> *Helpful spirits of earth,*
> *Assist me in my real estate venture!*

Place it back in front of the brown candle, and pick up the crystal in front of the yellow candle. Empower it by saying,

Crystal marker of the east,
Helpful spirits of air,
Assist me in my real estate venture!

Put the stone back in front of the yellow candle, and pick up the crystal in front of the red candle. Empower it by saying,

Crystal marker of the south,
Helpful spirits of fire,
Assist me in my real estate venture!

Set the stone back in front of the red candle, and then pick up the crystal in front of the blue candle. Empower it by saying,

Crystal marker of the west,
Helpful spirits of water,
Assist me in my real estate venture!

Then set the stone back in front of the blue candle, and pick up the center stone in your dominant hand. Empower it by saying,

Crystal marker of spirit,
Mother and father of all the elements,
Help me make my real estate venture a success!

Leave the crystals on the altar overnight, and allow the candles to burn down safely on their own. As you drift to sleep, imagine that you have already made the deal and bought the property or sold it at a good price.

In the morning, record your dreams, pull up the circle, and release your dream guardians. Put the top stone into an envelope and label it *North* with the brown felt pen. Put the crystal in front of the yellow candle in an envelope and label it *East,* and so forth. Carry the central crystal in your right pocket or purse.

If you are selling your property, take the four envelopes outside. If you are buying, take the envelopes with you and visit the property. Determine the north, east, south, and west directions of the property using the sun or a compass, and then put the corresponding crystal into the ground at these points. If there is a house on the property, you can place the stones around the house in a cross formation. As you put each of the stones in place, say,

Help me buy this property now!
So be it! Make it so!

If you are selling the property, empower the stones as you set them in position by saying,

Help me sell this property now!
So be it! Make it so!

Once you have bought the property in question, leave the crystal markers permanently in place while you own the land. If you are selling, pull up the crystal markers once the property has sold, clear them out, and use them again for another purpose. Also, once you have purchased a piece of property, immediately plant a tree on the land in honor of the dryads. This draws their protection and blessings to you and your property.

◖ Tonight's Magical Adventure: Nice Neighbor Dream Spell

This dream spell can be used to keep your neighbors nice instead of nasty. The best night for doing this spell is Wednesday night on or just before a full moon.

LIST OF ITEMS NEEDED: Sandalwood incense and censer ★ 1 blue candle ★ 1 white candle ★ 13-inch length of white cord or string

✳ Spinning the Spell

Draw a sacred circle and call in your dream guardians. Light the incense and then the candles. Sit or lie back for a few minutes while holding the ends of the length of cord in your hands. Imagine a bright blue ball of light encircling you. Once you are fully surrounded in the blue light, say,

Light all around, above, below, and beyond,
Protect me at night, all day, at dusk, and dawn.
So be it! So shall it be!

Next take the cord and knot it once in the center. As you do, say,

By knot of one, this spell has now begun.

Tie a second knot and say,

By knot of two, its power will stay true.

Tie a third knot and say,

By knot of three, tonight I take this opportunity.

Tie a fourth knot and say,

By knot of four, to bind negativity from my door.

Tie a fifth knot and say,

By knot of five, let wellness and positivity arrive.

Tie a sixth knot and say,

By knot of six, all problems resolve and fix.

Tie a seventh knot and say,

By knot of seven, release neighborly peace within.

Tie an eighth knot and say,

By knot of eight, make all days and nights great.

Tie a final ninth knot and say,

By knot of nine, keep my neighbors nice all of the time.
By these nine knots of power, so be it! So shall it be!

Then hold the knotted cord in your hands, gaze into the candle-light, and say,

Forge this spell in the fire.
Weave it well, craft it higher!
None shall pass my property line
Unless I so will it at the time.
So be it! So shall it be!

Put the cord on your altar overnight, and allow the candles to burn down safely on their own. As you drift to sleep, imagine having perfect neighbors with all the qualities you like in people.

In the morning, pull up the circle and release your dream guardians. Take the knotted cord and tie it on something just out-side your front door to reinforce the power of your Nice Neighbor Dream Spell.

☾ Tonight's Magical Adventure: Question/Answer Dream Ritual

The dreaming state is conducive for tapping into the cosmic consciousness of Oneness and in the process finding the answers to pressing questions. When you are dreaming, your mind sheds its cause-and-effect mask of rationality and becomes more malleable, open, and primed for magic. The best time to spin this spell is on a Monday or Wednesday night just before a full moon.

LIST OF ITEMS NEEDED: Piece of citrine ★ Rosemary oil ★ Your imagination

✴ Spinning the Spell

Draw a sacred circle, call in your dream guardians, and invoke Artemis, the Greek Goddess of the moon, by saying,

> *Artemis, Lady of the night sky,*
> *With your silvery white beams,*
> *Shine upon this circle tonight*
> *And unlock the sacred doors of dream.*
> *Blessed be Artemis, Come, I pray you!*

Next anoint your body with the rosemary oil by applying three drops to the top of your head, hands, and feet. Then rub three drops of the oil into the piece of citrine. Merge with the stone, and empower it by saying three times,

> *Questions I ask,*
> *Answers I seek.*

Now lie back in bed, holding the stone in your left hand. Take three deep breaths by breathing in to the count of three, holding your breath for three counts, and then exhaling completely. Now close your eyes and begin to imagine yourself slowly descending a beautiful stairway. With each step you take, you feel more and more comfortably relaxed and in tune with your surroundings. As you reach the bottom of the stairway, you notice a very long hallway with colored doors all along both sides of the corridor. Behind each of color-coded doors is an answer to one of your questions. Behind the pink doors are answers about friendship, romance, and love, with the red doors holding answers about sex and your lover. Behind the green doors are answers about prosperity, fertility, creativity, and healing. Behind the yellow doors are answers about new opportunities, business matters, and pursuits in learning, while the orange doors open to questions regarding courage, strength, and luck. Behind the blue doors are answers to questions concerning healing, protection, and travel, whereas the purple doors contain answers to questions about your higher self and psychic abilities. The brown doors open to questions about the home, your pets, and power animals, while the white doors open to questions of a spiritual nature. Now imagine yourself very slowly walking down the hallway of colored doors, thinking of one question at a time and opening the appropriate door for the answer. For example, if you have a question regarding your lover, open a red door for the answer. For questions regarding your spirituality, open a white door. Match the door to the nature of your question. Be sure to make a mental note of the answers you receive, or, better yet, jot them down on a piece of paper or tape-record them. Keep asking questions and opening doors until you drift to sleep.

In the morning, write down your dreams in your journal and thank Artemis, the moon Goddess. Then pull up the circle and release your dream guardians. Keep the citrine on your altar, and repeat this work whenever you need answers to pressing questions.

☾ Tonight's Magical Adventure:
Nothing but the Truth Ritual

I love this ancient story about truth:

Truth and Falsehood bathed together in sparkling waters, and when they came ashore, Falsehood put on Truth's clothing and ran ahead, leaving Truth the choice of either putting on Falsehood's garments or nothing at all. Truth chose to go skyclad.

Because Truth refused to wear false garments, we now speak of "the naked truth."

In modern times, truth isn't so much naked as nonexistent. The value of the truth has been degraded to such an extent that lying has become fashionable. Politicians do it, prominent people do it, your family and friends do it, and even Hollywood glorifies lies and deception in films. If you don't agree that lying is a trend, just try telling the absolute truth for one day!

Since falsehood is so widespread, it is often difficult to know whether or not someone is telling the truth. This simple ritual will help you distinguish truth from falsehood. It is best done on a Monday night under a waxing moon.

LIST OF ITEMS NEEDED: 1 candle (any color) that represents you ✶ 3 white candles ✶ Sandalwood incense and censer ✶ Quill or ballpoint pen ✶ Honeysuckle oil

✳ Spinning the Spell

Wash the candles in cool saltwater, dry them, and place them on the altar. Draw a sacred circle, cutting an energetic door so that you can go outside later in the work. Then call in your dream guardians and invoke a favorite Goddess and God of wisdom, for example, Hypatia (Greek) or Odin (Norse). Take a few minutes to think about what truth you want to learn. Focus completely on your question. Then use the quill or pen to inscribe the word *Truth* on each of the white candles. Inscribe your initials on the colored candle, and dress all the candles with the honeysuckle oil. Anoint yourself with the oil, applying three drops to your third eye, three drops on your hands, and three drops on your feet. Wipe your hands, and place the candles on their holders on the altar, with the white candles in a triangle surrounding the colored candle. Then light the colored candle and say,

> Great Goddess and God,
> This candle represents me.
> As it burns, I do see
> The truth in all things!

Use the lit candle to light the white candles that surround it. As you do so, say,

> Symbols of the truth, circle me,
> Reveal the secrets that I seek!

Gaze at the candles, merging with their light for a few minutes. Then go over to a window, or step outdoors through the energetic gate you cut earlier in the spell. Looking up at the moon, say passionately,

> Moon queen and king of lunar power,
> Come to me at this enchanted hour.
> Reveal the naked truth in my dreams,
> So I will know what is, not what it seems.
> Moon lady and lord with beauty bright,
> Rise bright and clear tonight.
> Shine on the Earth and sky and sea,
> And reveal the skyclad truth in my dreams.
> So dream it! As I will, so mote it be!

Again, take a few minutes to focus on what truth you want to learn. Now go back inside and lie back in bed, quietly contemplating the matter. Allow the candles to burn down safely on their own, and as you drift to sleep repeat silently to yourself, "Reveal the naked truth in my dreams."

In the morning, record your dreams in your dream journal. Thank the God or Goddess of wisdom, pull up the circle, and release your dream guardians. You can repeat this spell for three nights if you need more clarity or whenever you want to know the truth.

◖ Tonight's Magical Adventure: Finding Your Magical Dream Number

Since the beginning of time, numbers have been viewed as sacred symbols with mystic significance. This work shows you how to find your magical dream number by converting the letters of your birth name and magical name to numbers and then adding them together with the numbers of your birthday.

Each person has a birth name, and most people who practice the art and craft also choose a magical name. This name is a reflection of you and can be changed whenever you choose. It can be the name of a Goddess or God or totem animal or any other name. This work can be done on any night, and you can use your magical dream number whenever you choose.

LIST OF ITEMS NEEDED: Your birth name ⋆ Your craft or magical name ⋆ Pen ⋆ Sheet of paper

✺ Spinning the Spell

Find your birth number by adding together the month, day, and year you were born. Treat the year as a succession of four digits, and reduce it to a single digit. For example, if you were born in 1967, you add 1+9+6+7 and get 23. Then you reduce that number by adding its digits together: 2+3=5, so the number you use for the year is 5. If you were born on November 1 of that year, you add 11 (November is the eleventh month) to 1 (the day you were born) to 5 (the year), again reducing that number to a single digit:

11+1+5=17, and 1+7=8. Your birth number would be 8. If your number is 10 or more, reduce again by adding the digits.

Next find the numerical value of your first name (birth name) and then the numerical value of your magical name using the table below. Simply match the letters in both of your names to the corresponding numbers in the table and add them up.

1	2	3	4	5	6	7	8	9
A	B	C	D	E	F	G	H	I
J	K	L	M	N	O	P	Q	R
S	T	U	V	W	X	Y	Z	

For example, someone named Anne would add like this: 1+5+5+5=16, and 1+6=7. And if your craft name is Lugha, the numbers would be 3+3+7+8+1=22, and then 2+2=4. Next add your birth number, in this case 8, plus your birth name number, in this case 7, plus your magical name number, in this case 4. The total of 8+7+4=19, and 1+9=10, and 1+0=1. Your magical dream number is then 1. Now close your eyes and focus on your dream number and its basic qualities. Do this for at least five minutes. Then silently repeat the number until you drift to sleep. Do this for at least twenty-one nights, recording your dreams every morning. During this time, also post your dream number where you will see it regularly, for example, on your desk, front door, the dashboard of your car, or your bathroom mirror. This will trigger dream recall and also reinforce the magical power of your dream number. Following is a brief listing of the basic qualities of dream numbers.

1—Oneness, individuality, beginnings, independence, initiation, and creativity

2—Partnership, balance of polarities, the marriage of two elements into one, working with others, weaving elements together

3—The threefold nature of divinity, a number of divine power, the Otherworld, communication, expansion, expression, and optimism

4—A number of foundations, the four sacred directions, construction, productivity, strength, structure, organization, and unity

5—A magical number of the pentacle, associated with curiosity and travel, excitement and change, power, adventure, and resourcefulness

6—Home and family, love, compassion, beauty, the arts, and children

7—Wisdom, the seven chakras, birth and rebirth, good luck, contemplation, and spiritual faith

8—Material prosperity, the number of infinity, abundance, reward, success, and leadership

9—Universal compassion, tolerance, completion, knowledge, and humanitarianism

There are also three master numbers in numerology. Refer to the following if your dream number adds up to any of these three master numbers:

11—Intuition, telepathy, spiritual healing, and psychic abilities

22—Unlimited potential of mastery in all areas and endeavors, physical, mental, or spiritual

33—Oneness, where all things are possible

◖ Tonight's Magical Adventure: Dream Interview Charm

This charm can be used for luck and confidence in a job interview. The best night to make it is on a Thursday night during the waxing moon.

LIST OF ITEMS NEEDED: 1 green candle ★ Bayberry oil ★ Bayberry incense and censer ★ Your résumé ★ Green felt pen ★ 16-inch length of gold ribbon

✴ Spinning the Spell

Draw a sacred circle. Then select a favorite God or Goddess such as Lugh or Bridget (Celtic), and dedicate the incense and candle to this deity as you light them. Place a copy of your résumé on the altar, and then apply three drops of the bayberry oil to the index finger of your dominant hand and draw a large pentacle (five-pointed star) across your résumé. Apply three more drops to your index finger, and draw a clockwise circle on your résumé around the pentacle. With the green felt pen, write the name of the company who will be interviewing you inside the pentacle, and then write the name of the position you desire and the name of the person or persons who will be conducting the interview. After doing this, merge with the paper, pentacle, and writing, and say,

> *Star and circle, seal this request,*
> *Help me succeed on my job quest,*
> *As I will, so shall it be!*

Neatly fold the paper three times, and then seal it with the candle wax from the green altar candle. Tie the gold ribbon around the paper as you would a gift, and then, knotting the ribbon eight times, say,

> *With each knot the energy doubles,*
> *Drawing me closer to that perfect job,*
> *So be it! So dream it so!*

Leave the charm on the altar overnight, and allow the candle to burn down safely on its own. As you drift to sleep, imagine yourself at the actual interview, and go through some of the questions you will be asked. See and sense yourself being confident and positive, answering all the questions easily and completely. In the morning, pull up the circle and thank the God or Goddess who assisted you. Put your dream interview charm inside your briefcase, wallet, or purse, or carry it in your right pocket when you go to the interview. This will ensure that you get the job.

◖ Tonight's Magical Adventure: Decision-Making Dream Pouch

Use this pouch to help you make better decisions. It is most powerful when made on a Monday or Wednesday night on or just before a full moon.

LIST OF ITEMS NEEDED: 1 purple candle ★ Jasmine incense and censer ★ 4 pinches mugwort ★ 4 pinches dandelion ★ 4 pinches sweet basil ★ 4 pinches rosemary ★ 4 pinches mint leaves ★ 4 bay leaves ★ 4 cloves ★ Small piece of citrine ★ Spearmint oil ★ 4-inch by 4-inch purple pouch

✳ Spinning the Spell

Draw a sacred circle and call in your dream guardians. Next select a God or Goddess of wisdom, and call them into your circle. As you light the candle, chant the deity's name three times. Light the incense, using the candle flame, again chanting the name of the Goddess or God three times. Bathe the purple pouch in the incense smoke for a few minutes to purify it of any unwanted energies, and then do the same with the piece of citrine. Next open the pouch and put in the pinches of mugwort, dandelion, sweet basil, and rosemary along with the mint leaves, bay leaves, and cloves. Put the piece of citrine inside the pouch on top of the herbs, and then drop eight drops of the spearmint oil on top of the stone and close the pouch. To empower your decision-making dream pouch, hold it in your hands and say three times,

> *Dream pouch of wisdom,*
> *Show me the best decision.*
> *So be it! Dream it so!*

Put the pouch inside your pillowcase. Let the candle burn down on its own, and as you drift to sleep, repeat, "Dream the best decision."

Upon waking, thank deity, pull up your circle, and release your dream guardians. You can keep the pouch inside your pillowcase for up to eight weeks. After that time you will need to assemble a fresh dream pouch by replacing the herbs and oil. You can reuse the citrine and pouch. The energies of the items in your pouch will help you make better and more appropriate decisions about your life, while dreaming and awake.

☾ Tonight's Magical Adventure: Pet Protection Moon Spell

This spell will help you protect your pet. Most of us feel that our pets are part of our families because they are near and dear to us, much like our children. Many of us who practice the craft feel this bond even more acutely as many times pets become familiars, helping with our magic and dreaming with us. This is all the more reason to make sure our pets are protected, healthy, and happy. As the caretakers of our pets, we are responsible for ensuring that our loving familiars have the best life possible. Cast this spell on the first full moon after a sabbat, especially after Bridget's Day, for the strongest protective powers.

LIST OF ITEMS NEEDED: Rose water ★ Your pet(s)

✳ Spinning the Spell

To work this spell, sit or recline with your pet outside under the bright moon or in your bedroom where you can see the moon and stars outside. Talk with your animal companion, using kind words of praise. Tell your animal friend just exactly how much you care for him or her. Most of us have little nicknames and words of endearment for our pets. Use those now, and then imagine a protective egg of bright white light surrounding your pet. Next take the rose water, and anoint your animal friend with nine drops, stroking the water into the animal's fur or skin. As you do this, merge with your pet and say,

I call upon the Moon Goddess and Horned God,
I call upon the starspun powers of Oneness,
I call upon all the living creatures of the earth,
By divine will, by earth, air, fire, and water,
I ask that you work this goodly protective spell,
Please guard (insert name of pet) while sleeping and
waking,
And protect this animal from all negativity and harm.
Bless my bond of love and friendship with this animal.
May our bodies, minds, and spirits always know each other,
In all worlds, in all times! So be it! Blessed be!

Tell your pet how much you love him or her, and then let the animal do what he or she wants to after the protective blessing. Clap your hands three times, and then enjoy the rest of the evening. I also suggest using brown or blue dog collars with a hematite ring and a tag of identification securely fastened to the collar. I haven't had much luck using collars with my cats. They always manage to pull them off no matter how well fastened. Before you go to sleep at night, to reinforce the protective energy of this protective spell, take a few minutes and imagine your pets, yourself, and other loved ones being surrounded with protective, divine white light. This will help keep them safe from harm.

chapter nine

Divine Dream Magic

The following dream came to me just prior to my initiation into the Druid tradition. I still recall this dream vividly, and it is one of the main reasons I made the Celtic God Gwydion my sponsor and teacher. I describe it as if it were happening right now, in the present tense, which is usually the best way to write down your dreams.

It's midnight, and the sky is completely dark except for the moon and stars. The air feels moist. Crickets sound in an evening song, and an owl hoots three times and then is silent. Occasionally dogs bark in the far distance, and their cries seem to echo eerily off the hills. In the stark light of the full moon, I can see three earthen mounds in the valley below. I look out over the valley for a few minutes, the countryside aglow with moon fire. Then I turn around and walk toward the stone circle that stands close by on a small ridge. I walk by a giant upright stone that marks the entrance to the circle and then stop, looking up at two mighty dol-

mens with a large capstone hanging on top of them. I get the impression that giants at one time must have dined at this immense rock table. The placement of the capstone is high enough for me to easily pass underneath. After passing under the stone table, I find myself in front of a large rounded stone with a large hole in the center. The sun and the moon are carved into the face of the rock. I crawl through the hole, and the passageway creates a shifting or gap between worlds.

I hear someone whispering my craft name, and I see a man approaching me, Godlike in his demeanor. He wears a midnight blue tunic and pants. His hair glows golden like the sun and contrasts with his dark attire. He also wears a black blindfold, and only his eyes show through. His eyes are so dark that the pupils blend with their dark sapphire blue irises. I ask him his name, and he tells me that his name is Gwydion. He says that he is my friend and teacher. He bows to me, being both playful and serious. He moves quietly like a cat and for a moment shifts into a sleek black jaguar, and then, in an instant, he is the man in midnight blue once again. I stand completely still as Gwydion dances before me, moving in a circular motion and creating a vortex of bright cobalt blue light. His movements flow like a soft breeze embracing me. I gesture for him to remove his mask, but he refuses. He laughs and spins around, and when I look into his eyes again, I am staring into my own eyes. I feel startled but at the same time not surprised. Then Gwydion smiles and takes off his blindfold and proceeds to show me my three faces of maiden, mother, and crone by showing me my life like a movie flashing across a screen. I whisper Gwydion's name and then the names of the Goddesses and Gods. He then leads me over to the standing stones, and I can see the carved faces of three laughing maidens, a mother and child, and an old woman, as well as the faces of a horse, wolf, and a stag staring at us in the moonlight from the stones. The immense dolmens seem to sing in a midnight serenade. I touch the stone closest to me and watch as a bluish glow pushes at my hand. The *power of the light grows stronger and warm on my palm, and then I wake up.*

This dream showed me where I was going spiritually, although its significance wasn't totally apparent on the night I had the dream. An important aspect of dreams is that they often unfold as your own awareness unfolds. You only understand the depth of your dreams as your awareness expands.

Dreams can point you in the right direction, and magic can make it happen. Use the following spells and rituals to expand your spiritual self by getting in touch with the divine part of yourself, with Goddess and God. What better way to do this than with dreams, a meeting place of all levels of mind, bridging the conscious and unconscious? In this way, dreams create a pathway for you to move seemingly magical things from the dream world into "ordinary" reality.

☾ Tonight's Magical Adventure: Prophetic Dreams Pillow

European dream pillows, once called comfort pillows, can help you sleep more peacefully and at the same time stimulate prophetic dreams, connecting you with the divine.

LIST OF ITEMS NEEDED: ¹/₄ cup dried lavender flowers ★ ¹/₈ cup dried rose petals ★ ¹/₈ cup dried rosemary ★ 6-inch by 6-inch cloth bag

✳ Spinning the Spell

Make your dream pillow by filling the small cloth bag with the herbs. In a pinch, you can use a handkerchief or square of cloth tied with a rubber band. For a prophetic dream sleep mixture, combine the lavender flowers, rose petals, and rosemary. As you mix the bits of herbs together with the fingers of your power hand, charge them by chanting these words of power:

Prophetic dream mixture, come alive!
United energies now thrive
Show me what I need to see
As I sleep, so mote it be!

Let the mixture stand for a few minutes, and then put it into your cloth bag. After closing your dream pillow with a drawstring or stitching, tuck it inside your pillowcase for prophetic dreams. As you sleep, the movement of your head gently crushes the herbs, releasing their aromas. You will feel the effects of your dream pillow the first night you sleep on it.

◖ Tonight's Magical Adventure: Twinkling Magic

Twinkling is the practice of walking between the mortal and faery worlds. The faery realm mirrors our world but is one step away from ordinary reality, just out of our range of perception and normally but not always invisible. The portals between worlds are open on the eves of Beltane, Midsummer, and Samhain, the best times to try your hand at twinkling. One of the traditional ways of twinkling is to place your foot on top of a faery's foot, and by virtue of contact the Otherworld of the faery reveals itself to you. Since a faery foot is not always available, the following is a more accessible method of twinkling. A word of warning: *never,* under any circumstances, eat or drink anything in the faery realm, for to do so may cause you to remain stuck between worlds.

LIST OF ITEMS NEEDED: Upbeat Celtic music ⋆ 1 green candle ⋆ 5 small stones ⋆ Altar bowl filled with earth ⋆ Pinch of fresh or dried thyme ⋆ ½ cup warm milk with 2 teaspoons honey mixed in

✳ Spinning the Spell

Put on the music and draw a sacred circle, visualizing a pure forest green light flowing out of the tip of your athame. Light the candle.

Put the bowl in the center of the altar, and cover the top of the earth with the pinch of thyme. Then position the stones in a star or pentacle pattern around the bowl. Close your eyes for a few moments and see yourself descending a long natural rock stairway into the earth. At the end of the stairs is a circular doorway. Now open your eyes for a few moments and take the cup of milk from the altar. Pour the milk and honey over the earth and thyme in the bowl as you say,

> *To the woods and wild land,*
> *With a faery hand in hand.*
> *Mind and spirit, now set free,*
> *Open the faery door, so mote it be!*

Once again, close your eyes and see the circular doorway in your mind's eye. See and sense yourself opening the door and stepping into the magical world of the faeries. Allow the candle to burn down and music to continue playing as you drift to sleep. If you dream of faeries, your wishes will all come true.

In the morning pull up the circle and take the earth and stones and lay them in a clockwise circle around a plant while whistling or humming a little tune. When you are done, be sure to thank the faeries.

◖ Tonight's Magical Adventure: Blessed Be Divination Spell

In Wales and Ireland, small blue or green crystals (sometimes containing waves of blue, white, and red) are called "Druid Glass." The Druids acted as the diviners and augurs of the Celtic people. They excelled in the skill of divination, which was a mainstay of Celtic society. The Druid's or serpent's eggs most likely were forms of quartz crystal, and the "glain-nan-Druidhe" or "Druid's Crystal" is well known in Scotland.

This night spell is adapted from the traditional "Drawing Down of the Moon" and uses the watery, lunar energies of aquamarine crystal to bring out the Druid in you, enhancing your powers of divination. Spin it on a night of the full moon.

LIST OF ITEMS NEEDED: 1 white candle ⋆ 1 green candle ⋆ 1 red candle ⋆ Jasmine incense and censer ⋆ 1 thumb-sized piece of aquamarine ⋆ Chalice filled with juice or wine

✷ Spinning the Spell

Draw a sacred circle and set your dream guardians in place. Then call in your favorite moon Goddess, such as Artemis, Diana, or Arianrhod. Light the white candle, dedicating it to this Goddess, and position it in the center of your altar. Light the green candle from the white candle, placing it to the left side of the altar. Light the red candle from the white candle, and place it on the right side of the altar. Hold the aquamarine stone in your power hand, and then cross your wrists in front of you while holding them close to your chest. Merge with the Goddess and say,

> *Moon Goddess of the mysteries,*
> *Queen of the waves, tides, and sea,*
> *Beloved Lady, shine your silver light,*
> *I call you, bright star of the night.*
> *Beloved Mother of the womb and well,*
> *Next to your beauty, all others pale.*
> *I call upon your laughter and love,*
> *Beloved wise woman, spinner of life,*
> *Weaver of dreams and sacred wife,*
> *Fair Goddess of wisdom, I call thee,*
> *Moon Goddess of magic, come to me!*

Imagine the Goddess standing in front of you now. Uncross your wrists, and hold your hand with the stone outward toward her image. Look into her eyes and say,

Blessed be thy feet, which have walked the ancient pathways.
Blessed be thy legs, that have opened in birth again and
   again.
Blessed be thy sex, without which no living thing would be.
Blessed be thy breasts, formed in divine strength and
   beauty.
Blessed be thy lips, which utter the Sacred Names.
Blessed be the Goddess! Blessed Dreams! Blessed be!

Hold the stone over the chalice, and draw a triple X of white light. Then take the stone in your receiving hand, and hold the chalice upward with your power hand as if giving a toast, and say,

I call to you, Moon Goddess of light and wisdom,
With this drink, improve my powers of divination.
Blessed be! Divination dreams! Blessed be!

Now drink the contents of the chalice, all the while imagining you are drinking in the divine powers of the moon Goddess, including her abilities of divination and clairvoyance. Allow the candles to burn down on their own. Hold the stone in your receiving hand, and lie back in bed. As you drift to sleep, repeat, "Blessed be! Divination dreams!"

In the morning, write down what you recall of your dreams, and then thank the moon Goddess. Pull up the circle and release your dream guardians. Keep the aquamarine stone on your altar, and whenever you want to enhance your powers of divination, hold it in your nondominant hand as you drift to sleep. You will benefit from its magical energies immediately.

◖ Tonight's Magical Adventure: Creator/Creatrix Spell

Identified with mastery, the Dyad Moon is the sixth full moon after Yule. Each year on the Dyad Moon it is customary to ask the

Goddess to grant you a boon. A boon comes as a result of the good works you have done within the past year. The Creator/Creatrix Spell stems from the ancient tradition of the boon, bridging the present and the past and in the process igniting your creative energy. Cast this spell at midnight on the Dyad Moon.

LIST OF ITEMS NEEDED: 3 white candles ⋆ Sandalwood incense and censer ⋆ Bowl of dried vervain ⋆ Your dream journal ⋆ Pen

✳ Spinning the Spell

Draw a sacred circle and call in your dream guardians. Then call your favorite Goddess into the circle. Suggestions are Kerridwen or Anu (Celtic), Helen or Artemis (Greek), and Chandra or Akupera (Hindu). Next sprinkle the vervain over the altar surface to inspire creativity and mastery. Then position the candles side by side on the altar. Light the central candle, merging with the flame, and say,

> *Moon Goddess, Queen of the night,*
> *In all of your splendor bright,*
> *Send down your silvery beams*
> *And open the door of dreams.*
> *Moon Goddess, Queen of lunar power,*
> *Come to me at this enchanted hour.*

Use the base of your wand to knock nine times firmly on the altar table, and then stand before the before the altar, facing north, and say,

> *I am (state your magical name).*
> *Great One, I pray that you will grant me a boon.*

Next think about the good things you have done in the past. Merge with the candle again, and say,

I have done these good works in the past.
(State your good works out loud to the Goddess.)
You have seen my honest effort.
Please, Great One, grant me this boon of creativity
So I might create my deepest dreams.
Praise to you. Blessed be Great One!
Blessed be! Blessed be! Blessed be!

Continue gazing at the candlelight, and merge with your creative source. If you prefer, you can imagine going deep into a magical well and pulling up ideas and creative thoughts. Do this for at least fifteen minutes, noting any ideas or thoughts that come to you in your dream journal. When you are finished merging with your source, bow three times toward the altar, in honor of the Goddess, and lie back in bed with gladness in your heart. Allow the candles to burn down on their own. As you drift to sleep, merge once again with your creative source, and repeat the words "Creative dreams."

In the morning, write down your dreams and thank the Goddess for your boon. Then pull up the circle, release your dream guardians, and use your wand to knock three times on the altar. In the next few days, go over your notes, and continue jotting down ideas and creative thoughts that come to you. You will find that the source of your creativity is boundless, just waiting for you to tap into its Oneness. Within the next year, your deepest creative dream will come to fruition.

◖ Tonight's Magical Adventure: Divine Dreams Spell

Prophecy is part of the mythic story of all. Through the perception of universal and stellar powers and by tapping into the divine, the prophet is able to tell parts of our mythology that are not yet known to others. The prophet Finn Mac Cool of Celtic mythology was the last and greatest leader of the Fianna of Ireland. He was half faery and half god, and when Finn's father was killed, his mother put him in the protective care of a female Druid. While in her care, he acquired two magical skills. From the salmon of knowledge he gained his magic tooth, and by drinking a mouthful of water from the well of the moon he gained the power of prophecy.

Like Finn, you also can drink from the well of the moon on the full moon by using this Divine Dreams Spell. In doing so, you become divine, gaining the power of prophecy in your dream. The best time to do this spell is on a Monday night just before or on the full moon. Also remember, if incense smoke bothers you, convert the dried herbs into oils, and use a diffuser or cotton balls.

LIST OF ITEMS NEEDED: Cup of moon tea (recipe below) ⋆ 1 white candle ⋆ Chalice containing barley ⋆ Incense censer with charcoal block ⋆ Bowl ⋆ 5 bay leaves (fresh or dried) ⋆ 3 pinches dried saffron ⋆ 3 pinches dried rose petals ⋆ 3 pinches dried peppermint ⋆ 3 sticks of frankincense and myrrh incense (broken in small pieces) ⋆ Jasmine oil

✴ Spinning the Spell

Make a cup of moon tea using a chamomile tea bag plus one teaspoon mugwort and a pinch of cinnamon (or cinnamon stick). As the tea steeps, empower it by saying,

> *Moon tea of divine dreams,*
> *Bring me dreams of prophecy.*
> *So be it! So dream it!*

Then sweeten the moon tea with honey, and look at the moon while you sip it, imagining that you are drinking from the magical well of the silvery, high moon.

Next set the altar with the items listed, placing the candle in the center. Then draw a sacred circle around your bedroom and call in your dream guardians. Sprinkle the barley that is in the chalice on the altar in a triple, clockwise circle around the candle. Then light the candle, dedicating it to a favorite moon Goddess such as Arianrhod (Celtic), Artemis (Greek), Diana (Roman), Isis (Egyptian), or Akupera (Hindu). Chant the name of the Goddess nine times, and ask her to come into your circle. Next put the pinches of saffron, rose petals, and peppermint, together with the small pieces of broken incense, into the bowl, blending the mixture with the fingers of your power hand. Set aside two of the bay leaves, and also set aside for a moment the mixture in the bowl, and then light the charcoal block. Crush the three remaining bay leaves, and place them carefully on the ignited block. Inhale the smoke from the leaves, breathing deeply and completely. As you do this say,

Bay leaves of power and prophecy,
Tonight bring me divine dreams.
So be it! So dream it!

Next take the mixture in the bowl, and put a pinch of the blend onto the charcoal block, plus three drops of jasmine oil. Breathe deeply and inhale the smoke, and then say,

Magical mixture of prophecy,
Tonight bring me divine dreams.
So be it! So dream it!

Allow that pinch to ignite and smoke, and then put another pinch and three drops of oil onto the charcoal. Repeat the words

Magical mixture of prophecy,
Tonight bring me divine dreams.
So be it! So dream it!

Keep doing this until you have used up all of the mixture in the bowl. Then anoint yourself with the jasmine oil, applying three drops to your third eye, your throat, wrists, and ankles. Take the two remaining bay leaves, and hold one in each of your hands as you lie back in bed. Allow the candle to burn down on its own, and as you drift to sleep, repeat to yourself, "My dreams are divine."

In the morning, record your dreams in your journal. Then thank the moon Goddess, pull up the circle, and release your dream guardians.

☾ Tonight's Magical Adventure: Faces of Goddess and God Ritual

On the night of the full moon, select a Goddess or God you are very fond of, one with qualities and knowledge that would help you in some way. You can choose a God or Goddess from any spiritual pantheon. After selecting a deity, do this ritual to take on the aspects of that God or Goddess for one night. This experience can last from a few moments to several hours, depending upon your expectation, desire, and the depth of your merge. Keep in mind that during this experience, you become energetically or spiritually one with deity, where both you and deity benefit from this two-way exchange.

LIST OF ITEMS NEEDED: 1 white candle ★ Quill or ballpoint pen ★ Lavender essential oil ★ Wand ★ Amber incense and censer ★ Athame ★ Bowl with salt or clean earth ★ Chalice of fresh water ★ ½ cup almond, sunflower, or light olive oil

✴ Spinning the Spell

Set your altar with the items listed. Mix nine drops of lavender oil into the half cup of almond oil, and place the cup back on the altar. Wash the candle in cool saltwater, dry it, and place it upon the altar. Draw a triple circle of cobalt blue light edged in white, and set your dream guardians in place. Use the quill or pen to inscribe the name of the Goddess or God you have selected onto the candle body, and then dress the candle with the lavender oil and set it back in its holder upon the altar. Use the bottom end of your wand to knock nine times on the altar, in three series of three. Next take the bowl of salt or earth from the altar and hold it up toward the north point of your circle. Sprinkle three pinches toward the north and say,

> *Great Mother Goddess,*
> *Bless this bowl of salt unto your service.*
> *I call upon the powers of earth*
> *To protect this circle and witness this rite.*

Then set the bowl back on the altar. Next take the burning incense from the altar and hold it up toward the east point of the circle. Wave it back and forth three times and say,

> *Great Father God,*
> *Bless this burning incense unto your service.*
> *I call upon the powers of air*
> *To protect this circle and witness this rite.*

Set the incense carefully back down on the altar. Then hold the candle up toward the south point of your circle, and after carefully waving it from side to side three times, say,

> *Great Father God,*
> *Bless this burning flame unto your service.*
> *I call upon the powers of fire*
> *To protect this circle and witness this rite.*

Place the candle carefully back down on the altar. Then take the chalice from the altar and hold it upward toward the west. Sprinkle water three times, and say,

Great Mother Goddess,
Bless this chalice of water unto your service.
I call upon the powers of water
To protect this circle and witness this rite.

Place the chalice back down on the altar, and then stand in the center of the circle and begin to chant the name of the Goddess or God you selected for this rite. Next invoke the Goddess or God that you selected by chanting these words over and over:

O self of selves, arise and awaken. Attend unto me.

Repeat the words again and again, louder and louder, pulling the energies of the deity you have selected into the sacred circle. Keep repeating the chant. This causes the awakening of your many selves. As you chant, remove your clothing, any jewelry, and glasses if you wear them. Keep chanting the same words, and begin anointing your body, starting at your forehead, with the oil mixture in the cup. Continue anointing your body, rubbing oil on your arms, wrists, and hands, down your body and over your legs and ankles, ending at your feet and toes. While you are doing this continue chanting,

O self of selves, arise and awaken. Attend unto me.

When you are finished anointing your body with the scented oil, formally call in the Goddess or God you have selected to shapeshift with by saying,

(State the name of the deity), now enter into me,
So that I may see through your eyes this night,
Hear as you hear, taste and smell and sense as you do.
As you enter into me, I enter into you,
So that you in turn may see as I see this night,

Hear as I hear, taste and smell and sense as I do.
We are one. So be it! So dream it so!

Next build the energy of the experience to a peak, with the intention that the divine energy (Goddess or God) will descend and move into you. Draw the deity into the very cells of your body and into every facet of your awareness. Breathe the divine energy into your inner being, and then slide into the spirit of the Goddess or God. Allow the candle to burn down safely on its own, and lie back in bed. As you drift to sleep, repeat to yourself, "O self of selves, arise and awaken. Attend unto me."

In the morning, write down your dreams, and then thank the deity you selected. Pull up the circle, knock three times on the altar, release your dream guardians, and put everything away.

☾ Tonight's Magical Adventure: Dream Foretelling Ritual

Ancient peoples such as the Sumerians, Mesopotamians, and Egyptians had a sophisticated knowledge of the symbolic and metaphysical nature of dreams, often using dream messages to foretell the future. The Winter Solstice, also called Yule, is the longest night of the year and the perfect time to use your dreams to foretell the direction of your life for the upcoming year. In this ritual, you ask Nodens, the Celtic God of Dreams, to grant you insight and vision.

LIST OF ITEMS NEEDED: Warm mint tea ★ Clary sage essential oil ★ Your dream stone

✶ Spinning the Spell

Draw a sacred circle and call in your dream guardians. Make the tea, and sip it for a few minutes. Next anoint yourself with the essential oil, applying it to your third eye, to the "soft spot" on the back of your head, behind both ears, and on the insides of both your wrists and ankles. Hold your dream stone in your right hand and charge it with these words:

> *Nodens, guide and protect me, I pray you,*
> *Lord of Dreams, grant me vision and clarity*
> *Turn my bedchamber into a cloud of dreams*
> *And cause my soul to take flight tonight.*
> *Show me the future bright and clear,*
> *Tell me what I need to know of the coming year.*
> *Ayea, Ayea, Ayea Nodens! So mote it be!*

Now put the dream stone in your left hand. Lie back, and as you drift to sleep silently repeat one question: "What good things will the new year bring?"

When you awaken in the morning, be as still as possible. Don't move a muscle or open your eyes for a few minutes. Think back on your dreams, recounting everything you can remember. When you arise, immediately write down anything you can recall. These are your dream messages for the upcoming year. Thank Nodens, and then pull up the circle and release your dream guardians. Put your dream stone on your altar to use in other spells.

◖ Tonight's Magical Adventure: Shapeshifting Dream Magic Journey

One of my favorite dream adventures is this basic shapeshifting dream magic journey. Shapeshifting is an expression of your wild and free nature and an inherent human skill that has been all but forgotten except in folklore, mythology, and the craft. To shapeshift into someone or something else is to be privy to the secrets of a state of being where you can feel the inexplicable and mysterious. Human reason and logic do not necessarily apply. Shapeshifting allows for a richer and fuller perspective on life and experience. As a way to gather information and build magical skill, it connects you with your creative ability and spiritual center.

The shamanic art of shapeshifting is based on the idea of assuming the characteristics, traits, and talents of someone or something else, such as an animal, for a limited time and for a particular purpose. The ultimate potential for shapeshifting is to bring humankind closer to nature and animals so people can begin to understand that they do not stand apart from nature but are very much part of it. Take this dream journey during the waxing moon, on a Monday or Friday night. Remember, merging is the key to shapeshifting.

LIST OF ITEMS NEEDED: A stone you have found in a natural area ★ Your imagination

✴ Spinning the Spell

Draw a sacred circle of green light, and then call in your dream guardians. Next sit back or recline comfortably, holding the stone in your nondominant hand. Take a few deep breaths, relaxing a little more with each breath. Close your eyes, and continue to breathe slowly and rhythmically. Imagine yourself sinking into the stone in your hand. Start with your toes, moving up your body, your ankles, calves, knees, hips, stomach, back, arms, neck, and head, sinking even further into the stone. Let all your muscles go, and feel your flesh and bones sink completely into the lattice of the stone. Meld with the stone and become one with it. Abandon the normal structures of reality, and allow the stone to become fluid and soft, creating a gateway to Oneness, a threshold of awareness and creativity. Once you move through that threshold, you are transformed.

Now in your mind's eye, fully sense the animal you want to shapeshift into, before beginning to change shape. Make it an animal that you are very fond of, and see and sense the animal from every angle and move around it in your mind's eye. Imagine yourself becoming that image. For example, if your choice is a dolphin, say aloud at least three times, "I am the dolphin, the dolphin is me, we are one." Like a dolphin, see and sense yourself moving just below the surface of the water. Your body weaves in and out of the water, and your fins and tail move ever so slightly, changing your direction as you continue gliding along your way. The idea here is to feel yourself becoming a dolphin, pretending and using your imagination at first, if necessary, and paving the way for shapeshifting dreams about being a dolphin. See, feel, and sense the total experience. Be there completely. Merge and melt into the animal, into the other, and be one with it. Now take a deep breath and merge a little deeper. As you drift to sleep in this shapeshifted form, give yourself the suggestion to remember your dreams when you wake up. When you awaken, rub the stone in your hands, and write down or record those details you recall about your dreams. Then pull up the circle and release your dream guardians.

◖ Tonight's Magical Adventure: Dreaming with Your Power Animal

While standing at the checkout counter at the supermarket, I complimented the cashier on a pin she was wearing that was fashioned in the shape of a turtle. She told me she had always felt a strong connection to turtles, that she dreamed about turtles and saw them everywhere she went. Turtle power is all about the slow but sure way of accomplishing your goals, developing navigational skills, self-reliance, protection, and tenacity. This experience showed me how deep a connection many of us have with certain animals and how these connections often reveal our true nature and also empower us. Frequently we even resemble the animals we feel most connected to.

This work can be used to purposefully meet and dream with your spirit animal. The best night to do this work is on a Monday or Wednesday, during the waxing moon phase.

LIST OF ITEMS NEEDED: A drum ⋆ Your imagination

❈ Spinning the Spell

Draw a sacred circle and call in your dream guardians. Hold the drum, and begin playing it rhythmically for about five minutes. Stop for a moment and say,

> *Hail to my totems and power animals,*
> *On behalf of the powers of the moon,*
> *On behalf of the powers of the stars,*
> *On behalf of the Goddess and God,*
> *Come and dream with me tonight!*

Begin playing the drum again for a few minutes, and just merge with the tone and rhythm. Set the drum down when you feel the time is right, and sit back or recline comfortably. Imagine a mysteriously shaped tree in front of you, which you ascend slowly by climbing its branches. The branches are set at regular intervals to provide comfortable hand and foot holds. When you reach the top of the tree, you encounter a huge golden eagle who silently speaks to you, giving you a message of importance. The huge bird then flies away and disappears like a golden jewel in the distant sky.

You descend the tree carefully and look around, discovering that you are in a magical garden in the late afternoon. You feel completely comfortable and safe in this special garden, filled with green plants, stones, and mysteriously shaped trees. This magical place has a small pool with fragrant blossoms floating in the center, and you can smell the scent of the water and the flowers cradled on its surface. You breathe in deeply several times, relaxing even more in the magical garden. You sit by the side of the pool and look at the flowers and their reflection upon the pool's glassy surface. Every thought seems to float away, like the blossoms on the water, drifting in and out of your mind.

Suddenly you realize you are not alone. From the corner of your eye, you see a flash and then a strange shimmering. From the center of the shimmering light, your power animal emerges and stands on the other side of the small pool. You gaze at the magnificent animal for a few moments, in awe of its beauty and prowess. Without fear, you move over to it and touch it. As you do, it is as if all the knowledge and legacy of the animal passes into you in a positive and healing way.

Keep breathing deeply, relaxing more and more, seeing and sensing the experience with your power animal even more clearly. Ask the animal its name, and give yourself the suggestion to remember the name clearly. If you have any trouble discovering your power animal's name, repeat your question and wait for a response. Repeat your power animal's name over and over again to yourself. As you continue to touch your power animal in your mind's eye, all its strength and energy merges with yours, boosting your overall energy and well-being. Your power animal shares its powerful qualities and abilities with you completely, and you become one. Know that every night of your life, your power animal dreams with you. Know that every experience you have, your power animal is there to help, and you can communicate with it whenever you choose by calling its name silently or aloud, in waking or in dream.

Drift to sleep, and in the morning write down your dreams. Thank your power animal for its presence and help, and then pull up the circle and release your dream guardians.

☾ Tonight's Magical Adventure: Astral Dream Body Adventure

The astral dream body is able to explore other dimensions of existence in just the way mystics have claimed for thousands of years. There are many ways to transfer consciousness from the physical body into an etheric dream body, which allows you to float up through the ceiling or visit someone across the world. This also allows you to explore other realms with unusual beings, some with mythic and legendary status. Many times the astral body is viewed as a higher self. As you will discover, astral dreaming is just another one of the wonderful adventures in dream magic.

Take this adventure on a Monday night during the waxing phase of the moon.

LIST OF ITEMS NEEDED: 1 white candle ★ 1 purple candle ★ 1/4 cup almond oil ★ 3 tablespoons powdered mugwort ★ Dragon's blood oil ★ Bunch of mugwort ★ 13-inch length of white ribbon ★ 13-inch length of purple ribbon

✳ Spinning the Spell

Draw a sacred circle and call in your dream guardians. Rub nine drops of dragon's blood oil on each of the candles, and then wipe the oil off your hands. Next light the candles, dedicating them to a favorite Goddess and God associated with flying and birds, such as Rhiannon and Angus Og (Celtic). Then make some flying oil by putting the powdered mugwort and three drops of dragon's blood oil into the cup of almond oil, mixing it thoroughly with the index finger of your power hand. The dragon's blood oil adds strength to the work. Anoint each of your chakras with three drops of the flying oil, starting at your base chakra (at the base of your spine) and continuing to your second chakra (just below your navel), moving up to your solar plexus (directly below your ribcage in the center) and then continuing to your heart chakra, your throat, third eye (between your eyebrows), and finally ending at your crown chakra at the top of your head. As you anoint each of your chakras, say,

> *Dream oil of dragons, awaken and fly,*
> *Together our bodies, astral to the sky*
> *So be it! So dream it!*

Then take the ribbons and twist them together into one, and fasten the ribbon securely around the bunch of mugwort. Knot the ribbon nine times, putting three drops of the flying oil on each of the nine knots. Hold the bunch of mugwort in your hands and say,

Divine dream wort, make my body light
So I might float among the stars tonight.
So be it! So dream it!

Place the bunch of mugwort under your bed, and allow the candles to burn down safely on their own. As you drift to sleep, imagine a radiant white light moving down your chakras, from the top of your head to your feet. Then channel this radiant white light up through your chakras, imagining it to be a spinning vortex moving upward over your head, leaving your body dormant and sleeping as it does. Finally, imagine that only your mind is awake, and allow yourself to step free of your body and fly out into the night sky. Feel the delight in floating free, thinking yourself from one place to another, from one world to the next.

In the morning, thank the Goddess and God who helped you, pull up the circle, and then release your dream guardians. Leave the bunch of mugwort under your bed for three months to encourage astral dreams.

◖ Tonight's Magical Adventure: Time Travel Adventure

All aspects of reality exist—all times, spaces, and forms, both visible and invisible. Simultaneously and within the context of multiple incarnations, each life you experience deepens your connection with Oneness. Every lifetime happens simultaneously and only seems to occur at different times due to your vantage point. After all, if time has circular qualities, what exactly are past lives, future lives, ancestors, and descendants?

Each person is more than one individual and more than one incarnation. You are like the eternal time traveler, with your power lying within your lifetimes and experiences. I suggest you read over the following Time Travel Adventure and then record it, using your own voice, and play it back just before you go to sleep.

LIST OF ITEMS NEEDED: Sandalwood oil ★ Your dream stone

❊ Spinning the Spell

Begin by drawing a sacred circle and setting your dream guardians in place. Next light the incense. Apply three drops of the sandalwood oil to the stone, and then sit back or recline comfortably, holding your dream stone in your receiving, nondominant hand. Close your eyes, and breathe gently and deeply. As you breathe in and out slowly and rhythmically, begin to go back in time with each breath. As you breathe in, begin to imagine yourself about a year ago. With the next breath, imagine yourself five years ago, and then ten. As you keep breathing, you begin to imagine yourself as a child playing and laughing, remembering the house that you lived in. You can see around you the faces of some of the people you liked when you were a child.

As you take another deep breath, move even farther back in time, becoming an infant and discovering the world of color, light, smell, touch, and sound. As you breathe deeply once again, begin to remember being in your mother's womb, feeling watery and warm, secure and safe. As you take another deep and complete breath, move into free flow, into etheric space, breathing and feeling the energy of your true essence. See and sense yourself as light, as pure energy.

You begin to see the images of what seem to be tiny bubbles filled with holographs of golden keys. These bubbles float behind, beside, and in front of you. As you flow freely, you realize that these energetic keys unlock other lifetimes or worlds of your existence. You allow your essence, the part of you that is eternal, to select the one key that unlocks the door to one of your past lives, the one that you have most to learn from right now at this moment. Allow your attention to focus on the most appropriate key-filled bubble, and enter the bubble with your consciousness and take the key. Use it to unlock the door to the past, stepping through the threshold into a past life.

As you do this, merge into the lifetime you have entered. Do this by first looking down at your feet. What do they look like in this lifetime? Are you wearing shoes or are you barefoot? Very slowly, begin to move your attention carefully up your legs, seeing your ankles, knees, thighs, pelvis, buttocks, stomach, chest, neck, shoulders, arms, and then your face.

Are you a woman or man? What color are your eyes? What is the color of your hair? Is it short or long, coarse or fine? Are you bald? What color is your skin?

Slowly now in your mind's eye, begin to focus on your hands, studying your hands in this past lifetime. As you study your hands, looking at them carefully, notice if there are any rings on your fingers or distinguishing marks on your hands or arms. Pay close attention to the small details. As you breathe and relax even more in this lifetime, begin to become aware of what it feels like to be in this body. And as you continue to breathe deeply and softly and rhythmically, look closely at what you are wearing or not wearing. What are the colors and fabrics of your clothing? Feel the texture of the cloth.

Very slowly begin moving in this other body, observing your actions and noticing what you are doing in this body. Where are you? Begin to view your surroundings. Perhaps you know what country or region you are in. As you look around, start walking. You may become aware of other people and other sounds around you as well as the animals and plants.

Begin to interact with this past lifetime. Talk with people nearby. Experience the entirety of this lifetime. Keep using your deep breathing to clarify the images. Use your breath to move you forward, and very slowly and gently see this lifetime to its ending place.

Allow yourself to release all negative feelings, experiences, or traumas from this lifetime. Just let them go, breathing them out. View the negativity as though it is dissipating out into the universe and being recycled. Erase all negativity, pain, and unhappiness from this lifetime.

Using a deep and complete breath, get a clearer image, and begin to see, sense, and remember all the positive experiences and feelings from this past lifetime, with brightness and energy, using this positive energy and experience to strengthen you and your essence.

As you take another deep and complete breath, step out of this past life, moving once again into free flow and etheric space. Find yourself surrounded by the key-filled bubbles, as you feel more relaxed than ever before, lighter and empowered from your past life journey. Float freely with the bubbles, understanding that they represent the infinite lifetimes and worlds you can shapeshift into and experience.

Continue to breathe softly and quietly for a few moments; then very slowly begin to direct your attention back to your physical body. Slide back into your body, and enter the present moment in time, noticing light, sounds, smells, and the energy around you. Remember your entire past life experience as you breathe yourself back to the room, moving your hands and feet and slowly opening your eyes without really focusing. Complete the adventure by setting the dream stone down upon the altar and clapping your hands three times. As you drift to sleep, hold the dream stone in your receiving hand, and think about your experience. Repeat these words silently over and over again until you fall asleep: "Dreaming through time and space, and remembering."

In the morning, write down your dreams in your journal, pull up the circle, and release your dream guardians. Set your dream stone on your altar to use in again in other spells and rituals.

◀ Tonight's Magical Adventure: Divine Dream Magnet

This magical work attracts divine dreams, using a pentacle-shaped dream catcher and a magnet. The best time to make your divine dream magnet is on a Monday night on a new moon.

LIST OF ITEMS NEEDED: Sage and cedar smudge ⋆ 3-inch-diameter ring (preferably silver colored) ⋆ Silver crocheting thread ⋆ Beads, feathers, and other decorative items ⋆ Horseshoe-shaped magnet

✸ Spinning the Spell

Smudge your bedroom, yourself, and all the items listed before beginning this work. Next turn on some music, and begin to tie the silver thread onto the ring in the shape of a pentacle. Tie one end of the thread securely to the ring. Next wind the thread around the opposite side of the ring three times, not directly across from your first tie but at a slight angle, and pull it taunt. As a rule of thumb, every time you attach the thread to the ring, wind it around three times. Also, to decorate your catcher with beads, keys, shells, coins, or feathers, string them onto the thread and attach them where the string is wound around the ring three times. Now wind the thread around the ring three times a short distance from the first tie. Your threaded design should look something like an inverted V shape. Pull the string to the left side of the ring, and then wind it about the ring a little more than halfway up the side. Adjust it until it looks like the lower angle of the cross arm of the pentacle. Then stretch the thread across to the opposite side, and wind it about the ring three times. Next pull the thread back to the first tie you made. If you carefully check the angle of the thread each time you prepare to wind it at another point on the ring, it is possible to adjust and tighten the design. Finally, make a small loop for hanging the horseshoe magnet from the bottom of your dream catcher. Tie the magnet onto the ring three times, knotting the ends of the thread three times before trimming it off. Then make a loop of thread or cord for hanging your dream catcher, and attach it to the top of the pentacle. Hang your Divine Dream Magnet above the head of your bed to catch your dreams. It also helps you remember your dreams more clearly when you awaken.

◖ Tonight's Magical Adventure: Starwalking Dream Ritual

Stars serve as gateways between ordinary reality and the many realms of experience and spirit. The Druids paid particular attention to the stars Altair (the soul of Arthur), Cygnus (constellation of creation), Deneb (galactic home of the Celtic Gods), Vega (controlled the oceans), and Capella (lunar mysteries). Capella is at the rim of the galaxy and is one of the four constellations marking the four directions of the galactic plane. It is considered to be a sacred portal into the mysterious Golden Wheel of Life, which is a revolving doorway into another dimension.

As you will see in this unusual ritual, starwalking involves shifting your perception and moving through the dimensions of time and space to touch the stars. Expanding your perceptual awareness by starwalking through stargates allows you access to other dimensions of time and space along the continuum. The Lakota Sioux used stargates as such entryways. From these doorways, they walked among the stars, bringing back the star energy for the purposes of healing and prophecy. Interestingly, the Egyptians and Mayans also knew about these stargates, which are spread all across the universe. These stargates are doorways from one dimension to the next, transcending time and space.

The best time to do this starwalking ritual is at night during a new moon or at night before the moon rises, someplace outdoors that is private and safe, where you can see the stars. Keep in mind that seasonal influences have varying effects on the star patterns and your experience.

LIST OF ITEMS NEEDED: Piece of turquoise ⋆ 1 white candle ⋆ Silver chalice filled with fresh water ⋆ Sandalwood incense and censer ⋆ Your dream magic journal ⋆ Pen

✳ Spinning the Spell

Select a star or constellation of stars upon which you want to focus your awareness. Sirius and the Pleiades are excellent choices. Then gather together the four elements: the stone, candle, chalice with water, and incense and burner. Remember also to include matches or a lighter. Take everything outside, and then draw a sacred circle of white light around the area you are going to be working in. Ask a special Goddess and God to enter your circle for divine guidance and protection.

Begin by taking a deep breath. Hold the stone in your hand, and merge into the stone, becoming one with the stone for a few moments. Breathe the power of stone and earth into your body, mind, and spirit.

Next set the stone down on the ground, and focus your awareness and attention on the cup of water. Hold it in your hands, and merge with the liquid. Take a few moments and drink all the water in the cup, feeling the water shapeshift and become one with your physical body. Feel the power of water within your body.

Put the chalice back down on the ground, and move your attention to the candle. Light the candle and take a few moments to watch the flame as it moves, sways, and flickers. Merge with the candle, and become one with the flame for a few moments, allowing the power of fire to enter your being and ignite you.

Now set the candle back down on the ground, and focus your awareness on the incense. Light it, and watch the smoke flow upward. Merge with the incense smoke, and become one with it, ever flowing upward, higher and higher. As you flow ever higher, begin focusing your attention and vision on the star you have selected for this ritual. Feel yourself walking toward the star, closer and closer. Before you is what looks to be a holographic gate made entirely of energy. You find yourself walking through the gate, and as you do so, you sense a popping feeling.

Once you move through the stargate, there is a being of light waiting for you. This being is your star teacher and guide and will answer any questions you have or give you useful messages. You ask one question of your star teacher and then listen for the thought-form reply. Your star teacher then beckons you fully through the stargate. You realize that this is a gate that souls use to enter and exit the many dimensions of the continuum, including the earthly one. From this perspective, the star you are walking toward, and the stars all around you, are alive with energy, living beings who are on their own path of evolution.

Continue to focus on the star energy, and allow yourself to shapeshift into the star itself. You realize that you are one and the same. Your physical body is comprised of star stuff and serves as a universal link to all things. By starwalking through the skies, you reconnect with none other than your own self, your own stellar heritage and cosmic roots. Your stellar self becomes a source of energy, love, creativity, and enlightenment.

As you walk through the skies, you find yourself remembering things you were not aware you had forgotten. Your intuition grows stronger with every moment, and so do your healing abilities and creative powers. Continuing through the skies, you find yourself walking through more stargates, following the memory of a star map that dwells somewhere in your very cellular structure. Each time you will sense a popping as if you are entering and exiting the many gates of existence.

When you complete your starwalking experience, give yourself the suggestion to recall the details of your journey. Come back to the present moment, slowly open your eyes, and slide completely into your physical body. Take a few moments to thank your star teacher and the energies that have assisted you in your ritual. Write down your experience in your journal while you are still in a partially altered state of consciousness. After you are finished, pull up the circle and clap your hands three times soundly. Go back inside, and lie down in bed. As you drift to sleep, imagine yourself drifting up toward the stars and becoming one with them. In the morning, write down your dreams.

☾ Tonight's Magical Adventure: Watchtower Dream Spell

This spell is best done on a full moon. It can be used to call the Watchtowers of the four directions into your dreams. These Watchtowers are ancient beings who guard the four directions of your magical circle. They are powerful allies. This will empower your dreaming experience with the energies of the elements.

LIST OF ITEMS NEEDED: Bowl of salt ⋆ Frankincense and myrrh incense ⋆ 1 white candle ⋆ Chalice filled with fresh water

✳ Spinning the Spell

Draw a sacred circle, and call in your favorite Goddess and God. Light the candle, and then light the incense from the candle flame. Take a few deep breaths, and then hold the bowl of earth up and say,

> *Hail, Guardians of the Watchtowers of the north,*
> *Powers of earth, please dream with me tonight.*
> *I summon you!*

Put the bowl of earth down upon the altar, and pick up the incense and say,

> *Hail, Guardians of the Watchtowers of the east,*
> *Powers of air, please dream with me tonight.*
> *I summon you!*

Place the incense censer back upon the altar, and then carefully pick up the candle and say,

> *Hail, Guardians of the Watchtowers of the south,*
> *Powers of fire, please dream with me tonight.*
> *I summon you!*

Slowly put the candle back down upon the altar. Next pick up the chalice of water and say,

Hail, Guardians of the Watchtowers of the west,
Powers of water, please dream with me tonight.
I summon you!

Put the chalice back down on the altar, and then face the altar, holding both arms upward, and say,

Hear me, Great Watchtowers of the elements and quarters,
I stand before you under the moon and stars.
Grant me your universal strength and wisdom.
I ask that you please dream with me tonight.
So be it! So shall it be! Blessed dreams!

Allow the candle to burn down on its own, and as you drift to sleep repeat silently, "Watchtowers, dream with me tonight."

In the morning, record your dreams in your journal. Then thank the Goddess and God and the four Watchtowers, and pull up your circle.

◖ Tonight's Magical Adventure: Dream Spirit Guide Magic

The realm of spirit manifests itself through spirit guides, helpful beings who can assist you through life. Spirit guides are very real. Your guides can bring you joy and laughter, bridging physical reality with their pure spiritual energy and providing divine signs and messages when you need them most. Often when meeting your spirit guide, you experience a knowing from within. Your world becomes brighter, and there is a warm expansive feeling in the center of your being, accompanied by an infusion of love. Best done during the waxing or gibbous moon phases, on a Monday or Wednesday night, this magical work helps you meet your spirit guide.

LIST OF ITEMS NEEDED: Chalice of saltwater ★ 1 white candle ★ Sandalwood incense and censer ★ Soft music ★ Your dream magic journal ★ A pen

✴ Spinning the Spell

Place everything you will need on your altar, and seal all the openings to the room, closing all windows, doors, vents, and other openings. Then draw a sacred circle of cobalt blue light edged in white around your bedroom. Take the chalice, and sprinkle the saltwater over the energetic circle, starting and ending at the north point. Call in your dream guardians.

Next light the candle, and then light the incense from the candle flame. Sit back with your journal and pen on your lap, and take a few deep breaths, allowing yourself to become comfortably relaxed. Quiet your mind, be very still, and just watch the candle flame and the incense smoke for a few minutes. Any movement of the flame or smoke signifies a pulse in the energy field around you. Keep watching the flame and smoke, and focus all your attention on contacting your spirit guide.

Suddenly you realize you are not alone. You feel brighter and more expansive. You realize your spirit guide is there with you, speaking your name. The initial contact and the sound of your name may come as a thought, as a whisper, or as clear as a person speaking to you. Use deep, rhythmic breathing to get more details about your guide's features, mannerisms, and the tone of his or her voice. Ask your spirit guide his or her name, and then write it down in your dream magic journal. If you do not receive a name within a minute, discontinue contact. After you receive a name, say the name three times silently to yourself. Keep breathing slowly and rhythmically, and ask any questions you may have. Write down the response you receive from your spirit guide. Again, your guide may communicate through words, symbols, sensations, or thoughts. Just make a note of whatever kinds of answers and messages you receive without intellectualizing them.

You will know when your spirit guide is ready to leave. Be sure to express your thanks, asking your guide to visit you often so that you can communicate together.

Snuff the candle out, pull up your circle, and release your dream guardians. As you drift to sleep, reflect on your encounter with your spirit guide. In the morning, record your dreams in your journal.

☾ Tonight's Magical Adventure: Star Light, Star Bright Dream Box

Replicated from ancient amulet boxes of Tibet and the inscribed boxes of ancient Egypt, a dream box is a starspun box filled with dreams that are coming true. This magical work is best done on a clear evening on one of the first six nights after the new moon. To successfully perform it, you will need to go outside and find a shooting star.

The stars are connected to the existence and well-being of all living things on Earth, as everyone and everything is made of star stuff. Some of the oldest ceremonies and rituals are star related. In *The Divine Adventure,* Fiona Macleod writes, "Wind comes from the spring star in the East; fire from the summer star in the South; water from the autumn star in the West; wisdom, silence, and death from the star in the North." Elementally akin to these celestial star bodies, you are here to enjoy an original, ecstatic relationship with the universe. You are like a great cosmic bird, instinctually continuing your migratory pattern across planets, constellations, and galaxies as you soar through the cosmos. It is now time to spread your dream wings and ride the starry wind through the divine night.

LIST OF ITEMS NEEDED: 1 white votive candle in a fireproof holder ★ Small box ★ Star confetti ★ Piece of white paper ★ Pen ★ A shooting star

✴ Spinning the Spell

Place the items listed on your altar, and then draw a sacred circle of starlight around your bedroom. Cut a small energetic door where your bedroom door is so you can exit and enter the room during the work. Set up your dream guardians, and call in your favorite star Goddess into the circle. Examples are Arianrhod, Sirona, Nuit, Lilith, and Morning Star. Light the votive candle, and dedicate it to this Goddess, chanting her name nine times. Merge with the candle flame and say,

My mind is free, my heart is free,
My body is free, my life is my own.
On this night of all nights
At this place of all places
At this time of all times
I stand at the crossroads of worlds,
I stand before the Goddess and God,
I stand beneath the sacred stars,
Lifting the veil of stellar mysteries.
May the Shining Ones protect and guide me.
Blessed be the stars! Blessed be my dreams!
Blessed be! Blessed be! Blessed be!

Next use the pen to slowly and purposefully write down your most cherished dream on the piece of paper in oversized, large letters. Draw five stars around your writing, and then draw a clockwise circle around the whole thing. Check the candle to be certain it is safely burning and will continue to do so for a few minutes while you are outside. Otherwise, snuff out the candle for the time being. Then take the piece of paper with you and go outside. Watch the night sky until you see a shooting star. As soon as you see one streak through the sky, speak these words three times in a clear voice:

Star light, star bright,
First shooting star I see tonight,
I wish I may, I dream I might
Have my dream come true tonight.

State your dream aloud to the night sky, and then fold the paper nine times and sit down. Next hold the folded paper in your power hand, and squeeze it in your fist. Then close your eyes tight, and wish so hard that your dream comes true that it makes you light-headed and dizzy. Sit quietly for a few more minutes, gazing at the stars and concentrating on your dream coming true. Then go back inside, relighting the candle if necessary. Place the folded paper carefully inside the dream box, sprinkling star confetti on top of the paper, and then close the lid of the box. Empower the dream box by holding it in your hands and saying,

By the powers of the Goddess and God,
By the sacred light of the stars,
I bind the stellar power within this box.
This spell is cast and will hold fast.
So be it! So dream it so! Blessed be!

Place the box back upon the altar, and allow the candle to burn down on its own. As you drift to sleep, repeat silently, "Dream come true."

In the morning, thank the star Goddess, then pull up the circle of starlight and release your dream guardians. Keep your dream box on your altar to remind you that dreams do come true with a little help from the stars and your divine friends! Your dream will come true within the year.

c

List of Helpful
Dream Magic Goddesses

Rapport is a bond of energy between you and the Goddesses and Gods. The stronger the bond, the more powerful your magic. In Celtic spirituality, not only is each God and Goddess descended from the Mother Goddess, but each person with Celtic ancestry also stems from her. This points to the kinship between mortals and deities. Ancestral connections give an added dimension to divine rapport and can lead to your success in magic making and to a deeper communion with the spiritual and mystical realms

But ancestry and lineage need not influence divine rapport. For example, you can have a strong rapport with the Egyptian Goddess Isis yet have no trace of Egyptian ancestry. This is because all Goddesses and Gods respond to worthwhile efforts of love, warmth, and heartfelt honesty, regardless of your ancestry. If you are loving and warm in your feelings toward the Goddesses and Gods, then you will receive love and warmth in return. It is also because we are all one people, born from Oneness and part of the divine whole. From this perspective, attitude rather than ancestry is the key to divine rapport

To gain rapport with a particular deity, begin by selecting a name from the lists of helpful Goddesses and Gods in these appendixes. Select a divine name that you are especially drawn to, or choose one with which you are completely unfamiliar. By all means, use your intuition as well as common sense when making your selection. For example, Venus is a good choice for love spells, while Jupiter is an ideal selection for prosperity spells. Gods and Goddesses have traditional correspondences for the simple fact that they have domain over those specific energies. Also keep in mind that deities seek rapport with you just as you do with them, so make an effort to be aware of divine signs and messages in your waking life and in dreams.

After you have made a selection, for example, Lugh, one way to gain rapport is to repeat the deity's name over and over as you drift to sleep at night. You can also chant, "I am Lugh, Lugh is me, we are One," until you reach a merged state of consciousness. In addition, perform the spells and rituals in chapter 9 that are tailored to gain divine rapport, for instance, "Faces of the Goddess and God Ritual."

ABNOBA (Gaulish): Goddess of the hunt

ABTAGIGI (Sumerian): Goddess of desire and promiscuity

ADSAGSONA (Celtic): Goddess of the underworld and of magic

AGRAT BAT MAHALAT or IGIRIT (Jewish): Goddess of sex

AIFE or AOIFE (Celtic): Consort of the sea God Manannan

AILINN (Celtic): Goddess of affection, romance, and love

AINE (Celtic): Goddess of Earth and Sun, queen of the Faery, mate to Lugh

AIRMED (Celtic): Goddess of witchcraft and herb lore

AKUPERA (Hindu): Goddess of moonlight

ANADYOMENE (Greek): Sea-born Goddess of sexuality

ANAT (Assyro-Babylonian): Intense, warlike Goddess of passion and desire

ANDRASTE or ANDRASTA (Celtic): Goddess of fertility, warriors, and victory

ANNA PERENNA (Roman): Goddess of sexuality and fertility

ANNAPURNA (Hindu): Great Mother Goddess of abundance; giver of plenty

ANU or DANU (Celtic): Mother Goddess of knowledge, healing, and fertility

ANUKET or ANUKIS (Egyptian): Goddess of the river and fertility

AOBH (Celtic): Wife of Llyr, the sea God

APHRODITE (Greek): Goddess of love, pleasure, and beauty

ARDWINNA (Celtic): Goddess of the forests and woods

ARIANRHOD (Celtic): Stellar and lunar Goddess; her palace is the Corona Borealis, known as Caer Arianrhod (Northern Crown); consort to Nwyvre

ARTEMIS (Greek): Goddess of the moon and hunting, twin sister of Apollo

ARTIMPAASA (Scythian): Goddess of love, associated with the moon

ARTIO (Celtic): Goddess of fertility and wildlife, portrayed as a bear

ASTARTE (Assyro-Babylonian): Great Mother Goddess, associated with the planet Venus

ATHENA (Greek): Goddess of wisdom and warriors in battle

BADB or BADHBH, BADB CATHA, BAV, BOV, BODHBH (Celtic): Druidess of the Tuatha De Danann and Goddess of war, inspiration, fury, and wisdom

BANBA (Celtic): Goddess of the sacred land

BEBHIONN (Celtic): An Underworld Goddess of pleasure

BAST (Egyptian): Cat Goddess of fertility, pleasure, dancing, music, and love

BELISAMA (Celtic): Young Goddess of fire whose name means "like unto flame" and "the bright and shining one"; wife of Belenus

BELISANA (Celtic): Goddess of healing, laughter, and the forests; associated with the sun's warmth and woodland plants and animals

BLATHNAT (Celtic): "Little Flower," Goddess of sex

BLODENWEDD (Blodewedd, Blodeuedd) (Celtic): Beautiful and treacherous sun and moon Goddess, associated with the white owl, the dawn, primroses, broom, cockle, oak, and meadowsweet

BO FIND (Celtic): Goddess of fertility

BOANN or **BOI, BOANNA** (Celtic): Mother of the herds, Goddess of fertility, inspiration, and the River Boyn, wife of the Dagda

BRANWEN (Welsh): Goddess of love, called the White-Bosomed One and Venus of the Northern Sea; her name means "white raven"

BRIDGET or **BRIDE, BRIGHID, BRIGANDU, BRIGET, BREDE** (Celtic): Fertility Goddess of the sacred fire, the sun, hearth, and home; bride Goddess of inspiration, poetry, medicine, healing, and smithcraft

BRIGANTIA (Celtic): Goddess of nature and the sun, associated with the rivers, mountains, and valleys of the countryside

BRONACH (Celtic): Goddess of cliffs and precipices

CAER (Celtic): Swan maiden, wife of Angus

CAILLEACH (Pre-Celtic): Goddess of Earth, sky, moon, and sun, who controlled the seasons and weather

CALLIOPE (Greek): Muse of epic poetry

CHERUBIM (Hebrew): Goddess/God of sexuality and intercourse

CILLEAC BHEUR (Scottish): Goddess of winter, whose staff can freeze the ground and wither the crops

CLIODNA (Celtic): Bird Goddess and Faerie Queen associated with extraordinary beauty, shapeshifting, apples, and accompanied by three magical birds

COVENTINA (Celtic): Goddess of the well and the womb of the Earth, associated with healing springs, sacred wells, childbirth, renewal, and the Earth

CREIDDYLAD or CREUDYLAD (Celtic): Daughter of the Sea god Llyr

DAMONA (Celtic): Goddess of fertility and healing; her name means "divine cow"

DANA or DANU, DANNU, ANU, ANA, ANNA, ANN, DON (Celtic): The Mother Goddess from whom Tuatha De Danann were descended; Goddess of nature, wisdom, and creation

DEIRDRE (Celtic): "One who gives warning" or the older form, Derdriu, "oak prophet"; a humanized Goddess in the Red Branch tale of the Exile of the sons of Uisnach; daughter of the God Morgan

DEMETER (Greek): Goddess of fertility, marriage, and prosperity

DIA GRIENE (Scottish): The daughter of the sun

DIANA (Roman): Goddess of moonlight and the hunt

EDAIN or ETAIN (Celtic): Goddess of beauty and grace; wife of King Mider; one of the "White Ladies" of the Faery

ELAYNE or ELEN, ELEN LWYDDAWG (Celtic): Powerful Goddess of leadership and war

EOSTRE or OSTARA (Celtic): Goddess of spring and fertility

EPONA (Celtic): Goddess of fertility, power, and abundance

ERI OF THE GOLDEN HAIR (Celtic): Goddess of love and sexuality

ERIN (Eriu): (Celtic): The triple Mother Goddess of Erin, sometimes known as Ir, from which Ireland—the land of Ir—is derived; a shapeshifter and Goddess of sovereignty of the land

FAND (Celtic): Shapeshifter and Faery Queen of Ireland, associated with the sea gull

FELICITAS (Roman): Goddess of good fortune

FEN (Celtic): A war Goddess associated with Morrigan

FEND (Celtic): The sea Goddess and consort of Manannan mac Llyr

FINDABAIR (Celtic): Goddess of Connacht and the Otherworld, of beauty, grace, and love

FLIODHAS (Celtic): Goddess of the woodlands, protector of animals and forests, associated with the doe

FLORA (Roman): Goddess of fertility, sex, promiscuity, and spring

FORTUNA (Roman): Lady Luck, Goddess of love and sexuality

FREYA (Norse): Goddess of love, beauty, passion, and fertility

FRIGGA (Norse): Goddess of feminine arts, associated with hawks and falcons

HATHOR (Egyptian): Goddess of love, Mother of creation, and mistress of everything beautiful

HEKET (Egyptian): Frog Goddess of childbirth and creation

HELEN (Greek): Moon Goddess of childbirth, love, and fertility

HERA (Greek): Goddess of matrimony

HERTHA (Celtic): Goddess of fertility, spring, the Earth, rebirth, and healing

HYPATIA (Greek): Goddess of knowledge

ISHTAR (Babylonian): Goddess of love, beauty, and war; associated with Venus, the morning star

ISIS (Egyptian): Mother Goddess, embodiment of femininity

ISONG (African): Goddess of fertility

JUNO (Roman): Goddess of matrimony

KERRIDWEN or CERRIDWYN, CERIDWYN (Celtic): Goddess of knowledge and wisdom who possessed the cauldron of inspiration

KWAN-YIN (Buddhist): Goddess of compassion and beauty

LAKSHMI (Hindu): Goddess of beauty and good fortune

LETHA (Celtic): Midsummer harvest Goddess

LILITH (Hebrew): First wife of Adam. Winged, wind Goddess

LOFN (Scandinavian): Love Goddess who brings lovers together and smooths over love's difficulties

MACHA or EMHAIN MACHA (Celtic): Threefold sun Goddess of fertility, war, and ritual games; associated with the horse, raven, and crow

MARY (Christian): Daughter of Hannah and mother of Jesus; later became queen of heaven, with the greater portion of Christian churches dedicated to her, not her son

MAYA (Hindu): Goddess of creativity

MEDB or MAEVE, MAB, MEDHBH (Celtic): Warrior Queen and Goddess of sex, power, fertility, and sovereignty

MEI or MAI, MEIA (Celtic): Mother of Gwalchmei; a solar and Earth Goddess

MESKHENET (Egyptian): Goddess of childbirth

MODRONA or MODRON, MADRONA, MATRONA (Celtic): The Great Mother of Mabon (light)

MORGAN LE FAY (Celtic): Faerie Queen, sorceress, shapeshifter, and beautiful enchantress

MORGANA (Celtic): The Death Mother; Goddess of war and fertility

MORRIGAN or MORRIGANA (Celtic): The Phantom Queen or Great Queen, also a sea Goddess and triple Goddess of war; shapeshifts into a raven

MORRIGU (Celtic): Dark Gray Lady and Queen of the Sea; Goddess of life, death, and magic

NANA BULUKU (West African): For the people of Benin, she is the spirit of first creation.

NANTOSUELTA (Celtic): River Goddess

NEMETONA (Celtic): Protectress of the sacred Drynemeton; warrior Goddess of the oak groves; patron of thermal springs

NEPHTHYS (Egyptian): Goddess of dreams, divination, and hidden knowledge

NIAMH or NEEVE OF THE GOLDEN HAIR (Celtic): Goddess of love and beauty

NIMUE or NINIANE, NIVIENE, NYMENCHE (Celtic): Student of and teacher to Merlin, her consort

NUT (Egyptian): Great sky Goddess, sister of Geb

NYX (Greek): Mother Goddess; the personification of night and the offspring of Chaos

OMAMAMA (Cree): Ancestral Goddess of beauty, fertility, gentleness, and love

OSHUN (African): Goddess of love, pleasure, beauty, wealth, fountains, and dancing

PARVATI (Hindu): Goddess of marital blessing

PENELOPE (Greek): Spring Goddess of fertility and sexuality

PSYCHE (Greek): Goddess of love

RHIANNON (Celtic): Queen Mother, Queen Mare, or the Great
Queen

ROSEMERTA (Celtic): Goddess of fertility, beauty, and love

SADV (Celtic): Ancient deer Goddess of the forests and nature

SARAH (Hebrew): Goddess of beauty and sovereignty

SELENE (Greek/Roman): Moon and love Goddess

SHAKTI (Hindu): Great Mother Goddess, who embodies feminine
energy

SHEILA NA GIG (Celtic): Goddess of sex, birth, passion, and
laughter

SIRONA (Celtic): Solar and astral Goddess, consort is Borvo

TAILLTE (Celtic): Earth Goddess and foster mother to Lugh

TIAMAT (Mesopotamian): Great Mother Goddess, who took the
form of a dragon

TLAZOLTEOTL (Peruvian): Goddess of love

TRIANA (Celtic): The Triple Goddess; Sun-Ana, Earth-Ana, and
Moon-Ana; Goddess of healing, knowledge, higher love, and wisdom

VAR (Scandinavian): Love Goddess

VENUS (Roman): Goddess of love and sexuality

VIVIANA or VIVIAN, VIVIEN (Celtic): Goddess of love, birth, life,
mothers, childbirth, and children; consort is Merlin

VOLUPTAS (Roman): Goddess of pleasure and sensuality

appendix B

List of Helpful
Dream Magic Gods

ADONIS (Greek): God of beauty and love

AENGUS MAC OG or **ANGUS, ANGUS OG, OENGUS** (Celtic): God of love and beauty; healer of souls; associated with romance and courting

AMAETHON (Celtic): Agriculture and harvest God called the Harvest King; associated with the fruits and tools of the harvest

APOLLO (Greek): Sun God of poetry, creative arts, music, healing, and divination; twin brother of Artemis

ARAWN (Celtic): Death, war, and ancestral God; King of Annwn, the Underworld; associated with the swine, magical beasts, the ancestral tree, water springs, shapeshifting, and the cauldron

BEL or **BILE, BELENUS, BELENOS** (Celtic): Sun God of light and healing, referred to as "The Shining One"; husband of Belisama

BEL/BAAL (Assyro-Babylonian): Sky God of fertility

BHAGA (Hindu): God of marriage, fortune, and prosperity

BODB DERG or **BODB THE RED** (Celtic): Son of Dagda and Boann; bard to the Tuatha De Danann; king of the Sidhe

BORVO or **BORMO, BORMANUS** (Celtic): Healing God of unseen and concealed truth and inspiration through dreams; the golden God, associated with hot springs and a golden harp; consort of Sirona

BRAGI (Norse): God of poetry

BRAN or **BRON** (Celtic): God of music and prophecy; protector of bards and poets; associated with singing, the bard's harp, and the Sacred Head

BRES (Celtic): God of fertility and agriculture

BUDDHA (Indian): The energy of knowledge and wisdom

CAMULUS (Celtic): God of war

CHANGO (African): Great love God, drummer, dancer, king

CONDATIS (Celtic): Water God

CORDEMANON (Celtic): God of knowledge, ancestry, and travel, associated with the Great Book of Knowledge, stone circles, and sacred sites

CREIDNE or **CREIDHNE, CREDNE** (Celtic): Master sword maker named "The Bronze Worker"; associated with smiths, wrights, metalworking, and craftspeople

CROM (Celtic): God of storms, lightning, and thunder

CUPID (Roman): God of love

DAGDA (Celtic): God of abundance, love, pleasure, and plenty; husband of Boann

DEWI (Celtic): The Red Dragon God, the emblem of Wales

DIANCECHT (Celtic): God of herbalism and healing; physician to the Gods; associated with the mortar and pestle

DIONYSUS (Greek): From pastoral beginnings, associated with goat herding; became the God of ecstasy, sex, revelry, and pleasure

DUMIATIS or **DUMEATIS** (Celtic): God of creative thought and teaching

DWYANE (Celtic): God of love

DWYN (Celtic): God of love and mischief

EROS (Greek): God of passionate love

ESUS (Celtic): Woodland God associated with hunting, the sword, the Golden Bull (Tarvos), and the bow and arrow; pictured as a woodcutter

FAGUS (Celtic): God of all beech trees

FREY (Norse): God of fertility, joy, peace, and happiness

GEB (Egyptian): Earth God, whose sister is Nut, the sky Goddess

GOBANNON or **GOVANNON, GOIBNIU, GOIBHNIE, GOIBNLL** (Celtic): The divine smith and God of magic, also called "Gobban the Wright" and Gobban Saer, "The Master Mason."

GWALCHMEI (Celtic): God of love and music; son of the Goddess Mei

GWYDION (Celtic): Shapeshifter; God of the arts, eloquence, kindness, and magic

GWYN AP NUDD (Celtic): God of the Otherworld, the death chase, and the Wild Hunt

HEIMDALL (Norse): White God, known for his sight and hearing

HELLITH (Celtic): God of the setting sun and protector of souls of the dead

HERMES (Greek): God of flocks and music; guides travelers; divine messenger

HYPNOS (Greek): Mesmerizing God of sleep and dreams

JUPITER (Roman): God of the light sky, wielder of thunderbolts

KAMA or **KAMADEVA** (Hindu): God of love, "Seed of Desire"

KERNUNNOS or **CERNUNNOS** (Celtic): Father God of virility, prowess, and nature

KHNUM (Egyptian): God of fecundity and creation

KHONS (Egyptian): God of the moon; father is Amon-Ra

KRISHNA (Hindu): God of erotic delight and ecstasy

LLYR or **LER, LIR, LEAR, LEER** (Celtic): Sea God of music and king of the oceans; husband of Aobh

LUCHTA or **LUCTA, LUCHTAINE** (Celtic): Carpenter God and shield maker for the Tuatha De Danann

LUGH or **LUG, LLEU, LLEW LLAW GYFFES** (Celtic): Sun God and master of all arts; God of poets, bards, smiths, and war

MABON or **MAPON, MAPONUS** (Celtic): "The Divine Son" and "The Son of Light"; God of sex, love, magic, prophecy, and power

MANANNAN or **MANANNAN AP LLYR, MANANNAN MAC LLYR** (Celtic): Shapeshifter, teacher, God of magic, the sea, and travel; consort of Fend

MATH, SON OF MATHONWY (Celtic): Seasonal King God of magic, wisdom, enchantment, and sorcery

MERCURY (Roman): God of safe travel and communication

MERLIN or **MYRDDIN** (Celtic): Woodland and nature God, consort of Viviana

MIDER or **MIDIR** (Celtic): The Faery King, God of the Underworld, and consort to Edain; bard and chess player; associated with the Isle of Man, the faery hill of Bri Leith, the chessboard and game pieces

MIN (Egyptian): God of sex, fecundity, and crops

MITRA (Hindu): God of friendship

MORPHEUS (Greek): God of sleep and dreams; small pebbles were left by the bedroom door to welcome him

NODENS (Celtic): God of dreams and sleep

NUADA or **LLUDD, NUDD, LLUDD LLAW EREINT** (Celtic): The Good Father, first king of Tara; consort to Fea, the war Goddess, and to Morrigan

NWYVRE (Celtic): God of space and the firmament; consort to Arianrhod

ODIN (Norse): Father God of wisdom and inspiration

OGMA or **OGMIOS** (Celtic): "The Binder": God of eloquence, knowledge, and literature; invented the Ogham script or letters

OSIRIS (Egyptian): Father God of civilization and rebirth

PAN (Greek): Nature God of lust, love, play, and pleasure

PRYDERI (Celtic): Youthful shapeshifter God and son of the Goddess Rhiannon and the God Pwyll

PWYLL (Celtic): Prince of Dyfed and King of the Otherworld; a pack of hounds accompanies him

RA (Egyptian): Sun God, father of all Gods; has an all-seeing eye

ROBUR (Celtic): Forest King and tree God of the forests, particularly oaks

SHIVA (Hindu): God of creation; embodies masculine energy

SILVANUS (Roman): God of the forests and agriculture, especially woodland clearings

SMERTULLOS (Celtic): The Preserver and Lord of Protection; God of the abyss and the unmanifested

SUCELLOS (Celtic): River God and twin to the Dagda; shapeshifter and God of fertility and death

TALIESIN (Celtic): Son of Kerridwen; poet, prophet, and bard

TARANIS (Celtic): God of thunder, storms, and the seasonal cycle

TARVOS TRIGARANOS (Celtic): God of vegetation and virility

TETHRA (Celtic): Sea God of magic

THOR (Norse): God of thunder, protector from chaos

THOTH (Egyptian): God of writing; moon God; magician

TYR (Norse): God of war and justice

ZEUS (Greek): Leader of the Gods of Olympus

BIBLIOGRAPHY

Baumgartner, Anne. *A Comprehensive Dictionary of the Gods*. New York: University Books, 1984.

Beyerl, Paul. *A Compendium of Herbal Magic*. Custer, WA: Phoenix Publishing, 1998.

Blair, Nancy. *Amulets of the Goddess*. Oakland, CA: Wingbow Press, 1993.

Bowater, Margaret M. *Dreams and Visions: Language of the Spirit*. Freedom, CA: Crossing Press, 1999.

Bowes, Susan. *Notions and Potions*. New York: Sterling Publishing, 1997.

Briggs, K. M. *The Fairies in English Tradition and Literature*. Chicago: University of Chicago Press, 1967.

Buckland, Raymond. *Gypsy Dream Dictionary*. St. Paul: Llewellyn Publications, 1999.

Bulfinch, Thomas. *Bulfinch's Mythology*. Garden City, NY: Garden City Publishing, 1938.

Campbell, Joseph. *The Masks of God*. Vols. 1–4. New York: Penguin Books, 1977.

——. *Myth, Dream, and Religion*. New York: E. P. Dutton, 1970.

——. *The Power of Myth*. New York: Doubleday, 1988.

Castaneda, Carlos. *The Art of Dreaming*. New York: HarperCollins, 1993.

Cunningham, Scott. *Encyclopedia of Magical Herbs*. St. Paul: Llewellyn Publications, 1985.

——. *Living Wicca*. St. Paul: Llewellyn Publications, 1993.

De Grandis, Francesca. *Be a Goddess!* San Francisco: HarperSanFrancisco, 1998.

Delaney, Gayle. *Living Your Dreams: Using Sleep to Solve Problems and Enrich Your Life*. San Francisco: Harper & Row, 1988.

Devereux, Paul, and Charla Devereux. *The Lucid Dreaming Kit*. Boston: Journey Editions, 1998.

Donner, Florinda. *Being-In Dreaming*. San Francisco: HarperCollins, 1991.

Ellis, Peter Berresford. *The Druids*. Grand Rapids, MI: William B. Eerdmans, 1994.

Evans-Wentz, W. Y. *The Fairy Faith in Celtic Countries*. New York: Citadel Press, 1990.

Farrar, Janet, and Stewart Farrar. *The Witches' Way*. London: Robert Hale, 1984.

Farrar, Stewart. *What Witches Do*. London: Peter Davis Limited, 1971.

Ferguson, Anna-Marie. *A Keeper of Words*. St. Paul: Llewellyn Publications, 1996.

Ford, Patrick K., trans. *The Mabinogi and Other Medieval Welsh Tales*. Berkeley and Los Angeles: University of California Press, 1977.

Grabhorn, Lynn. *Excuse Me, Your Life Is Waiting*. Seattle: Hara Publishing, 1999.

Gackenback, J. I., and J. Bosveld. *Control Your Dreams*. New York: Harper & Row, 1989.

Gannon, Linda. *Creating Fairy Garden Fragrances*. Pownal, VT: Storey Books, 1998.

Garfield, Patricia. *The Dream Messenger*. New York: Simon & Schuster, 1997.

———. *Women's Bodies, Women's Dreams.* New York: Ballantine, 1988.

Gaster, Theodor, ed. *The New Golden Bough.* New York: New American Library, 1959.

Gimbutas, Marija. *The Language of the Goddess.* San Francisco: Harper & Row, 1989.

Godwin, Malcolm. *The Lucid Dreamer.* New York: Simon & Schuster, 1994.

Goldstein, Nikki. *Essential Energy: A Guide to Aromatherapy and Essential Oils.* New York: Warner Books, 1997.

Graves, Robert. *The White Goddess.* New York: Faber & Faber, 1966.

Green, Miranda J. *Dictionary of Celtic Myth and Legend.* New York: Thames & Hudson, 1997.

Grimal, Pierre, ed. *Larousse World Mythology.* London: Paul Hamlyn, 1965.

Heath, Maya. *Cerridwen's Handbook of Incense, Oils, and Candles.* San Antonio, TX: Words of Wizdom International, 1996.

Hopman, Ellen Evert. *A Druid's Herbal for the Sacred Earth Year.* Rochester, NY: Destiny Books, 1995.

Jung, Carl G. *The Archetypes of the Collective Unconscious.* Princeton: Princeton University Press, 1990.

Knight, Sirona. *Greenfire: Making Love with the Goddess.* St. Paul: Llewellyn Publications, 1995.

———. *Love, Sex, and Magick.* Secaucus, NJ: Carol Publishing Group, 1999.

———. *Moonflower: Erotic Dreaming with the Goddess.* St. Paul: Llewellyn Publications, 1996.

———. *The Pocket Guide to Celtic Spirituality.* Freedom, CA: Crossing Press, 1998.

———. *The Pocket Guide to Crystals and Gemstones.* Freedom, CA: Crossing Press, 1998.

Knight, Sirona, et al. *The Shapeshifter Tarot.* St. Paul: Llewellyn Publications, 1998.

Krippner, Stanley, ed. *Dreamtime & Dreamwork*. Los Angeles: Jeremy P. Tarcher, 1990.

Lazarus, Arnold. *In the Mind's Eye*. New York: Guilford Press, 1977.

Leach, Maria, ed. *Standard Dictionary of Folklore, Mythology, and Legend*. New York: Funk & Wagnalls, 1950.

LeBerge, Stephen. *Lucid Dreaming: The Power of Being Awake and Aware in Your Dreams*. Los Angeles: Jeremy P. Tarcher, 1985.

Linn, Denise. *The Secret Language of Signs*. New York: Ballantine Books, 1996.

Long, Jim. *Making Herbal Dream Pillows*. Pownal, VT: Storey Books, 1998.

Markale, Jean. *Merlin: Priest of Nature*. Rochester, VT: Inner Traditions, 1995.

———. *Women of the Celts*. Rochester, VT: Inner Traditions, 1986.

Mindell, Arnold. *The Dreambody in Relationships*. New York: Routledge & Kegan Paul, 1987.

———. *The Shaman's Body*. New York: HarperCollins, 1993.

———. *Working with the Dreaming Body*. Boston: Routledge & Kegan Paul, 1985.

Monaghan, Patricia. *The Book of Goddesses and Heroines*. St. Paul: Llewellyn Publications, 1990.

Monmouth, Geoffrey. *History of the Kings of Britain*. New York: E. P. Dutton, 1958.

Morrison, Dorothy. *Everyday Magic*. St. Paul: Llewellyn Publications, 1998.

Murray, Margaret. *The God of the Witches*. London: Oxford University Press, 1970.

Nahmad, Claire. *Cat Spells*. New York: Random House, 1998.

O'Donohue, John. *Anam Cara: A Book of Celtic Wisdom*. New York: HarperCollins, 1997.

Pajeon, Kala, and Ketz Pajeon. *The Candle Magick Workbook*. Secaucus, NJ: Citadel Press, 1991.

Paterson, Helena. *The Celtic Lunar Zodiac*. Boston: Charles E. Tuttle, 1992.

Pennick, Nigel. *The Complete Illustrated Guide to Runes*. New York: Barnes & Noble, 1999.

Polich, Judith Bluestone. *Return of the Children of Light*. Santa Fe: Linkage Publications, 1999.

Rector-Page, Linda. *Healthy Healing*. Sonoma, CA: Healthy Healing Publications, 1992.

Ross, Anne. *Pagan Celtic Britain*. New York: Columbia University Press, 1967.

Smith, Sir William. *Smaller Classical Dictionary*. New York: E. P. Dutton, 1958.

Starhawk. *The Spiral Dance: A Rebirth of the Ancient Religion of the Goddess*. San Francisco: Harper & Row, 1979.

Stewart, R. J. *Celtic Gods, Celtic Goddesses*. New York: Sterling Publishing, 1990.

———. *The Living World of Faery*. Glastonbury, Somerset: Gothic Image Publication, 1995.

Stewart, R. J., and Robin Williamson. *Celtic Druids, Celtic Bards*. London: Blandford Press, 1996.

Telesco, Patricia. *Future Telling*. Freedom, CA: Crossing Press, 1998.

———. *Magick Made Easy*. San Francisco: HarperSanFrancisco, 1999.

———. *Spinning Spells, Weaving Wonders*. Freedom, CA: Crossing Press, 1996.

———. *Wishing Well*. Freedom, CA: Crossing Press, 1997.

Wilde, Lady. *Ancient Legends, Mystic Charms, and Superstitions of Ireland*. New York: Lemma Publishing, 1973.

Williams, David, and Kate West. *Born in Albion: The Re-Birth of the Craft*. Runcorn, United Kingdom: Pagan Media, 1996.

Valiente, Doreen. *The Rebirth of Witchcraft*. London: Robert Hale, 1989.

———. *Witchcraft for Tomorrow*. New York: St. Martin's Press, 1978.

Van Over, Raymond, ed. *Sun Songs: Creation Myths from Around the World*. New York: New American Library, 1980.

Weinstein, Marion. *Earth Magic.* New York: Earth Magic Productions, 1998.

Worwood, Valerie. *The Complete Book of Essential Oils and Aromatherapy.* New York: New World Library, 1995.

Yeats, W. B., ed. *Fairy and Folk Tales of Ireland.* New York: Macmillan, 1973.

ACKNOWLEDGMENTS

I would like to gratefully acknowledge and extend a heartfelt thank you to David Hennessy, my editor at HarperSanFrancisco, for his vision, friendship, and continued faith in my writing abilities. Loving thanks to my agent, Lisa Hagan at Paraview, for her enthusiasm, honesty, and persistence. And brightest blessings and warmest thanks to Terri Leonard, Kathi Goldmark, Calla Devlin, Eric Brandt, Margery Buchanan, Rebecca Fox, and Jim Warner at HarperSanFrancisco, and especially to Steve Hanselman—you have all helped make my dreams come true! May your deepest dreams come true too!

Many thanks and blessings to Phyllis Currot, Trish Telesco, Dorothy Morrison, Raven Grimassi, R. J. Stewart, Z. Budapest, Starhawk, and Marion Weinstein for the work they are doing to help people understand the positive wisdom of Wicca. A special thank you to Michael Peter Langevin for his encouragement, and to all the people at *Magical Blend* magazine for their help. Bright blessings and thanks to A. J. Drew at Salem West, Nella at Pan's Grove, and to everyone at Triple Moon. I would also like to respectfully thank Mark Victor Hansen, James Redfield, Neale Donald Walsch, John Perkins, Cynthia Larson, and Dr. John Gray for the work they are doing to create a brighter future for humankind.

Much love and many thanks to Melissa Dragich for her generosity and friendship, and a special thank you to Jeff Beck for his kindness. Blessings to Donovan for his inspiring songs, and heartfelt thanks to Brandon Boyd and Crispian Mills for their visionary music and for restoring my faith in the future.

Loving thanks and lots of hugs to my family and friends, and to all those folks who have been so supportive in the writing of this book. In particular, much love to Michael and Sky for making every day bright and worthwhile, and to the Goddesses and Gods for their friendship, love, and guidance. Blessed be!

Sirona Knight
Midsummer's Eve, 2000